PACIFIC ORBIT

PACIFIC ORBIT

AUSTRALIAN-AMERICAN RELATIONS SINCE 1942
EDITED BY NORMAN HARPER

Published for the Australian-American Association
by F. W. Cheshire Melbourne Canberra Sydney

Library of Congress Catalog
Card Number 68-54764
National Library of Australia
Registry Number Aus 68-2012
Copyright
First published 1968
Printed in Australia for
F. W. Cheshire Publishing Pty Ltd
380 Bourke Street, Melbourne
Garema Place, Canberra
142 Victoria Road, Marrickville, NSW
by Wilke & Co. Ltd.
Registered in Australia
for transmission by post as a book

Contents

Prefaces *J. G. Gorton* vii

   Lyndon B. Johnson ix

PART ONE

1 The American Alliance *Norman Harper* 3
2 Partnership in Defence *T. B. Millar* 25
3 Partnership in Trade *J. G. Crawford* 43
4 American Investment in Australia *Ian Potter* 67

PART TWO

5 The American Impact on Education *A. G. Austin* 91
6 The American Impact on Australian Business *D. H. Merry* 108
7 American Culture in Australia
 (a) Literature *Grahame Johnston* 123
 (b) Theatre *Wal Cherry* 133
 (c) Mass Communications *Robin Boyd* 144
 (d) Architecture *John Buchan* 154

PART THREE

8 A Historical Perspective *Norman Harper* 167
9 Two Federations *Zelman Cowen* 189
10 The American Image in Australia *Bruce Grant* 207
11 The American Image of Australia *Frank S. Hopkins* 220

Appendix

The Australian-American Association:
A Brief History 1936-1968 *Patrick Hamilton* 243

Preface

This is the first book of its kind which sets out to tell readers how Australians and Americans get along together in all sorts of ways. It is written by experts and reflects great credit on the Australian-American Association, which sponsored it, and on its editor and contributors.

There has been real growth in the Australian-American relationship since the Association was formed after World War II to help foster the friendship which had been expressed so dramatically along the battle fronts of Asia and the Pacific. I am sure that friendship is lasting and will bring benefit to us all in the years ahead.

I see our friendship with America as a perfectly natural thing. It is natural because the pioneers of both countries came from Britain, from the same Anglo-Saxon stock, and built independent nations based on the inherited principles of democracy and the rule of law.

It is also inevitable because we are Pacific nations with a common interest in the region and a common purpose in the global community of nations which cannot be divided arbitrarily by the hemispheres and the oceans, or the colours, creeds and politics of the people who belong to it.

In the past twenty-five years, Australian-American co-operation has developed into a partnership of very great significance. It takes many forms, as this book shows, and I am sure it has an enduring quality.

Twice in recent years, the President of the United States has visited Australia and by his presence has set a firm seal on the relationship between the two countries. Australian Prime Ministers have paid many visits to Washington. This relationship flows out from these levels to all the people of both countries.

The Australian people respect America for her courageous leadership of the free world. We acknowledge that our own security rests heavily on an American presence in this part of the world, and we aim to pull our weight, according to our strength and resources, so that the partnership is never one-sided.

The association of the two countries is broadly based. It carries with it the capacity for instinctive liking, spontaneous friendship, frank speaking, tough trading, healthy sporting rivalry and common interests in cultural matters.

There has never really been a need for introductions between Australians and Americans. We started off as friends because we had never been enemies. But there is always something to do to help us know each other better. The foundation of the Australian-American Association was one example; publication of this book is another. The book deserves to be widely read because it is contemporary history.

J. G. Gorton
Prime Minister

The friendship between our two countries rests, I believe, upon the many things we have in common. Our countries are both young and richly endowed with natural resources. Our political systems are both free and democratic. We are both melting pots, with peoples drawn from many lands. We have both attained a standard of living undreamed of when our nations were founded. We share a distinctive historical background: the pioneering of vast open spaces and the hard task of hammering out a federal union.

As a result of these similarities in national experience, we are today the same kind of people — self-reliant but neighbourly, idealistic but pragmatic, peaceful but always ready to stand up for what is right. Most of all, our peoples share the conviction that the future will be better than the present, and that we have an obligation to make it so.

It is because we have so much in common that we are close partners in world affairs. We have often been comrades-in-arms but we also work closely together in peace. There is a flourishing trade between us. We co-operate in scientific research and in economic aid to the developing nations of Asia. As pioneer nations, we are today co-operating especially closely on mankind's newest frontier — the exploration of outer space.

Since the Battle of the Coral Sea, our partnership has grown into a vital force for peace, progress and freedom in the Pacific. One of the major aims of my administration has been to strengthen it still further.

Lyndon B. Johnson
President

Part One

1 The American Alliance

On 27 December 1941, the Australian Prime Minister, Mr John Curtin, made a dramatic appeal for American assistance as British power suddenly collapsed in the Far East after Japan had attacked Pearl Harbour.

The Australian Government . . . regards the Pacific struggle as primarily one in which the United States and Australia must have the fullest say in the direction of the democracies' fighting plan. . . . Without any inhibitions of any kind, I make it quite clear that Australia looks to America, free of any pangs as to our traditional links of kinship with the United Kingdom. We know the constant threat of invasion. We know the dangers of dispersal of strength. But we know, too, that Australia can go and Britain still hold on. We are therefore determined that Australia shall not go, and we shall exert all our energies towards shaping a plan, with the United States as its keystone, which will give to our country some confidence of being able to hold out until the tide of battle swings against the enemy.[1]

In one sense Mr Curtin's appeal may be regarded as a turning point in Australian-American relations. For more than a decade there had been constant friction between the two countries, friction developing over Australia's large adverse trade balance with the United States and Washington's refusal to revise its tariff policies. The friction was aggravated by pin-pricking over landing rights in Australia for Pan American, cabling facilities between North America and Australia, and entry and residence rights for Australian business men in the United States. Trade hostility between the countries reached a peak with Australia's ill-considered 'trade diversion' policy in 1936. The American Consul-General in Sydney, Pierrspont Moffat, commented in 1935 that 'We have never made any attempt to deal with Australia as a political entity, and anti-American feeling is fairly rife.'[2]

A rapprochement began with the revision of Australia's 'trade diversion' policy and a re-assessment of the role of Japan in the changing balance of power in the North-West Pacific. Australia became increasingly conscious of her isolation in a Pacific where British naval power was still dominant but which Britain tended to regard as peripheral. Mr Menzies commented in 1941 of Churchill that 'the more distant the problem from the heart of Empire, the less he thought of it'.[3] The appointment in February 1940, of Mr R. G. Casey as the first Australian Minister to the United States and the arrival in Australia in the following July of the first United States Minister, Mr Clarence E. Gauss, were important steps in improving diplomatic relations and in establishing more effective lines of communications for the discussion of common problems. The two appointments were strikingly successful in helping to convert friction into alliance and in creating a more favourable image in both Washington and Canberra.

Mr Curtin's appeal involved a reorientation of Australian policies towards both the Commonwealth and the United States. While he declared two days later that 'our loyalty to the King goes to the very core of our national life, I . . . consider . . . Australia an organic part of the whole structure' of the British Empire, he was at the same time asserting a new concept of Commonwealth relations.[4] This reconciled full dominion autonomy and equality with British Commonwealth co-operation. The emphasis from an Australian point of view was on equality in determining policy and the assumption of greater responsibilities flowing out of that equality of voice. It did not cut the umbilical cord with London nor pave the way for the dissolution of the Commonwealth. It was both a realistic appeal to the United States for support in a critical military situation and a declaration to Washington that Australia was not merely an associate of Great Britain: she had independent interests in the Pacific and an intention of discussing policy directly with Washington and London.

Australian claims for a primary responsibility in shaping Commonwealth policies and strategy in the Pacific war were increasingly recognised by both the United Kingdom and the United States. War-time collaboration between Australia and the United States was close. The American fleet played a major part in halting the Japanese advance towards New Guinea and Australia: the battle of the Coral Sea was of critical importance.

It was fought on 4–8 May 1942. A Japanese convoy was sent to attack Port Moresby but was intercepted by an American squadron. The battle was the 'first major fleet-air battle in history'. Not a shot was fired by the opposing ships which did not sight one another and the engagement was fought by aircraft based on carriers and on the land. The battle led to the return of the Japanese convoy to Truk and so checked a dangerous Japanese attack on Australian territory.

Australia became a spring-board for a combined offensive against Japanese positions in South-East and East Asia. General Douglas MacArthur used Australia as his headquarters for his northern advance. With Japan's surrender on 2 September 1945 and the dissolution of the South-West Pacific command, the close collaboration ended. Friction had been developing in 1944-45 over Dr Evatt's insistence that Australia be treated as a principal power in determining policy towards Japan. His firmness led to American agreement that Australia should sign the instrument of surrender with Japan.

The war brought with it a respect for American power and a recognition of the crucial role played by the United States in protecting Australia against Japanese attack. Australia's contributions to the joint effort in the Pacific made it clear that she did not intend to 'creep into safety' behind American power. It had also established close ties of sentiment between thousands of people in both countries, ties which strengthened the growing tendency in Australia to look eastwards across the Pacific as well as westwards towards Europe.

The future of the Australian-American alliance was central to

Australian defence and foreign policy thinking after 1945. W. K. Hancock's earlier view (1930) in his brilliant historical essay on Australia,[5] that American importance for Australia should be heavily discounted, no longer influenced government, academic, or popular opinion in any significant way. At the heart of the problem lay the analysis of the Pacific situation made in Canberra and in Washington, the assumptions about the nature of national interests, and the kinds of policy being formulated on the basis of these analyses and assumptions.

In 1945 the power structure in the Pacific had been drastically changed. The defeat of Japan and the collapse of her empire, the revival of Nationalist China relieved of the Japanese threat but bedevilled by a struggle for power between nationalist and communist forces, the emergence of nationalism in South and South-East Asia and the demand for independence by all the colonies from Karachi to Manila: these were the new facts of Asian life. Secondly, the defeat of Japan had been accompanied by a weakening of all the western colonial empires in Asia. British power had contracted dramatically and the Pax Britannica had ceased to exist east of Suez. The Dutch and French colonial empires were in process of dissolution and the United States carried out its war time promise of independence for the Philippines. War time developments had led the Soviet Union to emerge as a more important element in the Pacific balance. The crucially important change was that the United States had become the dominant power in the Pacific and in East Asia: economically, industrially, and militarily. In a sense, a Pax Americana was beginning to replace the Pax Britannica.

With the traditional pattern of security vanishing during the war, Australia faced the problem of attempting, as a small middle power, to reconstruct in the Pacific area a new framework of security. To her South-East Asia was of central importance. Within a radius of three thousand miles from Darwin lie Tokyo and Rangoon, Manila and Saigon, Hanoi and Taipeh, Bangkok, Guam and Wellington. Djakarta is closer to Darwin than Sydney is, and Hobart is further from Darwin than is Singapore. Peking and New Delhi lie close to this three thousand mile perimeter. Australia's centres of population and industry are within easy flying distance of South-East Asia, and with revolutionary changes in aircraft design, distances have been rapidly shrinking. Geographically and strategically Australia is part of Asia: every Australian post-war Minister for External Affairs from Evatt to Hasluck has recognised this geopolitical fact although they may have drawn slightly different conclusions from it.

In East and South-East Asia, an area of rapid political change and of relative instability, there was a danger that a partial political vacuum might develop. There was the further danger of external intervention which could increase instability and lead to new conflict. Whence came the threat to peace in the area? In the immediate post-war years, the Australian Government felt that it could come from the revival of Japanese power, a recrudescence of Japanese imperialism. It therefore supported a tough occupation policy designed to eliminate militarism and to break the economic and political power of the Zaibatsu. With these went a whole-hearted support for the democratisation of Japan. Australian fears of a resurgent Japan were shared for a short period by the United States, but towards the end of 1946, the United States adopted a less draconic occupation policy towards Japan. By 1947, Japan was being economically reconstructed and converted into 'the workshop of East Asia'. Australia reluctantly followed the new American policy and signed the Peace Treaty with Japan in 1951 with some misgivings. Over the long period, Washington's assessment of Japan's role in East Asia has been more accurate than Canberra's.

The long-term threat to Asian stability and to Pacific peace has, in the eyes of the two governments, come from Chinese expansion, ideological or imperialistic. A reassessment of the internal struggle for power in pre- 1949 China had led to a shift in American policy towards Japan. The seizure of power by Mao Tse-tung in 1949 intensified American apprehension about Chinese expansion in Asia. This was reflected in the provision attached to the SEATO Treaty providing for mutual assistance against communist aggression. It was expressed more than a decade later by Secretary of State Dean Rusk (16 March 1966):

The Chinese Communist leaders seek to bring China on the world stage as a great power. . . . Peking's use of power is closely related to what I believe are its second and third objectives: dominance within Asia and leadership of the Communist world revolution, employing Maoist tactics. Peking is striving to restore traditional Chinese influence or dominance in South, South-East and East Asia. Its concept of influence is exclusive. . . . Where Peking is present, it seeks to exclude all others.[6]

The Australian Government has periodically made its own assessment of the threat to peace in South-East Asia. As the threat from Japan receded by 1951–52, its analysis centred upon communist pressure on and threats to the small States of the region. Mr Spender made this clear in his first speech as Minister for External Affairs after the change of government following the elections of 1949. As the military threat appeared to ease, Mr Casey in 1958 emphasised the danger of communist subversion which was 'like a deadly snake in a dark room'. Sir Garfield Barwick in 1962 pointed out the danger from the 'rapid world-wide extension of Communist imperialism'. In his first Parliamentary survey of international relations after becoming Minister for External Affairs, Mr Hasluck emphasised the threat to Asia from the expansive policies of Communist China: 'What we are concerned with is to achieve an international climate in which threats against and pressures against other states and peoples are removed, whether those threats arise from aggressive nationalism or aggressive Communism or perhaps a mixture of the two.'[7] Anti-communism has thus been a central theme in Australian foreign policy since 1950. Government policy has been subjected to severe criticism from sections of the Australian Labor Party and from academics who find an alternative explanation for Communist China's foreign policies.

Australian foreign policy has been formulated in a context which changed drastically between 1939 and 1945 and which has continued to change since 1950. In analysing that changing context, Australian governments have implicitly adopted the basic Morgenthau assumption that power is the main determinant of international relations and that 'anyone engaged in foreign affairs must recognise and study the facts of power and also recognise the reality of power politics'. (Hasluck.) They have also assumed that as one of the newer Asian powers, Australia has a significant diplomatic and strategic role to play in the Pacific. At the same time, there was the recognition, sometimes belatedly, that 'in terms of power politics, Australia is a small country. However much we may resemble the United States in our way of life and in our outlook, we are not a world power. The United States, as a world power whose security can be directly threatened by developments anywhere in the world, has to adopt a political, economic and military policy that encompasses the whole globe. Australia has in large measure to direct its own efforts nearer home.' (R. G. Casey, 1958.)[8] Australian industrial potential is considerable and her military resources are limited: a small middle power cannot develop a two-ocean navy or formulate a global strategy.

Mr Menzies, in 1955, restated the objectives and principles of Australian foreign policy, objectives and principles which have hardly changed over two decades: basically, security and peace with the raising of living standards 'not only for ourselves but for all those other nations that are struggling towards a life that we have been privileged to enjoy for a long time. . . . If we are to become involved in war, we must see to it that in such a war we have powerful and willing friends.'

As a small emerging power, formulating an independent foreign policy for the first time after 1941, Australia has always been compelled to rely upon 'powerful and willing friends'. Traditionally and for sentimental reasons, Australia depended wholly upon British military and naval power for her security: Britain provided the post-war shield to protect her against real or imaginary threats from Asia. But the post-war power shift meant that Britain could no longer provide that security: in reality power lay with the United States. Hence the dilemma facing the Australian Government in 1941: the competing pulls, of sentiment and reality, towards London and Washington. As a matter of practical politics, Australian Ministers for External Affairs have been compelled to use every possible source of power. They resemble jugglers attempting to keep in the air simultaneously a number of balls: Great

Britain, the Commonwealth, the United States, the United Nations, Asian friendship.

An essential objective of Australian foreign policy since 1945 has thus been to preserve the close war-time alliance with the United States. This produced a healthy mutual respect and close personal ties. At the same time, the hard fact was that the South-West Pacific and South-East Asia were areas of peripheral interest for the United States even though they were of central interest to Australia. The post-war British defence line ended at Singapore; the American defence perimeter extended from Alaska to Manila. Australia occupied the exposed gap between the two different defence terminals.

Friction between Australia and the United States developed over the policies to be pursued by SCAP in Japan, differences over the timing and degree of changes: economic levels of production, the revival of Japanese trade, the recovery of the Japanese mercantile marine, the nature of land reforms. Distrust of American policy in Japan was increase by a fear that General MacArthur would in fact give Japan a *de facto* peace which would become a *de jure* peace after the signature of an American drafted peace treaty.

The signature of the Japanese Peace Treaty at San Francisco in September 1951 was a signal triumph of the patient diplomacy of John Foster Dulles. Australia signed the treaty somewhat reluctantly and Australian misgivings were vigorously expressed during the debate on its ratification. Dr Evatt bitterly criticised what he regarded as a 'deadly delusion': the assumption that a rearmed Japan would use its force wholly in the interest of the Western powers. Much as Australians might dislike the Treaty, there was no practicable alternative to its ratification and the acceptance of American policy.

The ANZUS Treaty of 1951 was a necessary condition for the ratification of the Japanese Peace Treaty: it was in a sense a *quid pro quo* that sweetened the Japanese pill. Ever since 1937, Australian and other governments had groped their way towards a broadly based regional pact to replace the defunct 1921–22 Washington Treaties. There was no American interest in such a pact 'until present conflicts in Asia were resolved'. (Dean Acheson.)

The United States was more interested in a net-work of bi-lateral pacts with other countries as a means of consolidating security in the Pacific and of limiting her obligations. Australia, like New Zealand, was anxious to pin down the United States in advance to accepting specific commitments against any form of aggression in South-East Asia.

The Treaty was in a sense 'an historical milestone' in Australian-American relations: it did in fact give a treaty basis to the vague and sentimental relationship that was a legacy of the war-time alliance. It did rest on a broadly common assumption that the chief threat to Pacific security came from Communist China rather than from a rearmed Japan. To Washington the primary purpose of the Treaty was to contain communism. To Australia its value lay in the formal American commitment to protect Australia against external attack and in the opportunity it gave for direct access by Australia to American leaders and top level experts. 'ANZUS gives Australia access to the thinking and planning of the American Administration at the highest political and military level. . . . ANZUS ensures that our own interests, both political and military are kept before the United States.' (R. G. Casey.)[9]

There were some doubts in Australia about the practical effectiveness of the ANZUS Treaty, especially in view of the deteriorating situation in French Indo-China. American strategy in South-East Asia appeared to oscillate between a continental and an 'off-shore' policy, between economic and limited military aid and the use of the fleet as a potential striking force. The hard fact was that there was no clear-cut military arrangement between countries with a vital interest in stability in Asia and a capacity to undertake firm military commitments. For three years Australia tried to secure an enlargement of the ANZUS Pact to include other governments interested in maintaining peace and stability in South-East Asia. The collapse of French power at Dien Bien Phu in 1954 produced the Geneva settlement and pointed the way to the loosely drawn South-East Asia Collective Defence Treaty, the SEATO or Manila Pact of September 1954.

The SEATO Treaty brought together the United States, Australia, France, Great Britain, New Zealand, Pakistan, the Philippines, and

Thailand in a loose regional pact. Like the ANZUS Pact, it provided that in the event of armed aggression against any member, or against any State or territories unanimously designated in the treaty, members would act to meet the common danger 'in accordance with their constitutional processes'. There was no binding commitment in advance to any military action in specified circumstances and the assumption was, or quickly came to be, that no action could be taken except by the unanimous agreement of members. The Treaty area was carefully defined to exclude Hong Kong, Formosa, and Japan; Laos, Cambodia and Vietnam could come under the SEATO umbrella provided their governments requested action by SEATO.

By 1954 the Australian-American alliance had come to rest legally upon the two separate treaty commitments between the two countries. The collapse of French power in Indo-China had pointed to the need for collective action to stabilise the situation in South-East Asia. To the United States it underlined the danger of communist expansion, a danger already indicated by the Korean War. The American commitment under SEATO was exclusively against communist aggression: it did not cover aggression by one South-East Asian country against another country in the region. It did not cover the contingency, for example, of an Indonesian threat to Australia.

The Australian Government shared America's concern over the threat posed by communism to the small countries of Asia. It was partly for this reason that Australia sent troops to Korea in 1950, when North Korea attacked the Republic of Korea. Australia interpreted its obligations under the United Nations charter to resist aggression in the same manner as the United States and maintained forces there until the armistice of 1953. But to Australia, neither the ANZUS Treaty nor the SEATO Pact provided adequate security against external attack. The two pacts did not close the Singapore-Manila defence gap. Their membership was limited, and while there was a clear understanding of the constitutional difficulties that prevented the United States from giving a binding commitment in advance, it was felt that the treaties really lacked teeth. Much of Australian policy since 1954 has been directed towards converting the SEATO Treaty from 'an insurance policy and a deterrent' (Casey) into an effective military shield.

The military effectiveness of SEATO, and to a lesser extent of ANZUS, has been limited by differences of objective and of interpretation between the member states. At no stage did the alliances involve close strategic and tactical planning and integration of military forces of the NATO kind. Little progress was made towards a definition of mutual obligations or towards a strengthening of military effectiveness. The existence of the regional pacts gave some credibility to the intentions of their members and contributed to the stabilisation of South-East Asia. At least, no major threats to the regional balance of power took place for six or seven years after the conclusion of the SEATO Pact. During these years infiltration and subversion rather than frontal military attacks became the major concern of the treaty states and of neutralist states in South-East Asia.

Changes in weapons and military strategy, and shifts in the internal struggles for power in South-East Asian states modified the context within which the SEATO and ANZUS Pacts could operate. Tension between Indonesia and the Netherlands over West New Guinea reached a peak towards the end of 1961 and there was a distinct probability that Indonesia would use force to resolve the issue. The build up of Indonesian military strength with Soviet arms was an indication of intent. Australia was reluctant to see a transfer of West New Guinea to Indonesia without allowing the indigenous people to be consulted. As the administering authority in Papua-New Guinea, it preferred to have temporarily a buffer state between Indonesia and East New Guinea. Diplomatically it had supported Dutch proposals for a United Nations settlement of the problem that would have permitted the people of West New Guinea to exercise their right of self-determination. American policy towards Indonesia was directed towards stabilising the rather precarious balance of power and preventing either the development of a power vacuum or the emergence of a communist oriented Indonesia under President Sukarno. As Indonesian nationalism became more truculent over West New Guinea, American policy gradually changed from a cautious neutralism to a cautious acceptance of Indonesian claims. Australian and Dutch attempts to secure United Nations action failed because of a lack of American support. It also became evident that there was no military support for the Netherlands should Indonesia launch an attack upon Dutch controlled West Irian. The Bunker plan, providing for a transfer for West New Guinea to Indonesia in 1963 after a transitional period of United Nations administration, was a diplomatic triumph for the United States, but a triumph that necessitated a reorientation of Australian policy on this issue.

For the first time Australia had a common political boundary with a foreign power, and one with very substantial ground forces. With the shift in direction of Indonesian interest to Malaya and the development of confrontation between Indonesia and Malaya, Australian concern about the possibility of military conflict with Indonesia was intensified. The firm Australian military commitment to Malaya and the presence of Australian troops in Malaya and Borneo as part of the British Commonwealth reserve under the ANZAM arrangement increased the risk of conflict. A more precise definition of mutual obligations under the ANZUS Pact became important for Australia.

When the ANZUS Treaty had been drafted it had been regarded by Australia primarily as a re-insurance against Japan and by the United States as a treaty to contain communism. A re-definition of obligations took place at the Canberra (1962) and Wellington (1963) meetings of the ANZUS Council. The American Secretary of State, Mr Dean Rusk, attended the Canberra meeting, the first to be held for three years. The communiqué issued at the close of the meeting made it clear that the obligations under Article v of the Treaty 'applied in the event of armed attack not only on the metropolitan territory of any of the parties but also on any island territory under the jurisdiction of the three governments in the Pacific'. Mr Rusk declared that 'you can expect complete solidarity from the United States for Australia and New Zealand's responsibility in the Pacific'. At the Wellington meeting, Mr Averill Harriman declared quite simply that should New Guinea be attacked, 'the three parties would be in it together', and the communiqué announced that 'anything that happens in the Pacific area is of vital concern to all three, and that a threat to any of the partners in the area, metropolitan and island territories alike, is equally a threat to the others. The ANZUS Treaty declares in simple and direct terms that in matters of defence, Australia, New Zealand, and the United States stand as one.'[10] Australian attempts to extend the ANZUS umbrella to Sabah during Indonesia's confrontation of Malaysia were quietly but firmly rebuffed.

Two days after the conclusion of the ANZUS meeting in Canberra, Mr Menzies announced that the United States would establish a naval communications centre at North-West Cape in Western Australia. On 22 May 1963, the House of Representatives passed a Bill incorporating an agreement between the two governments to lease a twenty-eight acre site to the United States for a minimum period of twenty-five years. With the development of the inter-continental ballistic missiles and of nuclear-powered submarines carrying missiles with limited range, it was essential for the United States to establish land bases to communicate with Polaris submarines in the Indian Ocean. These would bring parts of the Soviet Union and the Sinkiang province of Communist China within missile range (a double-edged process), and at the same time counteract the presence of a Soviet submarine fleet in the Indian Ocean. The North-West Cape was placed under sole control of the United States but was to be used only for purposes of defence communications unless the Australian Government gave express permission to the contrary. Australian forces would be able to use the facilities of the communications centre.

The signature of the treaty aroused considerable political controversy in Australia but was endorsed wholeheartedly by the Government and by a majority of the members of the ALP opposition. Sir Garfield Barwick, Minister for External Affairs, repeatedly pointed out that the setting up of the new base would increase 'the individual and collective capacity' of the ANZUS partners to 'resist armed attack'. The debate over the base in Parliament and the press centred round the questions as to whether Australian sovereignty was being infringed and whether sole American control of the station would involve Australia in a nuclear war without its consent. The Australian Labor Party, by a majority, accepted the Bill as 'a grim and awful necessity' but indicated its intention of re-negotiating the details of the treaty should it subsequently be returned to power as a government. (In 1963 the Government had an effective majority of one, a majority that was increased to forty at the 1966 elections.) The North-West Cape base agreement was in fact an important turning point in the evolution of the ANZUS alliance.

This firm American commitment to Australia meant a considerable strengthening of the Canberra-Washington alliance. It was at the same time closely linked with a re-definition of obligations under the SEATO Treaty. The revival of civil war in Laos and Pathet Lao successes against the conservative Boun Oum Government in 1960–61 increased concern in Bangkok over the security of Thailand. Attempts to secure SEATO action in Laos had broken down and Thai leaders became sceptical about the effectiveness of the SEATO guarantee. As a matter of convention, SEATO Council decisions had always been unanimous, thus allowing an effective veto on action to any member (e.g. France in 1961). Serious threats to north-eastern Thailand early in 1962 led to a bi-lateral agreement with the United States following the Rusk-Khoman talks in March 1962. The United States gave a firmer guarantee of Thai security which made it clear that it was prepared to act alone if necessary against communist aggression in Thailand: the SEATO obligation was both individual and collective, and if agreement could not be reached on collective action then members were free to act individually. Australia supported this drastic re-interpretation of the Manila Treaty. Three months later American marines, Australian and British air detachments and New Zealand paratroopers were flown into Thailand at the request of the Thai Government.

The re-interpretation of ANZUS and SEATO obligations (March-May 1962) arose out of the changes in the regional and global situations since the treaties had been concluded. Further re-assessment of obligations became necessary with the increasing instability in the protocol states designated in the annexe to the SEATO Treaty: Laos, Cambodia, and South Vietnam. Cambodia had adopted a firm neutralist policy under Sihanouk and tended to gravitate towards Peking. The intensified civil war in Laos led to the holding of a second conference at Geneva and the adoption of a Declaration on the neutrality of Laos. This barred the Laotian Government from entering into any military alliance inconsistent with its neutrality and provided for the withdrawal of all foreign troops with the exception of a handful of French military instructors. The significant thing was the withdrawal of the SEATO umbrella from Laos and the frank recognition that SEATO had been powerless to check subversion or infiltration or to intervene with military force to assist the Laotian Government. It meant some contraction of America's strategic perimeter in the area and a concentration on South Vietnam as the focal point in American policy of containing communist aggression in South-East Asia.

The re-interpretation of SEATO obligations, the leasing of a base at North-West Cape, and the firm ANZUS commitment to assist Australia in the event of an attack on Papua-New Guinea were part of the fuller American commitment to South-East Asia. The weakening of Ngo Dinh Diem's regime in South Vietnam was accompanied by an intensification of pressure from North Vietnam and by the setting up by Hanoi in December 1960 of the 'Front for the Liberation of the south' which subsequently became the National Liberation Front. A year later, President Diem appealed to Washington for increased military assistance. South Vietnam was one of the protocol States designated in the SEATO Treaty, and America's decision to commit further troops was taken primarily in accordance with her unilateral declaration of 21 July 1954 at the close of the Geneva Conference. The decision was one that foreshadowed the Rusk-Khoman statement three months later. It also foreshadowed a request from Washington to Australia for assistance in South Vietnam. Mr Rusk's announcement of a clear definition of ANZUS obligations during his visit to Canberra for the ANZUS Council meeting in May 1962 coincided with the decision of the Australian Government to send a small group of thirty military instructors to South Vietnam.

This token force was in a sense the first Australian reciprocal military commitment under the developing Australian-American alliance. It was not increased until the beginning of 1965 when it was trebled in size to 100. On 29 April 1965, the Australian Government announced its decision to send an infantry battalion of 800 men to South Vietnam after a request for aid had been received from the South Vietnamese Government. This was subsequently raised to 4,500 and then to 8,000 men as the war escalated and massive American forces were sent to South Vietnam. A small New Zealand detachment and substantial Thai forces were also despatched to Saigon. Other members of SEATO decided not to give assistance to the South Vietnam Government.

The Australian decision to commit troops to South Vietnam was one that was taken on requests made by both Saigon and Washington in terms of the SEATO Treaty. It followed logically from the Australian view that 'the [SEATO] Treaty obligation is individual as well as collective' (Barwick), and from the Australian estimate of the changing balance of power in South-East Asia:

. . . [T]he analysis of the situation made by the Australian Government . . . has brought us to a belief that the United States action is necessary for the defeat of aggression against Asian peoples and is also an essential step towards the building in Asia of the conditions of peace and progress. . . . In South and South-East Asia, it is American armed strength which is the reality behind which the countries in that area have retained their liberty to choose their own courses. (Hasluck, 23 March 1965.)[11]

Mr Menzies as Prime Minister vigorously repudiated the idea that the United States might be allowed to go it alone, and declared that 'the take-over of South Vietnam would be a direct threat to Australia and all the countries of South and South-East Asia. It must also be seen as part of a thrust by Communist China between the Indian and Pacific oceans.' Nearly eighteen months later, Mr Hasluck told an American audience: 'Our own country is not in Vietnam because you are there. We are involved far more directly than you. If this area goes, where do you attempt to hold the line?'[12] This involved implicitly the acceptance, perhaps in a modified form, of the 'domino' theory.

The Australian Government's decision to extend its assistance to South Vietnam from communications equipment and military instructors to a substantial part of the Australian army (conscripts as well as volunteers) aroused increasing criticisms in Australia. It matched the mounting attacks on American policy in the United States itself. Mr A. G. Whitlam, then Deputy Leader of the Opposition, declared that 'the Australian people are more divided on the issue of this war than on any in which they have ever been engaged'. (10 March 1966.) The ALP at first regarded the presence of American forces in South Vietnam 'as necessary and justified as a holding operation' until such time as the people of South Vietnam could 'decide by their own votes on their own government and to ensure the physical independence of that government. . . . Co-operation between Australia and America in these areas is of crucial importance and must be maintained.' But two months later (April 1965), it strongly attacked the Government's policy of sending combat troops rather than instructors to Vietnam on political and military grounds.[13] The chief critics of government policy outside Parliament were churchmen, academics and students as well as some of the militant trade unions. 'Teach-ins' at several Australian universities generally followed the American pattern, but concentrated on broad moral issues and the situation in Vietnam itself rather than upon the Australian national interests involved or the realities of the Australian-American alliance. The federal election of December 1966, fought largely on the issue of Australian foreign policy and Australian involvement in Vietnam, gave the Holt Government a substantially increased majority over a divided Australian Labor Party. While there was little enthusiasm for the Vietnamese war, the Australian people were prepared to accept Australia's commitment to it.

The Australian-American alliance has never been a 'debatable' alliance in the broad sense of the term. From the ANZUS Treaty to Australian participation in the Vietnam war, a series of Australian governments led by Mr Menzies and Mr Holt has deliberately sought to establish closer relations between Australia and the United States. A prime factor in Australian policy has been to maintain stability in South-East and East Asia and to strengthen the American presence in this area. The Australian Labor Party initiated the war-time move towards close military collaboration with the United States and in its 1955 platform recognised that 'co-operation with the United States in the Pacific is of crucial importance and must be maintained and extended'. On 23 March 1965, when the Indonesian confrontation of Malaysia was at its peak and the war in South Vietnam was being escalated, Mr Calwell declared that 'we want the American presence, strong and powerful, in Asia and the Pacific. We want it because Australia needs it until all nations are prepared to disarm.'[14] Both Mr Calwell and his successor, Mr Whitlam, are sensitive to the charge that the Australian Labor Party is anti-American in outlook and policy. Both have indignantly repudiated Government charges to that effect.

The essential point of difference between the Government and its critics, inside and outside Parliament, has been the degree to which Australia can exert an influence on American policy and how far she can follow an independent policy of her own: how far as a middle power she must become a satellite of the United States in a world dominated by two super states. The fear was put bluntly by a member of the left-wing minority of the ALP in the debate over the ratification of the North-West Cape agreement: it 'involved a total and irrevocable commitment to the United States policy. . . . He [the Prime Minister] is binding this nation and tying it hand and foot to the United States Government, the remote men in Washington, throughout the unknown future for the next twenty-five years.'

The controversy has centred round the deductions to be drawn from the original premise of co-operation between Australia and the United States and over specific questions of policy. The cardinal point of difference has been over the role of Communist China in Asia and the means by which stability in Asia could best be maintained. The Australian Government has consistently refused to recognise Communist China or to support her admission to the United Nations. This stems from a belief that Peking is pursuing a policy of ideological or imperialistic expansion which threatens the security of the smaller states of Asia. This is a view shared by Washington but one which is contested in detail by sections of the Australian Labor Party. The Australian Government has conceded that there may be some strong reasons for recognising, *de facto* or *de jure*, the People's Republic of China but argues that recognition gave no diplomatic advantages to the United Kingdom as compared to the United States, which has consistently refused any kind of recognition. In addition, 'a consequence of recognition by Australia would be a fundamental breach of policy between Australia and the United States'.[15] At the same time the need to avoid such a breach at the diplomatic level has not prevented Australia from expanding her trade with China very considerably. That trade, primarily in wheat, does not include any important commodities on the strategic list compiled by the United States. Parallel policies have been adopted substantially towards Formosa with differences over the creation of the strategic and jurisdictional lines between Formosa and mainland China. An identical assessment, albeit an independent assessment, of China's intentions in South-East Asia lies behind the Australian Government's policy towards SEATO, Vietnam and Tibet. The ALP would prefer a significant shift from military action to economic aid in this region and the full implementation of the latent possibilities of the Pacific Charter, which was signed at the same time as the Manila Treaty in 1954.

On a number of issues there have been sharp conflicts of policy between Canberra and Washington. Professor W. Macmahon Ball and Dr Evatt had disagreed with SCAP over important aspects of occupation policy in Japan; the Japanese Peace Treaty of 1951 had been accepted with many misgivings by Australia. It reflected a Dulles rather than a Canberra line. The Suez crises of 1956 found Australia and the United States adopting diametrically opposed policies on almost every major aspect of the Canal problem. Mr Menzies attributed the failure of his Cairo mission to hostility in Washington, and on 2 November Australia was one of the minority of five opposing the American resolution urging an immediate cease-fire. Mr Casey's subsequent task in Washington was to try to repair the breach in Anglo-American relations and to restore friendly contacts between Australia and the United States. There were few differences over Lebanon, primarily because these did not threaten Australian interests in the Suez Canal and because there was joint action by London and Washington.

The collision of interests over Japan and the Suez Canal illustrated in part the strength of the traditional imperial attachment at a time when the world balance of power was rapidly changing. On a number of issues in South-East Asia, Australian policies diverged from those of the United States. In Laos, Australia supported the setting up of a broadly based neutralist coalition government under Souvanna Phouma to replace the right-wing government of Boun Oum. The American acceptance of a 'provisional government of national union', thus paving the way for the meeting of the second Geneva Conference 1962, was due in no small measure to quiet pressure from Canberra.

Indonesia reflected the differing assessment of long-term and short-term policy between the two countries. The initial American assumption that Indonesia could, over the long period, be the important stabilising factor in South-East Asia led for years to cautious support for President Sukarno and, on balance, a reluctance to effectively support the Netherlands over West New Guinea. On the other hand, Australia, while anxious to have a strong unified Indonesia as its nearest neighbour, regarded a peaceful solution of the West New Guinea question and self determination for its people as an essential condition of friendly coexistence. In the last analysis, Australia was compelled to accept the Bunker solution for West Irian when it became clear that the United States had no intention of using, or threatening to use, force against Indonesia. Both Australia and the United States were anxious to prevent Indonesian confrontation of Malaysia from opening a new theatre of war in South-East Asia. Mr Robert Kennedy's view that the dispute was largely a by-product of British colonialism and ineptitude was not shared by Canberra or by a majority of members of the State Department. The United States was primarily concerned with halting the spread of communism, while Australia was determined to preserve the territorial integrity and independence of Malaysia while at the same time continuing friendly relations with Indonesia. Washington saw the issue of Malaysia as largely a Commonwealth one with the Com-

monwealth making what defensive arrangements were necessary
for its survival. As President Sukarno moved further towards the
left, the United States gradually reduced its economic aid programme to a nominal amount by the time the 30 September—1
October coup took place in 1965.

The Australian-American alliance, then, has been flexible
enough to accommodate sharp differences of policy of the magnitude of Suez as well as the disagreements in assessments of the
situation in Laos and Indonesia. It has provided the means for
joint or parallel action in Thailand and Vietnam and towards
Peking. During the past decade, Australia has come to regard
ANZUS rather than SEATO as the more important treaty arrangement
partly because of its tighter security guarantees and partly because
it gives a more direct access to Washington.

It is difficult to determine how much room for manoeuvre there
is within the ANZUS and SEATO pacts. Britain's decision to contract
its forces east of Suez and to carry out a phased reduction of
forces or withdrawal from Singapore will limit Australia's freedom of manoeuvre. The vital limitation lies in the reality of
power. Australia is only a modest middle power with considerable
industrial potential and small armed forces. When the chips are
down on an important issue, then Australia has normally been
compelled to accept an American policy with which she disagrees:
the West New Guinea issue shows this clearly. The Australian-
American alliance, with the ANZUS Treaty as its core, does give
Australia opportunities to register differences of opinion and to
attempt to influence American policy. She can act as a bridge
between London or New Delhi or Kuala Lumpur and Washington. But these differences are normally expressed privately and
confidentially rather than in the public debate, by quiet diplomacy
rather than 'diplomacy by statements in the newspapers'. Differences are concealed not revealed and influence takes place below
water level of the iceberg. Mr Hasluck has summed it up: 'We are
an aligned state in the sense that we have allies and have committed ourselves to support certain causes, but we are more independent in our foreign policy that some nations that call themselves
non-aligned.' (Mr Menzies in 1958 was downright in his assess-

ment of the situation: 'But the fact is that we are not truly independent except in legal terms.' This is, of course, true of every State except the super-powers.)[16]

Norman Harper

[1] Melbourne *Herald*, 27 Dec. 1941.
[2] N. V. Hooker (ed.), *The Moffat Papers*, Cambridge, 1956, p. 124.
[3] C. Hartley Grattan, *The South-West Pacific Since 1950*, Ann Arbor, 1963, p. 151.
[4] Ibid., p. 164.
[5] W. K. Hancock, *Australia*, Jacaranda, 1964 ed., pp. 215-21.
[6] *Current Notes* (Department of External Affairs, Canberra), vol. 37 (1966), p. 211.
[7] Ibid., vol. 36 (1965), pp, 122-3.
[8] R. G. Casey, 'The Foreign Policy of Australia': an address to the University of Michigan, 8 Oct. 1958. *Current Notes*, vol. 29 (1958), p. 658.
[9] Gordon Greenwood and Norman Harper (eds.), *Australia in World Affairs 1950-55*, Melbourne, 1957, p. 197.
[10] *Current Notes*, vol. 33 (May 1962), p. 7; ibid., vol. 34 (June 1963), p. 5; Melbourne *Age*, 5 May 1962, 6 June 1963.
[11] *Current Notes*, vol. 36 (1965), p. 123.
[12] Gordon Greenwood and Norman Harper (eds), *Australia in World Affairs 1961-65*, Melbourne, 1968.
[13] *Commonwealth Parliamentary Debates (House of Representatives)*, 22 Mar. 1966, vol. 50, p. 446.
[14] *Australia in World Affairs 1956-60*, Melbourne, 1962, p. 233.
[15] Ibid., p. 233-4.
[16] Melbourne *Age*, 31 July 1958.

2 Partnership in Defence[*]

Since before World War II, fearing military threats from Asia,
Australia has sought to involve the United States in the defence of
the South-East Asia—South-West Pacific region. The major Japanese miscalculation of Pearl Harbour precipitated America into such
an involvement, and for the rest of the war the millions of American servicemen who visited or were stationed in Australia were
a direct manifestation of a *de facto* alliance between the two countries. The United States, by its presence and the successful campaign against Japan, ensured the security of Australia, even though
that had not come under major direct attack. America made it
impossible for Japan to invade Australia had she decided to do so.
Australia, for its part, by its existence, its food and industrial
capacity, its defence facilities, its friendship, made possible the
island-hopping operations which led back to the heart of the
Japanese empire, crumbling Japan's will and potential prior to
the *coup-de-grâce* at Hiroshima. The Australian armed forces were
perhaps small by American standards, but comprised ten per cent
of the population and played a skilful and important part in some
of the operations, especially in New Guinea. On the ground it had
been the Australian army which stopped the Japanese thrust
southwards.

World War II thus saw Australia and the United States partners
of necessity, each almost (but not totally) indispensable to the
other. In the occupation of Japan, Australia was a useful, some-

[*] Some of the points in this Chapter are taken from the writer's *Australia's
Foreign Policy*, Angus & Robertson, Sydney, 1968.

times irritating participant, making demands and expressing views not always acceptable to the Supreme Commander of the Allied Powers, but broadly supporting him in his role and task. During the late 1940's Australia, unrealistically, continued to fear what Japan might do to the peace of the area. The United States, unrealistically, saw the insurgencies through South-East Asia as being basically nationalistic reactions to effete and immoral imperialist domination. When Dean Acheson in January 1950 drew the American outer defence perimeter as lying off the Asian continent (from the Aleutians to the Ryukyus and the Philippines), he publicly excluded Korea, Hong Kong, Indo-China, Malaya and Australia. This was a warning to Australia that she should not hope for a mutual security alliance; it served notice to France and Britain that they could not expect to have their colonial chestnuts pulled out of the fire; it was an encouragement to the Chinese People's Republic to exert pressure outwards, to the nationalist-communist forces in South-East Asia to step up insurgency, and to Soviet-dominated North Korea to launch its attack across the 38th parallel.

The Korean War brought American forces onto the mainland of Asia, where they still are eighteen years later. It appeared to prove the inherently aggressive nature of 'communism', which had been contained in Europe by NATO but was operating in a partial power vacuum in Asia. President Truman did not wait for the Security Council to act before he despatched combat forces from Japan, in a specifically American reaction to the communist breach of the peace. Australia, with its Mustangs located in Japan, was quick to offer them (and naval units) in support of American ground troops, and a few weeks later was the first other state to decide to send an infantry force.

The formal alliance between the two countries and New Zealand (ANZUS) which was signed in 1951 was directly due to Korea—to the communist launching of the war, with all that implied, and to the trusty Australian response.[1] For the United States, ANZUS was only one of a series of mutual security pacts negotiated over a period of several years. For Australia, it was—as it remains—the principal guarantee of her security.

The coalition of the Liberal Party and the Country Party which came to power under Mr (later Sir) Robert Menzies in December 1949 had been preoccupied in its thinking on foreign affairs with the dangers of communism, and saw ANZUS in terms of combatting it. The Labor Party, which had been in office since 1941 and in any case included strong left-wing elements, was much more concerned with the potential threat of a rearmed Japan; ANZUS suited it accordingly. For the United States, ANZUS was the sugar coating on the pill Australia and New Zealand were being asked to swallow of a peace treaty which not only did not prevent Japan from rearming but specifically accorded her the right of 'self-defence', in terms of Article 51 of the United Nations Charter.[2] Presumably the American Administration saw some potential advantages to itself in the Australian commitment, and thought it extremely unlikely that the United States would in fact be called upon to defend Australia under the Treaty. But the main factor was to assuage Australian anxieties over (a) communist threats to the peace, and (b) enabling Japan to cease to be, of itself, a power vacuum which must be defended by the United States or go under to communist pressures from the Soviet Union and/or China. Since 1951, the Australian-American military partnership has been directly related to the threat of communism; without it there would almost certainly have been no partnership.

What is the significance of ANZUS today to Australia and the United States? Neither is committed, legally, to specific action of any kind other than consultation. The words deliberately allow considerable latitude:

Each party recognises that an armed attack in the Pacific Area on any of the parties would be dangerous to its own peace and safety and declares that it would act to meet the common danger in accordance with its constitutional processes . . .
. . . an armed attack on any of the Parties is deemed to include an armed attack on the metropolitan territory of any of the Parties, or the island territories under its jurisdiction in the Pacific, or on its armed forces, public vessels or aircraft in the Pacific.

The Preamble to the Treaty declared 'publicly and formally their sense of unity so that no potential aggressor would be under the illusion that any of [the Parties] stand alone in the Pacific Area'.

This adds up to a much more formidable moral than military commitment, but it is a moral commitment to military action. Certainly, nothing is automatic about the application of the Treaty. If any member invokes it, the others will consider the request in the light of the circumstances at the time, and their other commitments or preoccupations. But it is a totally unjustifiable assumption that the Treaty therefore has no binding force. In none of the three member states could a government avoid accountability for taking a reasonable measure of military action in the event of an armed attack on one of the others. Each, and especially the United States, has publicly reiterated on several occasions over the years that it would do so. But the nature of such action is left for each to determine.

Australians, for obvious reasons, mainly think and talk of ANZUS in terms of what the United States would do if Australia were threatened or attacked. Australian assistance to the United States will rarely be anything but marginal; American assistance to Australia could well be decisive. The United States is not likely to send forces to defend Australia or Australian dependent territories unless the situation is one which Australia cannot meet from her own or other resources. If there is a situation where Australia or Papua-New Guinea is under substantial attack, then both the Australian and American Governments understand that American military aid would be quickly rendered. Similarly one could not easily imagine Australia staying aloof if the United States were engaged in major operations of war threatening its survival. But doubt has arisen and could again arise, in the public mind at least, in a number of cases less clear-cut than these.

The first such case was in April 1954 when Australia (among others) was invited to consider participating in a joint Western intervention in the Indo-China war. She firmly declined.[3] The following year Australian ground and naval forces were sent to Malaya (there were already air force units there) to help combat the communist insurgency and for the external defence of the country. Before sending them, Menzies sought assurances from the United States of American military assistance of some kind in an emergency. From his later public statement on the subject, it would seem that he was only given assurances of the most general kind of such effective 'cooperation' as was 'implicit in the Manila Pact' (see below). ANZUS was not mentioned.[4] Very understandably, the United States was not going to accept responsibility for the security of a relatively small Australian force operating in conjunction with substantial British forces in a British dependency at a time when the insurgency in which they were involved was on the wane. There was no external threat to Malaya at the time. Once Malaya became independent (in 1957), the cooperation would scarcely be implicit unless Malaya joined SEATO, which she has not so far done. Later in the year, Menzies made it clear that he did not feel that the off-shore islands such as Quemoy, Matsu, and others were worth a major war, but he did not say that Australia would refuse to stand by the United States under ANZUS if she became involved in a war with China over the islands.

The dispute between Indonesia and the Netherlands over West Irian (West New Guinea) erupted into restrained but open conflict in late 1961 and early 1962. Australia had never formally taken sides in the dispute, but had sought and obtained assurances from Indonesia that she would not use force to obtain control of the territory. These assurances proved invalid. There was little doubt that the Australian Government and Opposition both preferred a Netherlands administration, and both saw West New Guinea as strategically of considerable importance to Australia. Whatever representations were made to the United States, the latter was plainly unwilling, ANZUS or no ANZUS, to support Australia or the Netherlands (a NATO partner) in physically resisting Indonesia's bid for control.

Indonesian confrontation of Malaysia was a different matter. Here was no hunted band of insurgents (as in the Malayan emergency), but—behind the points of contact—an army of 350,000, a navy larger than Australia's, an air force with the latest Soviet fighters, directly opposed to a country with which Australia had a direct military association. It has not been revealed at what stage Australia sought to have ANZUS applied or applicable to this situation. The Prime Minister announced Australia's commitment to the defence of all Malaysia (i.e., including the Borneo states) on 25 September 1963, but the decision to send ground forces (at first, engineers) to Borneo was not made until the following April, coinciding with a public declaration by the Australian Minister for External Affairs on behalf of a silent United States Government that Borneo was 'in the Pacific Area' for the purposes of ANZUS.[5] Sir Garfield Barwick, the Minister concerned, was enjoying a brief period in politics between two distinguished careers in law. Whether or not he was wise, diplomatic or responsible in making the announcement, it is highly improbable that he was inaccurate. This does not mean that the United States was ready to launch into the confrontation conflict on the side of the Australians. On the contrary, the American administration was at pains to indicate that Malaysia was a Commonwealth responsibility. But it does seem clear that Washington was warning Djakarta that, in the last resort, it would intervene if necessary to prevent an Indonesian take-over of Malaysia, as of Papua-New Guinea.

This point has become of greater moment with the announcement of the British timetable of withdrawal from its bases in Malaysia and Singapore. Australia has not yet clarified its future intentions in the area, including the role of its forces located in Malaysia or the waters nearby. At present the Suharto Government is preoccupied with internal problems and is determined to be internationally respectable. Apart from its own desires in the matter, it is under strong economic restraint, especially from the United States, not to launch any external military operations. This may not always remain the case. Neither the United States nor Australia, for sound political reasons, has ever hinted at what would be the American reaction to a renewal of confrontation once the British have withdrawn. But, other things being equal, if Malaysia were 'in the Pacific Area' for the purposes of ANZUS at a time when there were large British forces there, Australia could reasonably hope, in the absence of any declaration to the contrary, that it would be no less relevant to ANZUS after the British have left.

Papua-New Guinea is in a different situation. The wording of the Treaty clearly applies to it so long as it is an 'island territory under [Australia's] jurisdiction'. Yet it is likely to become an independent state within perhaps ten years. When it does, *it* ceases to be covered by ANZUS, unless the Treaty is amended. But should Australia maintain 'armed forces, public vessels or aircraft' in the territory, *they* would presumably still be covered, at least in principle.

Britain's departure from Asia raises the question as to whether the Western seaboard of Australia is 'in the Pacific Area'. Whatever the geographical terminological ambiguities of the South China Sea, the Indian Ocean is scarcely in the Pacific. Yet the United States is not going to mark a point on Australia's north coast and say that she would be happy to resist any attack to the east of that spot but would be unable to assist if the enemy were smart enough to land a few miles to the westward. In August 1965, the Australian Minister for External Affairs gave Parliament his 'confidential assurance that Western Australia certainly would be regarded as one of the regions coming within the ambit of the ANZUS Treaty'.[6] When it was first drafted, ANZUS did appear to leave (implicitly) to Britain a major responsibility for the defence of Australia's western seaboard and lines of communication. When Britain no longer has the capacity to exercise that responsibility, Australia must surely make greater efforts of its own. To expect American power to move right in and fill the vacuum is asking more than the United States has indicated it is prepared to accept. Under Article II of the Treaty, each of the Parties undertook to provide 'continuous and effective self-help', and an individual (as well as collective) capacity to resist attack. The United States thus reasonably required of Australia that she make an adequate attempt to provide for her own security. The more America is locked in a land war in Asia, the more self-help she would be likely to expect of Australia.

ANZUS has no headquarters, no permanent consultative machinery, no forces in being. Presumably a certain amount of contingency planning is agreed to at the regular meetings of the military representatives, perhaps also some allocation of responsibility or roles to the different forces of the three nations. But it is very much a commitment *in posse*, an undertaking to act in the future if threats are sufficiently large and circumstances are appropriate.

Australia has not simply been a consumer of security under ANZUS; she has also been a producer. The most obvious manifestation of this is the naval radio communications station at North-West Cape in Western Australia, which has the special capacity of communicating with submerged missile-firing submarines in the Indian Ocean. The station is maintained and conducted solely by the United States, although its facilities are available to Australian ships. Sole American control was a political issue for a time in Australia, the Labor opposition asserting that if it were returned to power it would renegotiate the Treaty. There was also the fear that the station might be used, without Australia's foreknowledge or consent, to launch a nuclear war. The Government's position was that the station's location was an Australian contribution under ANZUS, and the station itself would enable the United States better to perform her Treaty obligations. Without sole control there would have been no station, since no government can permit another to control or examine its secret radio messages. The station was not for initiating American policy decisions, but for relaying them, making it more likely that messages would be received as sent, thus reducing the risk of a war inadvertently launched.

By its nature, North-West Cape is presumably a planned target for Soviet and Chinese nuclear missiles. It is thus the most dramatic manifestation of the interlocking of American and Australian military strategies and activities. It fixes Australia within the American world-wide security system, providing added protection at the cost of added risk.

ANZUS, it is often said, has given Australia access to American military thinkers and planners at the top level. It does not give Australia access to all America's military secrets. Australia is very much a junior partner: ANZUS is one of many American treaties. But it assures the Australian Government of the opportunity for discussion on a wide range of political and military topics, for special pleading and private representations. It has never carried any assurance that such representations would be successful. As a treaty, the fact that it demands so little of its members in the present is probably an assurance of its continuity. It is only a part of the system of arrangements between Australia and the United States, but it is the basic part, the principal rationale, the public declaration of intent, the touchstone of good faith.

It is not easy to be sure of the present or future significance of SEATO. From Australia's point of view, it did one vital thing: it interposed the United States between Communist China and Australia's non-communist neighbours in South-East Asia. From America's angle, SEATO provided for joint efforts at containing communism north of the 17th parallel—it spread the responsibility and the effort. Yet SEATO was founded on the assumption of agreement as to objectives, priorities and commitments, and this assumption was proved wrong first by Pakistan, then France, then Britain. The Laos crisis of 1961 effectively demonstrated the limits which most if not all SEATO members placed on their readiness either to contribute forces to SEATO operations or to agree on joint measures to be taken. The Rusk-Khoman agreement of 1962 (officially echoed in Australia), by which responsibilities under the Treaty were deemed to be individual as well as collective, saved SEATO from atrophy but it became essentially a context, a rationale for individual action rather than a machinery for common endeavour. Its deliberations are notoriously insecure.

Even formally, SEATO is in many ways weaker than ANZUS. In the event of 'aggression by means of armed attack' against one of the Parties, the others undertake to 'act to meet the common danger in accordance with . . . constitutional processes'. There is no mention of attacks on island dependencies, armed forces, public vessels or aircraft. The Treaty specifically excludes Taiwan, Hong Kong, and the Chinese off-shore islands. The United States in a protocol to the Treaty entered a caveat that it would take action only if the attack were a communist one. Unlike ANZUS, SEATO provided for the Parties to meet and agree on measures to be taken where a member felt it was threatened by subversion. There is no evidence that effective measures have been implemented under this article.

SEATO provided the opportunity, as ANZUS did not, for a wide range of continuing contacts between Australians and Americans —between ambassadors, planning and research staff—and for periodic other meetings and joint military exercises. These contacts will often have taken place in a wider, multi-national context, but this has not reduced their bilateral importance. In fact the less confident relationship with other members (except the United Kingdom and New Zealand) has served to emphasise the more intimate inner grouping. SEATO thus put flesh and bones on the skeleton relationship of ANZUS; it increased the points of contact at all levels up to the Foreign Minister.

SEATO was designed in 1954 with the prime objective of saving what was left of Indo-China from being over-run by communist forces. The three states were not members of SEATO—they could not be under the terms of the 1954 Geneva settlement, but were covered by its provisions to the extent that they so wished. In 1961–62, the SEATO powers acquiesced in the *de facto* division of Laos also into communist and non-communist areas, thus assuring the North Vietnamese secure routes (the Ho Chi Minh Trail) for arms, equipment and men down through eastern Laos into South Vietnam. The second Geneva conference neutralised Laos, thus removing it from the provisions of SEATO. (Cambodia had removed herself several years earlier.) One can argue at length whether the early American actions in South Vietnam came strictly within the terms of SEATO. They did not contravene it, and were clearly within the spirit of the Treaty, as was the Australian contribution. As North Vietnam intervened overtly in the situation, the American and Australian operations were more surely a reaction to the 'aggression by means of armed attack' to which the Treaty referred. SEATO as an organisation at first acquiesced in and subsequently authorised these operations,[7] although it did not take a collective decision to take collective action for the simple reason that several members were not prepared to be committed to either.

As in Korea, so in Vietnam, Australia was the first country to range itself alongside the United States. New Zealand followed as did, somewhat later, heavily subsidised forces of South Korea (not a SEATO member), the Philippines, and Thailand. For Australia at least, although her contribution was comparatively small, and although it was justified by the Government in vague terms as 'flowing from' its SEATO obligations and as related to the demands made by Australia's 'alliances'[8] (i.e. presumably including ANZUS), it was a larger and less congenial bite than she had originally calculated to chew under SEATO. The United States had made the Treaty possible, had been its principal guarantor, but France and Britain were also committed. In the event, when operations of war became necessary if the Treaty was to mean anything, neither France nor Britain was prepared to do anything, and nor, for several years, were the Asian members themselves. Australia saw SEATO as engaging the protective power of the United States at one remove from the Australian continent, in the defence of small Asian States whose security was related to Australia's but not vital to it. She found herself involved in operations of war in the context of SEATO but not because of SEATO—rather through the urgent representations of the United States, and without the company of the Asian treaty partners (the Philippines and Thailand came in later).

In justifying its Vietnam intervention to its electors, the Australian Government has more than once asserted that Australia stands to gain more than the United States from American participation in the war. This is not, of course, how the American Government speaks of its intervention. The United States is not in Vietnam on behalf of Australia, or at Australia's request. The Australian national interest has been irrelevant to the American decisions to provide successively instructors, protective troops, combat troops, air and naval forces in increasing quantity, or to American pressure on Australia to go and do likewise. It may be true—though it is hard to see how one would measure it—that Australia stands to gain more than the United States from American successes in Vietnam. If it is true, then Australia conversely stands to lose more from any American lack of success.

In Vietnam, the Australian force first operated within an

American formation. Now, being larger, it has its own area of operations, except for the naval component. Perhaps the Australian Task Force would make its most effective contribution to the war if it were able to be deployed wherever the American commander so wished, but the Force itself and many Australians at home would take some convincing on this point. It is widely accepted that the Force, small as it is, and although it has not had to face strong North Vietnamese units, has been almost a model of what is required in this kind of warfare.

The SEATO organisation continues to function because the American Government wishes it to function. It is not totally ineffective: various kinds of military and technical aid are rendered under it. It is still the principal guarantee of the security of Thailand. It is still ostensibly the context, the wrapping for the Vietnam commitment, but the wrapping is getting thinner all the time.

If SEATO is today less effective and less plausible than it has ever been, is there a possible alternative? Occasional meetings of the non-Communist participants in the war—South Vietnam, the United States, Australia, New Zealand, South Korea, the Philippines, Thailand—provide opportunities to set (or announce) guidelines, to declare the aims, methods or limits of operations. They thus do one of the tasks for which SEATO was intended, but they do not constitute a replacement organisation for SEATO. It is unlikely for political reasons that a new treaty could be negotiated. Neither the United States nor Australia would seem keen to enter new commitments in Asia, or even into new formal statements of existing involvements.

ANZUS and SEATO are the principal defence treaties linking Australia and the United States, but there are many others of a specialised nature, not all of which have been made public. Australia adhered to the military standardisation agreement between America, Britain and Canada, and over the past five years has stepped up its purchase of American equipment. Project 'Mallard' is a programme for joint development of communications, whose details have not been released. Even more secret are the activities of a

Joint Space Research Facility at Alice Springs, in central Australia. Two major purchases have been of twenty-four F-111 aircraft and three *Charles F. Adams* guided-missile destroyers. Australia is not totally dependent on American equipment, having bought substantial items from Britain, France, and Italy. Whatever American industry may believe, it would be extremely unfortunate if Australia or any other country (except perhaps Canada) came to be wholly dependent on American military production.

Since 1949, the military partnership with the United States has been, in the eyes of the Australian Government, the *sine qua non* of continued and assured survival. A majority of the electorate probably shares this view, and accepts the need to 'stand and be counted' with the United States from time to time. Yet many Australians react against an over-effusive deference to anyone at all, even to so friendly and powerful an ally. In June 1966, the Prime Minister, Mr Holt, took up a slogan used in President Johnson's election campaign, and said at the White House that Australia was 'all the way with LBJ'. Later he declared that this related to Vietnam, but the public effect of his statement was to indicate a wider and more total identification. Even on his own terms, he implied that Australian policy on Vietnam lacked any flexibility, and that Australia was prepared to go along with whatever the United States did there. This is neither sensible nor correct. On other occasions, Australian ministers have displayed an adherence to some of the more rigid or more militant aspects of American policy. They have appeared to oppose negotiations with communist authorities under any circumstances, when some members of the American administration, as well as its critics, were advocating them. Australia has publicly encouraged the United States to continue bombing North Vietnam, despite the contentious nature of these operations, and their uncertain military and political value. The effect of these declamations by Australian leaders has been to suggest either that they are frightened to criticise the United States, for one reason or another, or that they are less interested in the outcome of the war than in keeping American forces engaged on the Asian mainland. By being so 'loyal', Australia may be gaining presidential or public goodwill, but it is also making it harder for the United States to change its policy should it wish to do so.

Querulous criticism of the United States, which is its common lot, has little point or purpose. But total acceptance of American policies can be equally counterproductive. An ally which does not warn against an erroneous policy is no friend and is a bad ally. Some American policies in South-East Asia have been erroneous and unfortunate. It would have been more helpful if the American Government has been told this by a close friend than by public critics with different loyalties or objectives. The first responsibility of each government is to its own people, and neither government has the right to forfeit independence of judgment or action, even where it fully believes the general policy of alliance to be in the national interest.

Australia is in Vietnam partly because it supports the right of the South Vietnamese people to choose their own form of government without being subject to communist terrorism. It is in SEATO partly because it believes that smaller countries such as Thailand and the Philippines—and Australia—have the right to survive. It believes also that the communist subjugation of these Asian States would constitute a strategic threat to Australia. But the main rationale of Australia's actions, of being in SEATO and ANZUS, of going 'all the way', is the assumption that Australia will thereby earn the support of the United States should an emergency threaten Australia at some time in the future. There is no way of telling whether this assumption is correct, but it would seem more reasonable than to believe either that, irrespective of formal alliances, Australia is vital to the United States, who will always protect her, *or* that Australia is entirely expendable.

Another consideration which weighs with both the Australian and the American governments is that America finds it easier to justify being involved in the defence of South-East Asia if countries in the region, including Australia, play their part. Yet the size of that part is also relevant. In 1967 there was thinly-veiled American criticism of Australia over the extent of its participation in the war. How do you assess what kind of contribution will satisfy the 'great and powerful friend' and ensure its practical sympathy in a situation ten years hence? There is no answer to this.

Australia and the United States have different priorities and preoccupations, and it is only natural that the United States should wish Australia to adopt the American viewpoint. At present the Vietnam war almost fills the horizon of American foreign and defence policy. Yet Australia has two other areas of concern which cannot be neglected for Vietnam. As British air and seapower moves out of the Indian Ocean, Australian air and seapower must prepare to move in. This is not because there is an immediate threat to Australia or its lines of communication across the Indian Ocean, but because there are several potential threats, notably from the Soviet Union and Communist China, against which preparations need to be made now. Australia has forces in Malaysia which are not now needed either to combat communist terrorism or to withstand Indonesian confrontation. But the situation is far from stable, and for Australia to withdraw her armed services from the area would be a factor making for instability, a gesture of renunciation. It would be much easier on some later occasion to make forces available if they are stationed in the area than if they have left and must return. However much advantage, therefore, either the American or Australian Government may see in Australia's concentrating its external effort on Vietnam, it would not in fact be in the best interest either of Australia or the security of the region.

Australia is very much the junior partner in the alliance—something many Australians tend to forget. Sometimes, as in the Mutual Weapons Development Programme Agreement of 1960, this juniority is unduly or unnecessarily emphasised. The United States does not drive its bargains any less hard with its allies. It patently took advantage of Australia's political situation and lack of negotiating expertise over the F-111 deal. It has sought a more privileged status for its forces than it is prepared to accord. It has pushed through sales of less than first-rate military equipment, and has brought heavy pressure to deter the production in allied countries of competitive items. These actions are a function of its size and political make-up, and the obligation lies on the junior partner to be equally hard-headed, sophisticated and expert.

The disparity in size, in manpower and economic power, between the United States and Australia is related to differences in military philosophy. An Australian commander who had at his disposal the pipeline of reinforcements available to his American counterpart might become equally unconcerned about high casualty rates. In fact he does not have that pipeline; he cannot afford to be unconcerned. Every man must be husbanded, must therefore be as highly trained as possible before he goes into battle. Similarly, the large-scale operations and the 'computer mentality' demand big results—big casualties inflicted on the enemy, big numbers of defections by him, big areas plastered with bombs or 'cleared' of insurgency. These demands place an immense strain on individual commanders at all levels, and result—in the Vietnam context—in things being done which may be productive of individual promotion but are counterproductive in terms of the overall situation. The American military machine has been developed and is geared, physically and mentally, to fight a frontal war on the plains of Europe. Australians may indeed be grateful that this machine has been brought to bear on an Asian situation, and that the United States is prepared to expend mighty effort and make large sacrifices in a situation so relevant to Australian defence. Unfortunately it still has to be shown whether the mistakes made will not outweigh the value contributed. This is why Australia must retain its separate contribution though equally involved, must maintain as far as possible its independence of action, tactics and approach.

Every military partnership has its problems, and the one between the United States and Australia has remarkably few. It is carried on in an atmosphere of unusual trust and goodwill, each treating the other as being in many respects less than foreign. Perhaps the disparity in power, which has its own difficulties, is on balance productive of better relations; the two states do not compete for influence, for the right to determine general policy, or for priority in manufacturing major items of equipment. They speak roughly the same language—literally and metaphorically—and have many important values in common, have similar basic objectives.

The interlocking defence relationship extends beyond purely military aspects, notably to the space tracking facilities established in Australia, which are part of the American programme of satellite surveillance of the earth and earth surveillance of Soviet satellites, some of which undoubtedly have a military role. The defence functions of these tracking facilities are likely to increase rather than decrease. The United States is also contributing to a small Australian space research operation.

Through these activities and the North-West Cape station, rather than specifically through ANZUS or SEATO, Australia has become an important part of the American defence establishment, making American protection more essential to America's own interests. But on the same basis, as mentioned, Australia has become much more certainly a target for Soviet or Chinese nuclear missiles in the event of global war. And to the extent that, in such a war, Australia would not be expendable to the United States, she is a potential hostage. Large numbers of American troops in Europe, plus their families, reduced the likelihood that the United States would consider to be expendable the countries where they have been stationed. There is only a handful of American servicemen in Australia.

Does ANZUS extend to protection against nuclear threat or attack? One must assume that the Treaty is *as* valid under nuclear as under non-nuclear circumstances, but no more. This is probably sufficient assurance for the Australian Government; it is insufficient for some Australians, who want to see their country develop or acquire its own nuclear deterrent, regardless of cost. In the present state of the partnership, and of American legislation, the United States would be unprepared to help Australia to do either. In Australian eyes, such understandable reluctance places upon the United States a larger responsibility for protecting Australia in a nuclear situation.

The partnership which began with a concept of conventional military assistance in the event of remote and almost hypothetical situations has moved right into the nuclear-space era of defence. It has matured with very little acrimony on either side. Because it has moved with the times and matured, it would probably survive almost any challenge, including an American withdrawal under pressure from the Asian mainland, or a change of government in either Washington or Canberra.

T. B. Millar

[1] This point is elaborated authoritatively by Sir Alan Watt, *The Evolution of Australian Foreign Policy 1938–1965* Cambridge, 1967, pp. 120–4.

[2] 'Nothing in the present Charter shall impair the inherent right of individual or collective self-defence if an armed attack occurs against a member of the United Nations . . .'. Japan was not of course a member of the United Nations until 1956.

[3] R. G. Casey in Parliament, 10 Aug. 1954. *Commonwealth Parliamentary Debates*, (House of Representatives), vol. 4, p. 97.

[4] *Com. Parl. Debs. (H. of R.)*, 20 April 1955, vol. 6, pp. 52–3.

[5] See official transcript of Sir Garfield Barwick's press conference in Sydney, 17 April 1964.

[6] *Com. Parl. Debs. (H. of R.)*, 18 Aug. 1965, vol. 47, p. 516.

[7] See final communiqués of SEATO Council meetings: 10 April 1963, 15 April 1964, 5 May 1965.

[8] See statements by the Minister for External Affairs on 20 October 1964 and the Prime Minister on 29 April 1965. *Com. Parl. Debs. (H. of R.)*, vol. 44, p. 2131, vol. 45, p. 1060–62.

3 Partnership in Trade

The title of this chapter seems to fit rather easily into a trilogy of political alliance, active collaboration in defence and of growing relations in the economic field. It seems right that political and military partnership should be matched by a partnership in trade. Moreover, when economic partnership is deliberately encouraged by the governments concerned, it is for the same reason as partnership developed in the political and military field: national interest.

Nevertheless, the word has to be used carefully. In the first place, partnership may imply a smoother relationship than in fact exists. Indeed, I have elsewhere described Australian-American trading relations as reflecting all too often bilateral conflict within agreement on general principles.[1] However, the fact that there may be strains in an economic partnership does not, except perhaps in degree, differentiate the economic from the political and military; for these latter partnerships are not without stress.

A difference of greater substance between the political alliance and military tie on the one hand, and the economic partnership on the other, is in the way they develop. The former normally come about by inter-governmental agreement, backed, both governments hope, by the necessary measure of public support expressed in Parliament and Congress. Trade, however, while much influenced by the 'climate' created by the governments, occurs because under any given set of conditions (tariffs, profit prospects, comparative costs, etc.) it pays individuals and companies to trade. Some part of our trade is influenced directly by government decisions (e.g. defence orders or purchase of equipment for public enterprises); but the greater part takes place because of decisions made by private entrepreneurs, exercising economic judgments in relation to profitability.

The United States could almost eliminate her foreign trade if she chose to do so; Australia could not. The value of United States' imports is only some 3 per cent of her Gross National Product; in Australia's case the percentage is about 14 per cent and is vastly more vital to her whole economic development programme. None of the giants—United States, Russia or the European Common Market—chooses to try to be completely self-sufficient. In Australia's case there are many goods—capital equipment and raw materials—which Australia cannot produce or can produce only at great and unwarranted cost in resources. Moreover, while producing most consumer goods for herself the range available is enlarged by imports. To pay for these imports, mostly essential, Australia uses her natural resources and skill to develop export industries. Thus Australia trades because it is in her interests to do so—as do all her trading 'partners', whether large or small.[2]

As already noted this trade is largely promoted by individual producers, companies and organised marketing boards. Nevertheless, Government policies provide a framework which can be encouraging or stifling and there is much in Australian-American trade relations to illustrate both forms. It is because governments provide a policy framework that examination of trade relations cannot usefully be confined to a study of the actual exchange of goods and services in any one period of time: there is need to know why the trade occurs and in what ways government policies influence decisions to trade. Australia's economic development calls for and benefits from trade with the United States; governmental policy is an important factor in the actual trade pattern; conflict often occurs when declared policies are stood aside by governments in favour of some 'national' interest which may often be sectional in character; and trading relations, like political and military relations, can be greatly improved by a bilateral treaty covering economic relations.

The general theme of the chapter is therefore one that accepts the title, but notes conflicts within the partnership. The chapter also stresses that trading partnership is not limited to the direct or bilateral exchange of goods but is also reflected in policy alignments or differences between Australia and United States *vis à vis* the rest of the trading world.*

In the 'thirties Australian trade relations with the United States were anything but cordial, being dominated by the Ottawa Agreement of 1932. The series of Ottawa Agreements† between the United Kingdom and the Dominions represented their reaction to the Great Depression. They greatly enlarged the existing policy of mutual preference in trade as a means of offsetting the disastrous collapse in prices in 1929 in the export markets in the United Kingdom for primary markets and the fall in associated exports of United Kingdom manufactures. The period was marked by a highly protectionist tariff, the Hawley-Smoot tariff, introduced in 1930 by the United States, and by hardly less severe barriers to trade erected by other countries, too.

Our concern is not with the details of the Ottawa Agreement[3] nor with its doubtful contribution to total world trade recovery, but with the principles of trade policy it appeared to establish as the basis both for the conduct of Australian trade and for the development of her industry. The United Kingdom was easily the major market for Australian goods, taking in the 1930-32 period over 47 per cent of our exports. It was also our major source of capital inflow, both publicly borrowed and private. Not unnaturally Australia looked to the United Kingdom for help when the prices of wool, wheat and other products collapsed. The Ottawa Agreement gave that help in the form of assured free entry for

* This latter relationship shows up in places like GATT—the organisation administering the General Agreement on Tariffs and Trade—and UNCTAD—the United Nations Conference on Trade and Development—as well as in the general political forum of the United Nations.

† These were all bilateral: United Kingdom-Australia; United Kingdom-Canada; United Kingdom-Australia; Australia-Canada, etc., but all reflected the system of mutual preferences especially directed, in effect, against non-British trade.

most of Australia's primary exports, supported in many instances by preferential advantages which were established or increased by imposing new or higher duties against competitive goods from 'foreign' sources such as the United States. These preferences have remained of considerable importance to certain Australian industries such as dairying, dried and canned fruit and canned meat. Indeed, it can be said that much irrigation settlement developed in the early post World War II period in Australia has been heavily dependent on these preferences.

It is doubtful if the Agreement itself lifted total trade in the 'thirties, any recovery in prices being due to recovery in investment and employment in Britain, Europe and America rather than directly to the Ottawa Agreements. They did however strengthen the Australian-New Zealand and Canadian competitive position in the United Kingdom at the expense of competitors like America, Denmark and Argentina whose reaction was understandably one of protest.

American hostility was not only directed to the grant of new and wider preferences by the United Kingdom to Australia (and the other partners to the Ottawa Agreements), but also to the considerable preferences extended to British exports in the Australian market. Moreover, the Australian policy of tariff protection was so shaped by tariffs and import controls as to minimise the effect on British exports, attempting to divert the main brunt to non-British suppliers.[4] Under the Ottawa Agreement Australia undertook to provide margins of preference of 15 per cent and upwards, according to a formula laid down.*[5] In fact preferences on a great many items of industrial manufacture remained greater than the formula required.

The other obligations assumed by Australia were to grant protection to Australian industries 'reasonably assured of sound opportunities for success' and to base the tariff on the principle that protective duties should not exceed such a level as would give United Kingdom producers full opportunity of reasonable com-

---

* Shorn of technicalities the 'margin of preference' can be regarded as the difference between duties payable on British goods entering Australia (British Preferential Tariff) and those paid by suppliers not enjoying a preferential position (mostly the 'Most Favoured Nations' suppliers). See later definition.

petition. This became, and has remained for almost four decades, a basic principle in Australian tariff making.[6] The preferential system ensured the minimum level of tariff against non-British sources once the British Preferential Tariff was determined. This system certainly operated strongly against American suppliers.

The principles of Ottawa were somewhat gratuitously and foolishly reinforced by the ill-conceived trade diversion policy implemented against the United States and Japan in 1936.[4] Again we need not be concerned with detail. The venture was fortunately short-lived. It reflected an effort through import licensing (especially directed against the United States) and by similarly discriminating tariff duties to develop Australian industry (and especially the automobile industry) without hurt to British interests. To justify this policy it was argued that Australia had an unfavourable balance of trade with the United States. This was a particularly poor argument since it overlooks that fact that the arithmetic that counts is total trade and that, in any case, it could be used by others (e.g. Japan) against Australia. The real intention was protective within the framework of marked preference for Britain.

Our pre-war story must stop here. By 1939 relations with the United States had improved a little and some concessions were made by the United Kingdom to the United States at Australia's expense (e.g. the preference for Australian wheat was abolished) and with Australian understanding.[4] Australia's readiness to be more conciliatory was dictated, in part, by hopes of concluding a trade treaty of its own with America. These hopes were at least suspended by war which, however, brought other great changes to the international framework of Australian trade policy, changes which have proved of great importance in understanding the development of American influence in Australian economic development. As we shall see there were already evident in the pre-war years strong reasons for the emergence of the United States as a major influence in Australian development. In 1937–38 the United States and Canada took only 8·3 per cent of Australian exports but despite the heavy discrimination against the States, Canada and the United States supplied 22·6 per cent of Australian imports. These were mainly producer goods and reflected the advanced technology of the States—a matter of great importance to Australia just beginning its development as an industrial nation.

The next part of our story commences with Article VII of The Mutual Aid Agreement between the United States and Australia of September 1942[7] which was based on an earlier and similar agreement between the United Kingdom and the United States setting out the conditions of mutual aid in prosecuting the war against Germany and Japan. It was, of course, vital to Australia which readily agreed to the declaration of post-war economic aims contained in the Agreement. The signatories agreed in Article VII to take action

directed to the expansion, by appropriate international and domestic measures, of production, employment, and the exchange and consumption of goods, which are the material foundations of the liberty and welfare of all peoples; to the elimination of all forms of discriminatory treatment in international commerce; and to the reduction of tariffs and other trade barriers.

There is little doubt that this article meant for the United States a pledge to bring discriminatory trade systems* like the Ottawa Agreements to an end. In giving the undertaking to join in the action prescribed in Article VII there is likewise little doubt that the Australian Government, in no position to refuse, feared that it could mean this. Indeed, one well informed group of observers considered that the requirements of the Article stood 'in flat contradiction to Australia's historic policy of protection and preference . . .'.[8]

The full story of the implementation of Article VII leading in

---

* The Ottawa Agreements were discriminatory: they differ from the Free Trade Areas and Customs Union systems allowable in GATT and represented by the Common Market (= a Customs Union) and European Free Trade Area (Austria, Denmark, Norway, Portugal, Sweden, Switzerland and the United Kingdom). The difference is that in the Ottawa Systems tariffs were raised against non-members while in the European examples to-day the members seek free trade among themselves by abolishing barriers between them *without* (at least in respect of industrial products) raising tariffs against non-members.

1947 to the General Agreement on Tariffs and Trade is too long to be retold here.[9] This Agreement has provided the principal international framework for Australian trade policy in relation to most other countries with which it trades. In particular the terms of the Agreement represent the point of reference against which decisions by the American or Australian Governments affecting the trade relations of the two countries are likely to be judged by the two partners.

Contrary to war-time expectations promoted by Article VII of the Mutual Aid Agreements in 1942, GATT did not abolish existing preferences but it did ban, and has effectively prevented, the development of new preferences. The 'no new preference' rule has been a factor in the 'retreat from Ottawa' a term I have used elsewhere to describe the course of Australia's post-war policy. The existing agreements were not killed, but new life could not easily again be injected into the Ottawa agreements. There were, in any case, other basic factors in the retreat from Ottawa. These can be summed up as: (a) the decline in significance of Great Britain as a market for Australian exports and as a supplier of its imports in the circumstances of Australia's dynamic growth (Britain did, however, remain an important source of capital); (b) the emergence of Japan as a major replacement of Britain as a market and, less dramatically, as a supplier of goods to Australia; and (c) the growth of the United States as a market and its development as the most significant supplier of capital goods, technological know-how and financial capital.

Other aspects of the GATT rules which are relevant to the rest of our story include its recognition of tariffs as an instrument of protection; its general ban on non-tariff devices (such as direct import restrictions) except in approved circumstances; its provision that any tariff concession made by one member of GATT to any trading partner must be extended to all members of GATT; and, not least, Article XXIV which provides for special trading blocks in the form of Customs Unions or Free Trade Areas.[10] Contrary to much popular belief GATT does not ban tariffs although it encourages their reduction and elimination by negotiation. Moreover, it makes no distinction, in its rules about tariffs and in its ban on import restrictions, between trade in agricultural and industrial products—a point of considerable importance in understanding the course of the American-Australian trading partnership.

In accepting Article VII and the consequent international machinery for governing world trade, Australia had set its back not only on further developments of the Ottawa system but also on fresh attempts at discrimination against the United States like that tried so ineffectively in 1936. But the United States also accepted the new principles and in understanding much of the conflict that has occurred between the two partners, this important point must not be overlooked.

We now examine the actual trade pattern that has developed between the two countries and look at some of the difficulties in their relations against the background of pre-war and post-war treaties and policies just outlined.

Tables 1–3 and Figures 1 and 2 give some idea of the course and pattern of trade between the two countries. It can be seen that pre-war the United States was an important market for Australian goods and an important supplier even then of capital goods. In the early post-war period it was not a strong market and was prevented from showing its strength as a supplier because of restrictions imposed by Australia on purchases requiring scarce dollar currency.[11] By 1966–67 the relative important of the United States as an export market had not fully recovered ground although, of course, the absolute monetary value of American imports had greatly increased.

The most striking post-war change shown in Figure 2 is the large rise in the American share of Australian imports—from 10·0 per cent in 1948–49 to 25·1 per cent in 1966–67. This reflects the abolition of all remaining Australian dollar import restrictions in February 1960 and the growing importance of the United States as a supplier of capital goods and components. This is due in part to the undoubted competitive ability of American firms in this field but also the growth of American investment in Australia and the purchase by Australian firms of American 'know-how'. Not all

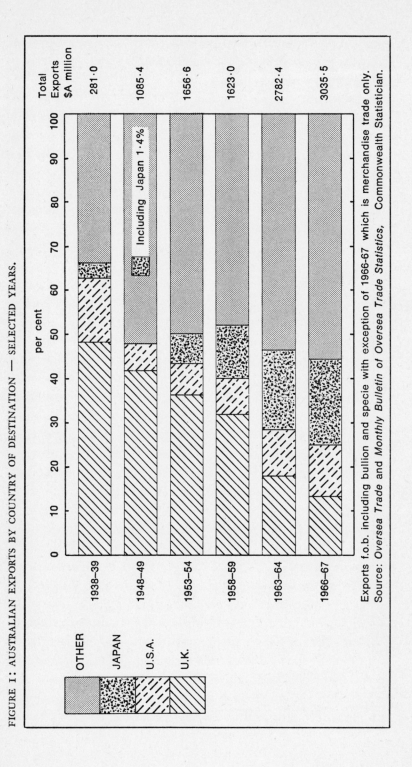

FIGURE I: AUSTRALIAN EXPORTS BY COUNTRY OF DESTINATION — SELECTED YEARS.

Exports f.o.b. including bullion and specie with exception of 1966-67 which is merchandise trade only.
Source: *Oversea Trade* and *Monthly Bulletin of Oversea Trade Statistics*, Commonwealth Statistician.

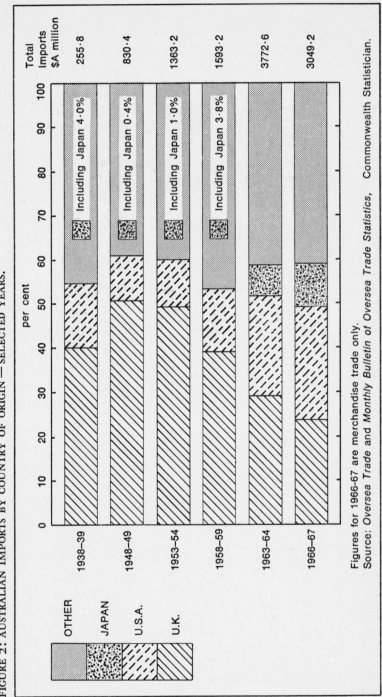

FIGURE 2: AUSTRALIAN IMPORTS BY COUNTRY OF ORIGIN — SELECTED YEARS.

Figures for 1966-67 are merchandise trade only.
Source: *Oversea Trade* and *Monthly Bulletin of Oversea Trade Statistics*, Commonwealth Statistician.

TABLE I: TRANSACTIONS BETWEEN AUSTRALIA AND NORTH AMERICA $A M.

	Aust. exports to			*Aust. imports from*			*Capital inflow (private investment) from North America to Australia*		
	U.S.A.	Canada	Total North America	U.S.A.	Canada	Total North America	Undistributed income	Other investment	Total
1938-39	39	4	43	37	19	56	n.a.	n.a.	n.a.
1948-49	65	9	74	83	24	107	4	4	8
1953-54	111	22	133	146	39	185	34	0·6	34·6
1958-59	123	40	163	217	46	263	63	31	94
1963-64	281	50	331	542	96	638	45	148	193
1964-65	264	40	304	692	117	809	40	194	234
1965-66	338	43	381	704	108	812	49	256	305
1966-67	360	52	412	783	117	900	n.a.	n.a.	n.a.

Source: *Oversea Trade* and information supplied by Bureau of Census and Statistics.

American financial investment is used to purchase American equipment but a good deal undoubtedly is.

As seen from Table 1, although Australian exports to the United States have increased from $A39m. in 1938–39 to $A360m. in 1966–67, our imports from the United States over the same period have risen from $A37m. to $A783m., resulting in a marked adverse balance of trade with that country. But private capital inflow from North America (mainly the United States) has also been steadily increasing in the post-war years. In 1965–66 it amounted to $A305m., and can be regarded as partially offsetting the unfavourable trade balance. However, since Australia's *total* balance of trade in goods and services (that is, her current account) is adverse, she must be interested in expanding her exports to any market. A natural Australian policy objective in these circumstances is to seek to break down some of the illiberal American import policies in respect of Australian goods. This objective will be pursued even more assiduously by Australia in the face of the American decision announced on 1 January 1968 to limit invest-

TABLE 2: AUSTRALIAN EXPORTS OF SPECIFIED COMMODITIES TO U.S.A.

$A.M.

	1938–39	1948–49	1953–54	1958–59	1963–64	1964–65	1965–66	1966–67
Wool	3	41	60	23	41	62	69	85
Meat	–	0·6	2	47	152	103	136	157
Sugar	–	–	–	–	20	18	20	19
Fish	–	0·8	3	7	11	14	19	n.y.a.
Lead	–	8	16	14	11	17	20	19
Zinc	–	0·1	–	1	0·1	0·2	4	n.y.a.
Titanium and Zirconium	–	0·6	1	3	6	11	11	n.y.a.
Manufactures	–	–	3	6	16	17	28	n.y.a.

Source: *Oversea Trade* and information supplied by Department of Trade and Industry.

ment abroad. In Australia's case it will be limited to some 65 per cent of new investment in 1965–66.

In looking at the pattern of trade between the two countries it is important to note that while the United States ranks largely in our export and import statistics, Australia is relatively 'small beer' for American trade. Australia ranks thirteenth as a supplier to the United States, her exports accounting for only 1.6 per cent of American imports: as a market for United States goods Australia ranks eleventh, taking 2.2 per cent of American exports. True, Australia is a valuable market for particular American industries and is rising in interest and acceptability as a place for investing American capital. But in trying to assess the reasons why difficulties occur in our trading relations with the United States it must be borne in mind that her economic relations with Australia are far less vital for that country than they are for the Australian economy.

In looking at the export and import position more closely, it is well to keep this last observation in mind. The United States has now become the largest supplier of imports into Australia, thus

TABLE 3: AUSTRALIAN IMPORTS OF SPECIFIED COMMODITIES FROM U.S.A.
$A.M.

	1938–39	1948–49	1953–54	1958–59	1963–64	1964–65	1965–66	1966–67
Tobacco, unmanufactured	4	7	17	21	16	12	15	16
Chemicals	3	3	3	9	50	56	77	90
Motor vehicles, components and parts	5	6	10	18	74	82	59	55
Aircraft and parts	6	5	6	15	24	54	42	64
Ships and parts	n.a.	n.a.	n.a.	n.a.	n.a.	n.a.	41	37
Electrical machinery and equipment	n.a.	3	3	14	26	33	41	48
Non-electric machinery	n.a.	21	47	62	149	206	201	202

Source: Department of Trade and Industry.

ending the United Kingdom's traditional pre-eminence. It is also our third export market (for a more diversified array of products than pre-war) ranking behind Japan and the United Kingdom. If we add exports and imports together it is our largest trading partner. If we add to this recent levels of capital inflow the United States is the largest single external influence in our economy—a point often overlooked in considering the more dramatic emergence of Japan as, for Australia, the 'new Great Britain' in the Far East. Questions of conflict and agreement in trade policy relations with the United States are accordingly of the highest importance.

Although exports of manufactures to the United States have grown (and are likely to grow further as we develop our mineral processing industries) our principal exports are still primary in origin. The order of importance can be seen from the tables: meat is now well ahead of wool and both these easily surpass sugar, lead and zinc, crayfish and the entire category of manufactures. In respect of all the principal exports (and one or two still-born post-war hopes like dairy products) there have been tensions. It is worth noting the nature of these and the rather ambivalent attitude of the United States in world trade policies affecting agricultural and other primary products. We can then ask whether an equivalent ambivalence exists on the part of Australia in respect of imports from the United States.

The high United States tariff on wool was a sore point in the bad relations of the 'thirties. The tariff of thirty-four cents per pound of wool (clean basis) was more than 100 per cent in *ad valorem* equivalent when first imposed in the Hawley-Smoot tariff of 1930 and remained a discouragement to wool consumption even when reduced to twenty-five and a half cents by agreement in the tariff negotiations held under GATT auspices in 1947. Efforts to obtain further reductions since have failed, despite the high promise of Administration assurances of 1960 and 1961 that bilateral or GATT negotiations could be held in reasonable confidence that there would be a successful outcome. This cause of resentment is aggravated by the fact that the United States continues to be the only country which imposes a tariff on raw wool. Australia does not object to protection for the American industry but feels strongly that the American wool industry is not large enough to warrant such a method of protection which increases the effective competition of synthetics by restricting the consumption of raw wool by American industry. Hopes were held for negotiations over this tariff in the Kennedy Round concluded last year but these were dashed when the United States, pressed by its own wool interests, tried to drive an impossibly hard bargain on the terms of entry of American tobacco into Australia as a *quid pro quo*. Moreover, primary producers in the United States have since pressed hard for high tariffs and quotas against other primary products from Australia and other exporters, so adding to the general sense of injury. Fortunately, President Johnson threatened to veto any Bill designed to implement these, thus recalling to Australian minds a similar situation at the GATT negotiations in Geneva in 1947 when Congress tried to pass a Bill to greatly increase wool tariffs only to have it vetoed by President Truman on the grounds that it

would be a tragic mistake. It would be a blow to our leadership in world affairs. It would be interpreted around the world as a first step on that same road to economic isolationism down which we and other countries travelled after the First World War with such disastrous consequences.[12]

This inconsistency between precept and practice is a major difficulty in trading with the United States. Now inconsistency is not confined to the United States but, for reasons already given, it is probably more serious for her trading partners than it is for the United States when her partners breach the rules in fact or in spirit. Inconsistency in the United States is a reflection of strongly organised pressure groups able to influence the United States Congress in which, for example, small rural States have the same number of Senators (two each) as the heavily populated and highly industrialised states like New York and California. This fact alone means that the country voice in the United States is probably more disproportionately represented in legislatures (and through normal political appointments in the Administration) than it is in Australia despite the great strength of the Country Party here.

This is very clearly evident in respect of dairy produce for which Australia negotiated concessions in the GATT in 1947.[13] Australia was to share in a large global quota at lower rates of duty, but before she could take proper advantage of this (she had bilateral contracts with the United Kingdom at the time), protectionist pressure in the United States won out. The American position was 'regularised' by a special waiver granted in GATT (March 1955) enabling the United States to default on its GATT obligations. Instead of a large quota Australia is now allowed to ship in nine tons! A complete embargo would have been better understood. It is not only in Australia that dairy interests have powerful influence. Restrictions of a similar order apply to cheese and despite efforts to exploit loopholes the total position is bad for both Australia and New Zealand.*

The imposition of quantitative import controls on lead and zinc in 1958 also hit Australia rather hard as it had become by then a principal supplier and its exports had risen considerably during the actual years used for fixing the base quota. However, the controls were lifted in 1965. The granting of special preferences to Cuba for sugar imports by the United States also worried Australia, but since 1962, following political differences between Cuba and America, Australia has been given an annual sugar quota which has risen considerably in recent years. Under ordinary competitive conditions it could probably be higher and is a clear case where the United States regulation of its imports is inconsistent with the spirit of GATT.

Under the Meat Agreement negotiated with the United States in February 1964 (the only bilateral agreement Australia has with America) imports are limited to set quotas, with provision for increases in these according to the rate of growth of the American market. The agreement came about following a sudden rise in

---

* For example, Australia exports junex, a butter fat-sugar mixture for use in making ice-cream which evaded American import controls on both butter fat and sugar. Many other countries exported similar products and eventually in 1967 the United States brought them under import control, but Australia is allowed to retain a voluntary quota which it had imposed prior to 1967 at America's request.

Australia's meat exports (principally for hamburger and processing use) over the years 1958–59 to 1962–63 from approximately $A6m. to $A152m. which seemed to cause harm to the American industry. Further pressure from the local American industry led to legislation later in 1964 enabling the President to set a global import ceiling for meat which, if estimated to be exceeded, would result in a lowering of import quotas for individual supplying countries. This could, at any time, result in curtailment of Australian exports of meat. The situation—at least until 1968—has not been seriously tested since the legislation because drought and the growth of other markets have eased the pressure of Australian supplies. Despite difficulties there is little doubt that the American market will grow with population and incomes there.

For some Australian exports the United States is a competitor in third markets. Wheat sales to Japan and Britain have been cases in point where Australia has had to negotiate for 'fair trade' (i.e. equal conditions of competition) with subsidised American wheat. America's surplus disposals policies under which she has sold large quantities of wheat on non-commercial terms to countries such as India, with consequent adverse effects on Australia's own wheat trade have also been a source of grievance. However, the virtual ending by 1966 of a long sustained and dangerous surplus stock situation in the United States has led to modified surplus disposals legislation which now emphasises the building up of cash wheat markets and the financing of food aid through long-term dollar credits rather than sales for foreign currencies. The recent International Grains Arrangement negotiated under the Kennedy Round of GATT negotiations should result in a 'partnership' approach between Australia and the United States and other GATT nations in providing food aid to developing nations. Under this scheme participating countries—importers as well as exporters— will finance a programme of $4\frac{1}{2}$ metric tons of wheat a year for developing countries. The earlier stridency of Australian protests on this issue has practically disappeared. It has become clear that countries like India need food but, because of foreign exchange shortages, are not viable commercial markets for the large quantities required. Moreover, Australia has had little trouble in selling its wheat, especially to China. The question of surplus disposals is no longer a major point of conflict between Australia and the United States.

Ambivalence in American policy has been mentioned. In the 'fifties it was most apparent to Australia in the relations of the two countries in GATT, especially *vis-à-vis* agricultural protectionism as practised by European countries. Consistently with its own barely defensible waiver, the American delegations soft-pedalled criticisms made by Australia and other countries of the failure of GATT to apply its rules to agricultural products as consistently as it enforced their application to industrial products. Nevertheless, softness in this case was not any recognition of inconsistency. The United States fully understood the good reason for Australia's increasing criticism of the protectionist common agricultural policies (CAP) being promoted under the Rome Treaty by the Common Market members. For political reasons, however (principally the *rapprochement* of France and Germany), Washington wanted to ensure a solid establishment of the Community and was more prepared to contemplate damage to its own agricultural export interests. This attitude changed by 1960 as the seriousness of the CAP threat became apparent. American interests joined with those of Australia and other temperate zone agricultural exporters in seeking to negotiate these problems in the Kennedy Round. Success was limited[14] and there is every reason to think that the inconsistency between American pressure against Common Market protectionism and its own restrictions against agricultural imports weakened its bargaining strength.

All told, the story of Australian exports to the United States is one of some progress but considerable impairment* as the result of restrictive policies followed by Washington. There is room for improvement in policies: this given, there could be a very considerable further growth in Australian export earnings even in the traditional primary products. Nevertheless, it is not unlikely that the greatest growth will come in minerals, semi-processed minerals

---

* It has been suggested by many people that Australia should retaliate for some of this impairment, a course allowable under the GATT rules for impairment of concessions negotiated under GATT. There are few dividends in this course. (See comment below.)

and specialised manufactures which utilise Australia's cheap raw materials and its increasingly skilled labour force.

There is little need to review the nature of Australian imports from the United States. With few exceptions they fit well into the needs of Australian economic development. They are mostly purchased for good economic reasons despite the handicap of the tariff preferences given to British exports. What then have been the grounds for grievance on the part of the United States? There have been several.

First is the continued existence of the preferential tariff structure established before, but especially enlarged by the Ottawa Agreement of 1932. The GATT 'no new preference' rule has not satisfied the United States which, as we have observed, hoped that the system would disappear altogether in the post-war period. Australia did reduce the most-favoured nation rates of tariff on some 800 items following the new 1967 Trade Agreement with the United Kingdom.[15] There was no great measure of thanks to the Australian Government on the part of Washington, despite the importance of these items (mainly producer goods) to American trade. The reason is simple: there is really very little case for continuing these preferences at all. They apply in the main to goods not produced in Australia and the duties payable on goods of non-British origin merely add to our internal cost structure.

Again we reduced the obligatory margins of preference to Britain[15] on protected items but have in fact taken very little advantage of our consequent freedom to reduce the most-favoured-nation rates payable by most non-British suppliers. There would be considerable scope here for further negotiations with Japan and the United States, especially if the United Kingdom enters the Common Market.[16] There is no doubt that the preferences are higher than obligatory and are open to reduction.*

A second difficulty has now disappeared. Pre-war, during the war and up to February 1960, Australia applied restrictions against the entry of dollar goods. During the first decade after the war,

---

* Whether this were done by raising the BPT rates or lowering the MFN rates would be an important issue in any negotiations. The United States would no doubt press its point of view that some Australian MFN rates are too high.

firstly during a period of a British Commonwealth dollar shortage and, later, during a period of recurrent 'crises' in the Australian balance of payments position generally, Australia heavily discriminated against American goods, such discrimination being permitted under GATT, Article XII. However, this descrimination which probably continued a year or two longer than strictly necessary has now ended with the abolition of Australia's general import restrictions in February 1960, and this has been an important factor in the recent upsurge of American supplies to Australia.

Australia's rather frequent use of other GATT articles which permit emergency tariff action or withdrawal from undertakings not to increase certain tariff rates has been criticised by America—perhaps as part of its general position that Australia is over-prone to use the tariff. Nevertheless, Australia's actions have been permissible under GATT and it is for Australia to judge whether her actions have been short sighted: there are not lacking in Australia critics who consider we should be more discerning in our tariff making.[17]

A particular point of difficulty has been Australia's protection of her raw tobacco production industry. Differential rates of duty are applied to tobacco imports, and the concessional lower rate is only allowed when a required proportion of Australian leaf is used in Australian manufacture, thus giving a 'double' protection effect. In the Kennedy Round negotiations the Americans demanded that the Australian protective duty be reduced by 50 per cent and an assurance given of access to one-half of the Australian market for leaf, with the right to share in the growth of the market and with the condition that even if consumption of tobacco were to fall in Australia, its growers 'would roll back so that the Americans' opportunities would not be reduced'.[18] The Americans had a case, but overstated it to an extent which does throw some doubt on their bona fides in this final stage of negotiations under the Kennedy Round in which a large reduction in the wool duty was sought by Australia. This is the more regrettable since Australia was asking only for a change in the form of wool protection in the United States not for abolition of assistance to that industry. There is no need to assume the cause completely lost, as success has been near at times during the period 1959–67. The flexibility of the Australian tariff structure and the prospects of import growth offer ample scope for renewed attempts to negotiate better entry into the American market.

We may conclude this section by noting again that the United States is our largest supplier, is participating in our growth and will continue to do so. There have been causes for tension on both sides but it would seem that grounds for grievance by Australia have been the more persistent. We may well ask whether conflict of the kind already noted is likely to continue.

It can be said that, despite the failure to produce any significant improvement in the mutual trading opportunities for the two countries, the worst in bad relations is over. From the Australian end, physical restrictions on imports from America applied for currency reasons have gone; and reductions in preferential discrimination against American goods have occurred and there is a willingness to negotiate more. There are sticky problems still, such as the Australian protection of tobacco, but it seems incredible that these should prevent future negotiations either within or outside the GATT framework. To America, Australia may still seem too unwilling to review its protective tariff and yet Australia clearly entered the Kennedy Round with a willingness and ability to negotiate on a wide sector of its industrial tariffs.

From the American end, as seen by Australia, there has been improvement in the matter of mineral imports and a reasonably sensible solution on meat imports, but dairy produce and wool remain more difficult than their importance to the American economy would seem to warrant.

Of the two partners America seems more in breach of the intentions of GATT than Australia, so much so that on occasion the question of Australian retaliation has been mooted. The grant of a waiver to the United States by GATT (i.e. permission to be in breach of the rules against import quotas on agricultural imports) does not take away Australia's right to retaliate against the breach.[19] Thus it is asked by some Australian interests, 'why purchase aircraft and large defence requirements from the United States when so many others are eager to supply?'. Where there is probably a strong case, on grounds of acquiring greater technological experience and skills, for deliberately building up some more defence industries in Australia, decisions by governments to import aircraft and naval ships from the United States must be presumed to be based on calculated assessment of cost or national interest. To retaliate would consequently mean (as it mostly does) increased costs or less satisfactory goods. Moreover, retaliation is a dangerous game to play internationally. Our pre-war experience in attempting to divert trade from Japan and the United States should have taught this. The United States at least would well survive any loss of trade with us and could feel more justified in continuing restrictions known to be serious to us. Where grievances exist they are not always one-sided and it is better to try to ameliorate problems by negotiation rather than retaliation.

As partners in GATT relations have been good. In the establishment of GATT and in the Review Session (1954–55) and in the routine sessions relations have been mostly marked by mutual respect and understanding. Again, however, conflict is not absent. We have noted that until 1960 the United States offered little support to Australia in its direct efforts to ease the impact on trade of agricultural protectionism in Europe. Again the American attitude to inter-governmental commodity agreements has not always been as strongly positive as Australia has wished. But, while this point is often made by Australian spokesmen, the fact is that Australia's own attitude has also been ambivalent. We are for a wheat agreement but with apparent inconsistency not for an international wool agreement.[20]

An area in which conflict was marked but has eased somewhat is in respect of unrequited tariff preferences to less developed countries (LDC's) as encouraged in the new Part IV of GATT. Australia has given a significant lead here by offering preferential entry to the LDC's on a long list of items of import, although at no great cost to herself. The United States has opposed even this type of preference on grounds of principle, that is, on grounds of its traditional hostility to preferences. This attitude has recently changed and, if European countries can be persuaded, there may be a general move in the direction started by Australia.

Altogether, experience of collaboration between Australia and the United States in international trade bodies, especially in GATT, encourages the belief that further progress can be made by direct talks and this article will be concluded on this note.

It is possible, but not highly probable, that in the next few years Australia and the United States may be involved in official talks and negotiations about economic collaboration in 'regional' organisations. A North Atlantic Free Trade Area is sometimes mooted (especially if the United Kingdom fails to gain entry into the Common Market) with Japan and Australia as members. Sometimes a South-West Pacific Free Trade Area is mentioned especially by Japanese interests. There is undoubtedly scope for Australian association with groups of this kind—although short of a complete free trade relationship—since she could offer reduction and eventual abolition* of British preferences on a large proportion of imports (possibly some 60-70 per cent) in exchange for gains in the market for her own exports. Nevertheless, the net gains need to be carefully calculated before judgment could be offered. Meanwhile the gains from direct and early bilateral talks with the United States need not be doubted. These, as with our treaty with Japan could be negotiated within the GATT framework knowing that any concessions offered by either party would automatically be extended to GATT members.

In my view a general treaty of commerce between the two countries would offer gains to both countries. It could incorporate existing understandings about double taxation treatment of capital investment (both by America and Australia) as well as direct trade matters. Speaking only of these last, Australia has a strong interest in ameliorating the present harshness of United States import policy on agricultural produce; gaining assurances against the re-introduction of mineral quotas; and securing improved access for wool as well as general encouragement to develop the United

* Complete abolition would be dependent on abandonment of the existing contractual preferences to Britain under the United Kingdom Australia Trade Agreement. Abandonment would be almost automatic if Britain entered the Common Market or a North Atlantic Free Trade Area.

States market for other products. In return Australia can offer improved access for American goods especially those where the United States is a principal supplier. The room for maneouvre exists because many preferential margins are beyond any obligation to Britain. Moreover, Australia must regard the present Treaty with the United Kingdom as overdue for further revision, regardless of the outcome of the British reapproach to Europe.

Despite the strength of protectionist interests in the United States there is no need to write off the liberal forces. A trade treaty or agreement would contain the protectionist forces (their strength would, of course, be tested in the negotiations) and would, to many influential Americans as well as Australians, be seen as a reasonable counterpart to the political and military partnerships already based on treaty relations. A strong economic tie is emerging without a treaty: it can be given greater force and assurance by American recognition of strong economic growth in Australia as a proper basis for future political alliance.

J. G. Crawford

[1] J. G. Crawford, *Australian Trade Policy, 1942–1966: A Documentary History,* A.N.U., 1968, Sections 5, 6 and 11.
[2] *Report of the Committee of Economic Enquiry,* May 1965, (Vernon Report), Vol. I, Ch. 12.
[3] D. F. Nicholson, *Australia's Trade Relations,* Cheshire, 1955, Ch. IV.
[4] Ibid., Ch. VII.
[5] Ibid., Ch. IV, pp. 57–8.
[6] Vernon Report, op.cit., Vol. I, Ch. 14.
[7] Crawford, op.cit., Section 1.
[8] Ibid., Section 1, Document 1:3.
[9] Ibid., Sections 1 to 3.
[10] For a further account of GATT see ibid., Section 5 and Vernon Report, Ch. 12.
[11] Crawford, op.cit., Sections 4 and 11.
[12] Ibid., Section 11 and Nicholson, op.cit., Ch. x.
[13] Nicholson, op.cit., Ch. x.
[14] Crawford, op.cit., Section 18.
[15] Ibid., Section 9.
[16] Ibid., Section 18.
[17] Vernon Report, op.cit., Vol, I, Ch. 14 and Crawford, op.cit., Section 18.
[18] Address by J. McEwen to the United Farmers' and Woolgrowers' Association of N.S.W. in Sydney on 17 July 1967. Roneoed document.
[19] See Articles XXIII and XXV of GATT as set out in Vernon Report, op.cit., Vol. II, Ch. 12 and Crawford op.cit., p. 144.
[20] Crawford, op.cit., pp. 218–19, 598–9.

4 American Investment in Australia

Preliminary Comment. Australia has become one of the major areas of American investment. According to the United States Department of Commerce, this country is the fifth most important area as measured by the American dollars invested here. Statistics in relation to private overseas investment are not available before 1948, but since that time, total foreign investment amounted to some $A5,000m. with an average annual inflow over the past five years of nearly $A500m. Until the post-war period the United Kingdom was the main source of overseas capital. This is historically in accord with the pattern of Australian development, which in the earlier years was financed almost exclusively from Great Britain. Since the war however, the momentum of American investment has increased, and if account be taken of the recent crescendo in overseas investment in Australian mining ventures, then the percentage of the annual inflow represented by American investment can be assumed to have moved ahead of the British.

It is interesting to study the fluctuations in the annual inflow of private overseas investment in companies in Australia. As the following Table discloses, there has been considerable year to year variation in amount and in the sources from which the capital has been derived.

In the following Table, Canadian investment is grouped with American, as although it is nominally Canadian it is ultimately of United States origin. It is also of interest to look at the manner in which the geographical ownership in which the aggregate of

TABLE 1: ANNUAL INFLOW OF PRIVATE OVERSEAS INVESTMENT IN COMPANIES, 1957-66 $A M.

Year ending June	U.K.	N.Z.	U.S. & Canada	Other	Total
1957	123	8	55	23	209
1958	122	9	55	21	207
1959	129	—1	94	26	248
1960	209	16	126	36	387
1961	224	6	176	64	470
1962	125	10	142	19	296
1963	207	5	184	65	461
1964	184	9	193	45	431
1965	255	14	234	62	565
1966	258	2	305	98	663

Source: *Bulletin of Overseas Investment,* Commonwealth Bureau of Census and Statistics.

$5,300m. introduced since 1948 is distributed. This is set out in the following Table which was recently compiled by Business International.

TABLE 2: FOREIGN INVESTMENT IN AUSTRALIAN MANUFACTURING, 1965*

Total assets owned from	$U.S. m.	No. of ventures
U.K.	2,575·3	490
U.S.	2,297·6	328
Canada	84·6	20
Switzerland	75·4	16
West Germany	75·0	16
Netherlands	60·5	7
Sweden	43·5	9
France	35·1	13
New Zealand	11·1	8
Japan	1·1	5
Other	39·6	24
TOTAL	5,298·8	936†

* Adjusted by BI to account for investment via third countries.
† Total exceeds actual number of Australian firms having foreign-owned equity interest because of duplication where jointly owned firms are held from two or more countries. Only the principal subsidiary, not its affiliates, is counted.

From this it will be seen that as measured in total assets owned, the United Kingdom was in 1965 slightly ahead of the United States, although the margin is reduced below $200m. if Canadian investment is grouped with American. Considering the large influx of American capital in 1965–66 as shown in Table 1, which is known to have extended through 1967, it can, I think, be said with some certainty that American capital now invested in Australia is at least equivalent to British.

Another interesting area of inquiry is the direction in which overseas capital, and especially American capital, has been invested in Australia. Table 3 shows how overseas ownership of Australian assets has been distributed throughout Australian industry. From this Table it is apparent that the main areas of United States investment have been in three important areas: oil refining, motor vehicles and non-ferrous metals. Quite large investments have been made in other industries, e.g. agricultural and construction equipment, domestic appliances, fertilisers, pharmaceutical products and rubber-plastics, but it could be said that it is in the first three groups above referred to that the major impact of American investment in Australia has occurred.

It is interesting to note that American investment is approximately 50 per cent greater than British in oil refining and some five times greater in motor vehicle manufacture. If these industries are eliminated however, it will be seen that British investment is still significant across the full range of Australian economic activity.

This concentration of overseas investment in such a limited number of directions has given rise to some comment in official circles. Dr H. C. Coombs, Governor of the Reserve Bank of Australia, has made reference to the unevenness in the distribution of foreign capital through the Australian economy. He pointed out that the areas of special influences of overseas capital have been in large scale enterprises, particularly in mining and large scale manufacturing. The reason for this concentration is apparent. These are the industries in the main which have the most to gain in access to technical know-how that is characteristic of large scale operations. It is natural that important American companies en-

TABLE 3: AUSTRALIAN MANUFACTURING FIRMS WITH EQUITY INTEREST OWNED ABROAD ($U.S. M.)

	No. of firms	Assets owned abroad	U.K.* assets	U.S.* assets
Founding, engineering, metal working	240	1,114·9	576·4	363·3
Iron, steel, metal shapes	13	154·5	130·3	6·6
Non-ferrous metals	21	579·3	353·6	194·6
Heavy engineering	43	76·2	54·2	19·8
Agric., Construction equip.	21	105·9	9·7	60·8
Pumps	9	20·1	7·0	12·9
Internal combust. engines	6	11·6	5·2	1·6
Hand tools	8	7·6	2·9	4·3
Control equip. meters, valves	17	14·5	6·8	7·7
Food processing equipment	8	12·4	5·1	7·3
Other engineering products	94	132·8	70·6	50·6
Vehicles, parts, accessories	53	781·2	153·8	438·8
Motor vehicles	18	677·9	79·5	422·9
Motor parts and accessories	28	84·4	57·9	13·5
Other transport	7	18·9	16·3	2·4
Electrical goods cables, etc.	89	374·7	194·5	104·5
Electrical and telecommunications	41	218·7	113·3	33·1
Domestic electric appliances	17	124·3	64·6	59·7
Other electrical products	31	31·6	16·6	11·7
Chemicals and oil refining	168	1,795·8	849·4	871·4
Industrial, fertilisers	33	359·2	249·1	95·7
Petroleum products	17	1,163·1	472·9	666·8
Paints, pigments, inks	16	61·4	57·8	3·2
Pharmaceutical and veterinary	43	107·2	24·8	73·6
Cosmetics and toiletries	20	21·5	4·4	14·9
Other chemical products	39	83·4	40·5	17·2
Food, drink, tobacco	76	605·7	427·6	132·1
Food, confectionery	57	486·2	318·4	122·4
Beverages	14	20·8	16·6	3·6
Cigarettes, tobacco	5	98·7	92·6	6·1
Other manufacturing	246	626·2	381·6	186·1
Pulp, paper, paperboard	5	59·9	40·2	12·6
Paper products, packaging	39	83·7	66·8	11·3
Bricks, tiles, glassware, etc.	23	36·3	30·9	3·8
Cement and building materials	34	76·7	66·8	1·7
Rubber and plastics	14	79·6	15·3	61·5
Furniture, floor coverings	18	25·3	23·7	1·5
Textiles, clothing, cordage	73	149·2	113·0	13·3
Other	40	114·9	24·9	80·4
TOTAL†	872	5,298·8	2,652·5	2,099·3

* Without adjustment for investments via third countries.
† Any discrepancy in totals and sub-totals due to rounding.

deavour to match the type of operation comparable with that which they conduct in the United States.

Dr Coombs pointed out that Australia has recently shown an increasing capacity to marshal financial and technical resources to participate directly in these large scale operations. Heretofore, the machinery of the Australian money market was inadequate to handle such projects, but recent developments culminating in the establishment of the Australian Resources Development Bank, have assisted greatly to this end.

These improvements in the machinery of capital mobilisation however, do not add to the total quantum of available resources unless we can find other avenues to which overseas capital may be attracted. An obvious area is borrowing for Governmental purposes. This however, is temporarily affected by the Interest Equalisation legislation of the United States introduced in 1964. It is suggested also that American capital might be attracted to housing projects which provide an important outlet for venture capital in the United States. Further development is also expected in the agricultural and pastoral industries which recently have attracted substantial amounts of American capital.

Profits and Dividends on Overseas Capital. Few will deny that the first impact of capital inflow is beneficial to the recipient country. It augments the international resources available to it, and in most circumstances it stimulates internal activity. The basic question is, however, whether the stimulus to internal activity will be sufficient in the long run to support the service of the overseas capital in the remittance of profits or dividends. It is extremely difficult to measure these things, but there is a good deal of apprehension as to whether the service of overseas capital ultimately may not become a serious burden upon Australia's export income.

However, the statistics available do not indicate that we have yet reached this situation as Table 4 shows. From this Table it will be seen that the ratio of investment income to Australia's external earnings while increasing steadily up to 1960, has thereafter declined quite appreciably so that the relationship today is approximately the same as it was ten years ago.

TABLE 4: ANNUAL INVESTMENT INCOME PAYABLE OVERSEAS BY COMPANIES, COMPARED WITH AUSTRALIA'S EXTERNAL EARNINGS

| Year ended 30 June | *Investment income payable to* | | | | Total External Earnings $A m. | Ratio of investment income to earnings % |
	U.S. & Canada	U.K.	Other Countries $A m.	Total		
1948	9	37	5	51	936	5·5
1949	9	31	5	45	1,182	3·8
1950	13	51	5	69	1,358	5·1
1951	22	62	5	89	2,146	4·2
1952	29	57	6	92	1,542	6·0
1953	31	59	5	95	1,908	5·0
1954	61	70	8	139	1,854	7·5
1955	57	79	9	145	1,770	8·2
1956	64	96	11	171	1,808	9·5
1957	66	99	14	181	2,270	7·9
1958	76	98	16	192	1,950	9·8
1959	96	112	22	232	1,954	11·9
1960	104	124	17	249	2,234	11·1
1961	99	109	25	240	2,270	10·6
1962	74	102	19	201	2,612	7·7
1963	89	140	23	259	2,637	9·9
1964	103	157	25	285	3,357	8·5
1965	100	161	33	294	3,280	9·0
1966	108	166	29	303	3,369	9·3
1967	N.A.	N.A.	N.A.	N.A.	3,740	N.A.

Source: Commonwealth Bureau of Census and Statistics.

This trend has falsified some of the forecasts made in the 1950's, which suggested that by this point of time profits accruing to overseas interests would absorb 25 per cent of export income. But the truth is that the expansion in Australia's export income has more than kept abreast of the cost of servicing overseas capital.

This is in part due to the rapid expansion of Australia's export earnings, but it is also due I believe, to the reduction in the profitability of overseas investment (particularly American investment) in Australia. This is illustrated in Table 5 which indicates that while the investment income payable to British-owned companies since 1948 has shown considerable stability, although tending to decline over the last few years, the yield on American and Cana-

TABLE 5: ESTIMATED 'EARNING RATES' ON NORTH AMERICAN, UNITED
KINGDOM AND TOTAL OVERSEAS INVESTMENT IN COMPANIES IN
AUSTRALIA*

*Investment income payable as percentage of total overseas
investment in companies in Australia.*

Year ended 30 June	U.S. & Canada (%)	U.K. (%)	All overseas countries (%)
1948	7·3	7·7	8·0
1949	6·9	5·6	6·3
1950	9·4	8·2	8·7
1951	13·9	8·5	9·5
1952	14·5	7·0	8·6
1953	11·7	6·6	7·6
1954	22·8	7·4	10·7
1955	18·7	7·6	10·1
1956	16·8	8·4	10·4
1957	14·8	7·7	9·5
1958	15·2	6·9	9·1
1959	17·3	7·3	10·0
1960	16·0	7·4	9·6
1961	12·8	5·8	8·0
1962	7·8	4·8	5·7
1963	8·2	6·3	6·8
1964	7·7	6·1	6·6

* Annual estimates of the value of overseas investment in companies in Australia
were reached by adding estimates of annual capital inflow to an assumed value
of private overseas investment at 30 June 1947. In each case the investment income
payable has been compared with the value of investment at the beginning of the
year in question.

Because figures showing the domicile of the overseas investor do not provide
a classification of direct and portfolio investment, the above 'earning rates' refer
to both types of investment combined. The approximate nature of the estimates
is obvious even from figures shown for 1947/48, where 'earning rates' for both
North American and British investment are shown as being below the average
for all countries, despite the heavy preponderance of investment from those two
areas.

Source: Commonwealth Treasury 1965.

dian investment after reaching a high plateau in the 1950's has
consistently fallen away since then.

Many reasons have been advanced for this trend, the more
important being: (1) the influence of import restrictions during
the 1950's and their subsequent removal, (2) reduction in Ameri-

ca's technological superiority over other countries in recent years, (3) the more selective character of American investment during the 1950's. All of these factors probably have some bearing on the situation, but I would like to suggest that probably the greatest factor has been the growing competition on the Australian manufacturing scene and in particular amongst overseas companies operating here. This is reflected in the financial results of companies operating in oil refining and marketing, in automobile manufacture and aluminium and in food. It is likely that Australian manufacturing will retain its competitive atmosphere. Since the removal of import restrictions in 1959, the Australian manufacturer has become a great deal more cost conscious than previously, and Australian tariff policy is likely to ensure that this attitude is maintained.

Sources of Capital. One of the most important elements in the quantum of overseas investment in Australia is the retention of profits by subsidiaries or branches of overseas companies operating here.

It will be seen that undistributed income of American and Canadian companies has represented a very considerable part of the total investment by these companies. In some years, e.g. in 1956–57 and 1958–59, it amounted to three or four times the amount of new investment made by companies in this category. On the other hand, in the difficult year of 1961–62, it fell away markedly and was only about one-eighth of the amount of new investment.

Over the last twenty years however, the retention of profits has been a very important element in capital inflow. Its *relative* unimportance in the last few years has been due mainly to the very considerable increase in new American investment here, especially in the field of mining. This trend is likely to be reversed again as these mining ventures reach the profitable stage.

Pattern of Capital Structure. It is difficult to get a complete picture of the capital pattern followed by American companies in financing their Australian activities. A recent study on this subject by

TABLE 6: INVESTMENTS OF UNITED STATES AND CANADA IN AUSTRALIAN
COMPANIES

Year ended 30 June	Distributed profits* $A m.	Undist. profits $A m.	Investments other than undist. profits $A m.	Ratio of undist. profits to total investment %
1948†	4·6	4·2	8·6	32·8
1949†	5·2	4·0	4·2	48·8
1950†	4·8	8·4	12·2	40·8
1951†	6·2	16·2	24·4	39·9
1952†	5·2	24·2	37·0	39·5
1953†	6·0	24·8	−20·8	620·0
1954†	27·0	34·0	·6	98·3
1955†	25·0	31·6	47·4	40·0
1956†	23·8	40·2	23·6	63·0
1957	25·0	41·0	14·0	74·5
1958	34·0	42·0	13·0	76·4
1959	33·0	63·0	31·0	67·0
1960	34·0	70·0	56·0	55·6
1961	38·0	61·0	115·0	34·7
1962	58·0	16·0	126·0	11·3
1963	62·0	27·0	157·0	14·7
1964	58·0	45·0	148·0	23·3
1965	59·0	40·0	194·0	17·1
1966	58·0	49·0	256·0	16·1

* Net of withholding tax on dividends.

† For these years a relatively small proportion of 'Undistributed profits' would
have been classified as 'Investment other than undistributed profits'. The difference in basis would mainly affect particulars for the United Kingdom.

Note: The table covers both direct and portfolio investment, except for undistributed profits on shares held by portfolio investors.

Source: Commonwealth Bureau of Census and Statistics.

Dr Donald T. Brash in his book *American Investment in Australian Industry* however provides considerable information on the
subject. Through private inquiry Dr Brash has accumulated quite
a number of interesting points which may be summarised as
follows:

In regard to the degree of American ownership, he found
that out of a group of 208 companies incorporated in Australia
at 30 June 1962, the percentage in terms of numbers was as
follows:

25%–49%	U.S. ownership		28
50%–74%	„	„	50
75%–99%	„	„	5
100%	„	„	111
Branches			14
			——
			208
			——

It will be seen that considerably more than half of these companies were fully owned by American capital. If we take as another measure the employees of these companies, we find that almost 75 per cent of the labour force employed by the 208 companies were employed by companies with 100 per cent American owner-ship. These figures reflect a strong preference for complete owner-ship or at least a controlling interest on the part of American companies operating in Australia.

Of these 208 American-affiliated companies, 101 of them were financed in 1962 as follows:

	$A m.
Ordinary Capital	240·1
Shareholders' Funds (including retained profits of 189·7)	660·4
Debt to U.S. Parent	191·4
Long and short term liabilities (mainly in Australia)	345·4
	——
Total Funds employed	1,197·4

To summarise, these 101 companies (who originally invested $A240m.) have apart from dividends remitted, now accumulated a total net worth of $660m. and have borrowed further substantial funds (some $320m.) to finance their activities. In other words, their Australian borrowings exceed their original capital by a sub-stantial margin. This has been a fairly consistent pattern of finance followed by American companies operating in Australia.

Australian Participation. The growing importance of overseas (and in particular American) ownership of Australian companies has given rise to a growing feeling that Australians should participate as equity shareholders in these enterprises.

Historically, in the earliest stages of American investment here, in the early post-war period, these was considerable enthusiasm for the establishment of industries by American capital. The general acceptance of the view that Australia should become rapidly industrialised as part of its long range policy of immigration and development, was the key-note of Australia's attitude to capital inflow. Taking as an example the establishment of the Australian automobile industry, there is no doubt that without the enterprise of General Motors, this industry, which is vital to Australia's economy, would have been long delayed. At that time, Australians regarded this development as a major international contribution to the country's economic future and nothing but praise was forthcoming for the American company that was responsible for it.

Similarly, in other industries (e.g. the establishment of oil refineries and of factories to produce tractors), the attitude of Australians was unreservedly favourable. Indeed this attitude was well founded as Australia had no industrial techniques upon which such industries could be based, nor did it have industrial units with reserve capital or technical personnel that would enable them to embark upon projects of this magnitude.

Some years elapsed before any critical comment regarding capital inflow was forthcoming. In fact, most of the Australian States were vying with one another for overseas industries, and were offering important benefits to American companies as an inducement to them to establish themselves within their boundaries. It was not until General Motors-Holden began to generate profits of a major order early in the 1950's, that some questioning first arose in the minds of Australians as to whether this order of profitability accruing to overseas companies may not after all be too high a price to pay for rapid industrialisation. Nevertheless, this feeling was not of great importance at that stage and the pressure to encourage investment from overseas still far out-weighed any opposition.

As time went by however, the weight of opinion against 100 per cent overseas ownership and in favour of some Australian participation in ventures that were originally entirely owned abroad grew, and as a result it can be said that there is now a much more objective attitude towards overseas investment as such. There is no political suggestion however, that American companies already established here should be compelled to share their equity with Australians. Indeed, very little positive thinking has been devoted to working out ways and means of achieving Australian participation even if the American companies were to co-operate completely in the matter (which is unlikely). In order to provide the funds necessary to purchase a substantial interest in large American-owned companies for Australian investors, very considerable problems could arise in relation to Australia's balance of payments. To acquire a 25 per cent interest in wholly-owned subsidiaries of American companies, an amount of some $400m. at least would need to be found which in itself would constitute a substantial drain on the money market, quite apart from the effects on our overseas balances.

As it happens the attractiveness of investment in the subsidiaries of overseas companies has diminished in recent years. I have already referred to the decline in the profitability of American companies since 1960. Competition between American companies in the field of automobile manufacture, has for instance, reduced considerably the demand for participation in share capital of companies operating in this area. The profits of General Motors-Holden have stabilised and the earnings of Ford and Chrysler have been far from spectacular. British Motor Corporation and Volkswagen have also shown unsatisfactory profit positions. The same is true in the field of chemicals, oil refining and other areas of manufacture. For these reasons, it can be said that the pressure for Australian participation in wholly-owned subsidiaries of American-owned companies is not likely to reach a higher pitch, indeed it is likely to diminish.

From this conclusion however, we should probably exclude the mining industry. There is currently a strong feeling, which is in part emotional, that profits earned from the extractive industries which are mainly based on export, should at least be shared with Australians. Even though the ore reserves of the companies operating in this area may have a very long life, it is felt that the extraction of this ore means a net loss of a physical asset that cannot be replaced.

But against this argument have been advanced some very strong views by several eminent authorities. Perhaps the best known of these is Sir George Fisher, who in his Presidential Address to the Australian Institute of Mining and Metallurgy in June 1967, strongly supported the use of overseas capital in Australian mining, and advanced strong arguments to support his case. Sir George bases his argument upon the historical truth that Australian mining from the outset—over 120 years ago—depended upon overseas capital and technical assistance. He examines the phases of mining development in Australia and illustrates that in each of these phases overseas investment took a leading part even though at a later stage, this investment was largely bought out by Australian investors.

Such companies as Mount Morgan, Mount Isa and even the Broken Hill Proprietary Company in its mining days, were largely owned abroad. But it is not only because it makes capital available that Sir George advocates overseas participation in Australian mining ventures. He speaks also of the great importance of overseas technical knowledge in mining upon which Australia has relied very extensively in recent years. He points out that in the 1930's, Australia had only eleven geologists, and all of them came from abroad.

This reliance upon overseas capital and techniques, in the view of Sir George Fisher, is equally true of today. He refers to the overseas leadership (both American and British) in the development of the iron ore reserves of Western Australia, and to the part that overseas capital has played in the development of bauxite and aluminium industries. Sir George's arguments are very compelling and cannot be readily controverted. He does however, concede that opportunity should, if possible, be provided for Australian equity in mining provided that this includes investments during the period of high risk. While this is an argument that can be justified on equitable grounds, there is an equally strong argument to permit Australian participation in Australian mines owned abroad, at a later stage when mines are developed and producing but on a basis that compensates the overseas owners substantially for the risks (or the proportion of them) that they have already borne. Indeed, this practice has now become established as witnessed by several mining issues during 1967 and it may be expected to continue.

Australian Attitude to United States Investment. It can now be said I think that the Australian attitude toward overseas investment has stabilised. There are still some conflicts of viewpoint, but both attitudes are expressed in moderate terms. The current official attitude is expressed in 1962 in a Commonwealth Government publication in which these words appear:

The Australian Government welcomes overseas investment in Australia, particularly where it is of a kind likely to be held in the balanced development of Australia's resources and brings with it the skill and 'know-how' needed for the successful fulfilment of the project in which the investment is made. . . . There are no provisions (such as exist in some countries) requiring local participation in the capital or management of companies set up in Australia by overseas interests, but many overseas companies have found that their aims are best achieved in association with an Australian enterprise. There is a great diversity of arrangements in existence, and although no rules are laid down by the Government it is considered desirable that there be Australian participation in ownership and management.

More recently the then Australian Prime Minister (Rt Hon. Harold Holt) expressed himself on the subject as follows:

Let me give you eight good reasons why we should not be shy about foreign capital:

1. It gives us the margins we must have for growth and for the security in our balance of payments.

2. It fills the gap that our domestic capital raising cannot fill and on

some occasions is prepared to take great risks which Australian investors are not willing to accept.

3. It ensures the importation of new technology and new management skills.

4. It creates employment and special attractions for migrants.

5. It provides revenue by way of taxation and royalties.

6. It provides profits, some of which are re-invested and contribute to further growth.

7. It gives us new towns, ports and sources of power.

8. It helps us diversify our exports.

I have spoken in some detail on this because I believe it to be important and because we should not take for granted an inflow of foreign capital at anything like recent levels. The trend of our balance of payments has been down and capital inflow helps very much to keep the movement within acceptable limits.

There is more to foreign investment here than 'Come on in—the water's fine'. We are not 'selling-out', and in any case are dealing with the 10 per cent plus segment of our total capital investment. But we must take care not to discourage the foreign investor—who is sensitive enough to the hazards and uncertainties of enterprise beyond his national boundaries. We prefer to use 'guide-lines' and get a response in a voluntary way. Not every investor wants to come here, and those with capital for export are finding it harder to venture and less rewarding when they do because of the recent restraints imposed by their own Governments. This may, or may not last, but the fact that it is happening has done two things. It has reduced our capital inflow, with the inevitable effect on our balance of payments, and it has injected question marks into our forward planning because we do not know how long it will last, or whether it will vary in degree. It makes good sense to me to keep on saying we want it and can make valuable use of it.

From the negative viewpoint, perhaps the most authoritative opinion is that of the Vernon Committee, set up by the Australian Government to review the future of the Australian economy. In its Report published in May 1965, the Vernon Committee had the following to say on the question of foreign investment:

Once an economy has a substantial body of overseas investment, it is in a sense 'on the tiger's back' unless the trade balance is improving sufficiently to meet the additional income payable overseas. The continuation of capital inflow becomes seemingly more and more desirable as a means of offsetting the increasing payments on the latter account. As the annual amounts become larger, the immediate consequences for the economy of an interruption of the capital inflow, either contrived or occurring by reason of external circumstances, become more and more serious.

The Committee recommended that a ceiling be imposed on the amount of capital inflow into Australia each year. The Labor Party solution would require foreign firms to admit a 30 per cent minimum Australian ownership.

But what is the measure of Australia's need for overseas capital? The most authoritative reference on this aspect is expressed in information recently compiled officially in regard to funds available for capital expenditure in Australia. This is set out in Table 7 from which it will be seen that the percentage of total funds available provided by capital inflow has fluctuated considerably over the last ten years or so but over the whole period has averaged something to the order of 11 per cent. This percentage is lower than was previously generally assumed to represent the actual importance of overseas investment in the capital supply. Furthermore, the percentage overall has not shown much tendency to increase over recent years, mainly due to the high rate of internal generation of funds, especially in the form of personal savings and surpluses.

A study of the Table would indicate that over the past decade Australia's demand for overseas capital has steadily increased, but if the peak point of 1965–66 is excluded, it can be said that the rate of growth of the inflow has not been spectacular. I have already referred to the importance of overseas capital in mineral development in Australia. It is probably to this area that the inflow of overseas (and especially American) capital will be directed. Industrial expansion as such will probably be able to finance itself from cash flows internally generated, supplemented by periodic internal borrowings on a modified scale.

TABLE 7: AUSTRALIAN FUNDS AVAILABLE FOR CAPITAL EXPENDITURE

	Depreciation Allowances	Increase in Dividend & Tax Provisions	Undistributed Company Income Accruing to Residents	Retained Investment Income of Life Insurance Funds, etc.	Personal Savings	Public Auths. Current Surplus & Grants Towards Private Capital Expenditure	Sub-Total, Domestic Savings		Withdrawal of Oversea Monetary Reserves	Net Apparent Capital Inflow		Total Funds Available for Capital Expenditure
	$m	$m	$m	$m	$m	$m	$m	% of Total	$m	$m	% of Total	$m
1957/58	895	-131	284	105	457	918	2528	89·1	82	227	8·0	2837
1958/59	959	27	330	122	685	723	2846	88·1	-16	401	12·4	3231
1959/60	1038	131	392	137	691	870	3259	87·7	-15	474	12·7	3718
1960/61	1136	-52	321	158	773	1100	3436	82·3	80	657	15·7	4173
1961/62	1201	-104	316	193	907	883	3396	99·9	-176	178	5·2	3398
1962/63	1268	106	393	218	881	903	3769	88·9	-146	615	14·3	4238
1963/64	1433	137	474	245	1231	1059	4579	98·9	-450	503	10·9	4632
1964/65	1578	9	642	269	1296	1426	5220	87·0	297	480	8·0	5997
1965/66	1735	-69	615	306	1214	1398	5199	85·6	-61	937	15·4	6075
1966/67	1900	27	659	337	1572	1337	5832	90·0	125	530	8·2	6487
Total 10 Years												
—$m	13143	81	4426	2090	9707	10617	40064		-280	5002	·	44786
—% of Total	29·3	·2	9·9	4·7	21·7	23·7	89·5		-0·6	·		100·0

Source: Australian National Accounts.

Much of the criticism of overseas investment in Australia has been based on the possibility that Australia may have difficulty later on in servicing this investment through dividend payments or remittance of profits. There have been various estimates as to the likely percentage of Australia's export income that may be absorbed by the service of overseas capital. If however, we take the latest official forecast of the Australian balance of payments through 1969–70, and allow for the probable additional income from minerals, it would seem likely that the increase in Australia's international reserves will approximately balance the rate of capital inflow. In this event, it would seem that Australia would no longer be dependent on overseas capital, and indeed may have reached the earlier stages of a capital exporter.

Technical Benefits of Capital Inflow. Quite apart from the importance of capital inflow upon the balance of payments and upon the availability of resources thus made possible, it is generally recognised that the provision of technical and scientific knowledge and know-how is one of the most important benefits to Australia arising from American investment here.

Indeed, it can be said with some certainty that the major industrial developments in Australia leading to the manufacture of entirely new and complicated products such as motor cars and chemicals, have in the main been due to overseas investment here in the early stages. Latterly, mainly due to overseas affiliations either through an equity link or by technical agreement, has come the main stream of innovation in Australia's industrialisation. To a degree this is also true of the mining industry.

An objectively dispassionate look at Australian industrial development since 1945, makes it obvious that access to overseas (and in particular American) technical information has been a vital element in our economic growth. This technical information has covered both products and manufacturing processes. In addition to the provision of technical information, these affiliations have made possible the exchange of personnel, thus ensuring a proper knowledge of American techniques on the one hand, and of Australian production problems on the other.

Some concern however, has been expressed that Australia has become too dependent upon overseas know-how. A plea is made for a greater degree of research in Australia. Although some progress has been made in this direction, it is nevertheless true that the amount of original research in the field of manufacture in Australia is very limited. Furthermore, of such research as is conducted, apart from one or two significant exceptions, it is probably true that a great proportion is carried out by American companies operating here. It cannot be assumed that as a general rule American know-how is entirely suitable to Australian conditions. Many major errors have occurred arising from the application of American techniques to the much smaller output volume experienced in Australia. In these cases, it is found that Australian improvisation and adaptations of American methods may give a better result than the unqualified acceptance of American methods.

Effect Upon Exports. A large part of the comment regarding overseas ownership of Australian industry is directed to the likely effect of such ownership upon Australian exports. Since manufacture is such an important factor in population absorption, it is part of Australian policy to develop export trade in manufactures. Results of this policy are already evident, so that now 16 per cent of Australia's exports are composed of manufactured goods having doubled in value over the past six years. Examination of the export activities of American affiliated companies does not suggest that these firms are prominent in the development of such exports. It may be that American companies merely reflect the lack of export consciousness which is true of Australian industry as a whole. In any case, American companies generally have invested in Australia largely to overcome tariff barriers and the existence of such barriers does not suggest export potential.

Nevertheless, the development of exports is essential in some cases to lift the volume of production in certain Australian industries to a level that will permit economies necessary to meet competition abroad from countries organised for high volume output.

However, there is considerable evidence of restrictions upon export freedom imposed by American parent companies upon their Australian affiliates. This is by no means true of all American companies, but any limitation must have some negative effect upon export volume. This has given rise to much critical comment against American control of large sections of Australian industry.

The situation may be expected to alter as time goes by. In fact, in the last two or three years there has been a substantial increase in exports made by American-owned companies operating in Australia. Products exported have, in the main, been motor cars, electrical equipment and engineering products. To some degree these exports have resulted from pressure by the Australian authorities but they have also been stimulated by tax concessions offered as incentives for exports. Further stimulus has come from the growing use of Australian subsidiaries to enable American companies to qualify for British preferential tariff in Commonwealth markets. More recently, the growing magnitude of the Australian market itself has enabled economies to be introduced that were previously impossible.

The pressure to develop exports will undoubtedly continue and Australian companies with overseas ownership will be expected to take a full share of this responsibility. One area to which considerable attention may be directed is in the food processing industry which is now very largely in overseas, mainly American, hands. This industry was formerly a large contributor to Australian exports, and considerable anxiety is expressed that this contribution may not increase—or may in fact decline as a result of international marketing policies of the overseas owners. Because farming as well as manufacturing interests are involved in the food industries, they have a particular significance in the Australian political scene.

Conclusion. In our survey the influence of overseas capital, and especially American capital upon Australia, we have been primarily concerned with economic aspects. From time to time however, we have referred to facets of the matter that have significance in other directions. We have referred to its importance to Australia's policy of rapid growth. This policy in itself, has overtones related to defence, since the strategical problem of holding the country depends primarily upon an increase in numbers in a minimum of time.

From the defence view point also, there would seem to be advantages in having a large American investment committed in Australia. The greater the American economic involvement, the greater is likely to be the degree of common interest in defence policy in the Pacific area.

But in the final analysis, the benefits or disadvantages of capital inflow must be economic. The favourable arguments may be summarised briefly:

Overseas capital influences growth and capacity to absorb population.
It fills the gap between domestic saving and total capital needs.
It provides immediate benefit to the balance of payments.
It enables the importation of new technology and new management skills.

On the other hand, the main negative arguments are:

The ultimate cost of servicing capital in dividend and interest remittances or repayment of loans.
The control of large sections of Australian industry or enterprise by non-Australian interests.
The unpredictable character of capital inflow which fluctuates violently from year to year with factors beyond Australia's influence.
The danger that it may inhibit the development of exports of manufactured goods which may be essential to maintaining growth.

There is no real doubt that historically Australia has on balance benefited greatly in the post-war period from overseas investment (and especially American investment) in Australia. It is unlikely that the negative factors mentioned will at any stage outweigh these benefits. If they should, the Australian authorities have available to them correctives, which however, they would be loath to apply except in extreme emergency.

Having accepted the most obvious arguments for and against the use of overseas capital, it is perhaps proper to conclude by considering some of the more subtle consequences that are not immediately apparent. One is the gearing effect overseas capital has upon the overall rate of growth. Australia is expanding at a rate of about $27\frac{1}{2}$ per cent of GNP and of this $27\frac{1}{2}$ per cent, 3 per cent is generated from overseas capital. Although it represents a relatively small part, this 11 per cent addition to available resources lifts Australia into an area of high growth and tends to magnify the stimulus to further expansion. The association of technological know-how with foreign capital adds further to its importance. Another indirect benefit of capital inflow has been the growing competition in Australia between overseas manufacturers established here. Outstanding examples are the motor car and chemical industries, which ten years ago provided highly remunerative investments for overseas companies, but which now yield relatively modest profits. The main beneficiaries have been Australian consumers as the decline in profitability is generally reflected in lower prices.

But on the other side of the ledger has been the influence of foreign ownership of Australian industry in inhibiting the generation of research and developmental activities which undoubtedly would have been necessary had Australia developed these industries entirely from her own resources. It is agreed that the immediate availability of technical know-how from overseas has been of vital significance, but the consequent dependence upon overseas sources of technical information is a seriously adverse aspect of the Australian economy.

As Australia passes through the phase of import replacement to the development of exports of manufactures, augmented by greatly increased mineral exports, it seems probable that the consequent development of large international reserves will enable her to adopt an increasingly independent attitude with a greater insistence upon the development and use of Australian research facilities. If this is combined with an increasing Australian participation in ownership of industries now controlled abroad, the result could be a true partnership both in profits and technology which would seem to be the proper philosophical objective of international investment.

Ian Potter

Part Two

5 The American Impact on Education

The American educationist who ventured into Australia after the end of World War II exhibited, after a few weeks' stay, all the signs of a man who had been deeply shocked; disbelief was written on his face, and a sense of professional, if not moral, outrage was apparent in what he said.

To some extent the American visitor deserved sympathy. The Australians had written so little about their educational system, even at a descriptive level, that the visitor was probably entitled to assume that the superficial similarities he observed between the two societies betokened a similarity between the educational systems which had moulded them. If he had more than a passing acquaintance with modern pedagogical history he probably knew that the revival of Herbartianism, which spread from Europe to England and then, with far-reaching consequences, to Australia in the early years of the twentieth century, had rested, in part, on the scholarship and enthusiasm of Americans such as Charles de Garmo. He might also have known that some American progressive educationists, notably Colonel Parker of Quincy fame, were being widely read in Australia in those same early years of the century. Snippets of knowledge such as these, reinforcing a superficial impression of cultural similarity, could have misled him into the belief that Australian education would look like American education, writ small.

However, if he had been keeping up with his reading, he should have been a little better prepared for what he saw. One of his compatriots, John F. Cramer, a Superintendent of Schools in

Oregon, had set out his impressions in *Australian Schools Through American Eyes* (Melbourne, 1936), and there he could have read of 'a general sameness' about all Australian schools, 'ponderous organisation', 'rigid inspection', failure 'to develop local interest in the schools', 'inbreeding', 'mechanical excellence of the performance', and the secondary school remaining 'largely a preparatory school for the university, hedged round with restrictions and made very selective'. Also available to the post-war visitor were the proceedings of the New Education Fellowship Conference which was held in Melbourne, Victoria, in 1937 (K. S. Cunningham and W. C. Radford (eds.), *Education for Complete Living*, Melbourne, 1938). This conference had been strongly influenced by the Americans present (Hart of California, Kandel, Rugg and Brunner from Columbia Teachers' College) and they made no secret of the deficiencies they saw in the Australian system. Hart, in a succinct summary of his impressions, stated categorically (pp. 661-3):

The major barriers to educational progress in . . . Australia . . . as I see them, are:
1. The complete and universal absence of a feeling of ownership or control of the schools by the people . . .
(a) A uniform standardized syllabus of instruction imposed by central authority on all children regardless of differences in ability, interest or outlook . . .
(b) The system of internal examinations . . .
(c) The system of inspection . . .
2. Seniority as a basis of promotion . . . almost equivalent to senility as a basis of promotion . . .
3. An over-emphasis on the employment advantage of an education. . . .

Nevertheless, even a visitor as distinguished as Freeman Butts of Columbia Teachers' College, having Cramer's and Hart's impressions available to him, was obviously disturbed by what he saw in Australia in the latter half of 1954. In his report (*Assumptions Underlying Australian Education*: Australian Council for Educational Research Melbourne, 1955) he carefully stated his own assumptions about education and, in the light of these, challenged almost every Australian procedure: centralised administration, élitism ('Everywhere I went I found a uniform hierarchy of schools, a hierarchy of courses, and a hierarchy of subjects'), external examinations, emphasis on 'orderliness, discipline and development of skills', the teachers' security of tenure, the inspectorial system. 'I would say,' he concluded, 'that Australia needs a great educational revival and awakening of interest in education.'

Although Butts, James Bryant Conant (who visited Australia in 1951), and others, were all careful to point out, in Conant's words, that it is 'extremely difficult to say what is a good educational procedure except in terms of a particular society'[1] they nevertheless seemed unprepared for the extent to which the administration of public education in Australia, being only an aspect of public administration in general, was geared to the geographic and demographic realities of the country's short history; they also seemed unprepared for the extent to which Australian pedagogy (including school organisation, curriculum and methodology) was based upon social and psychological theories which, though repugnant to most American minds in the 1950's, had a respectable parentage. This failure to appreciate the Australian background and environment left them open to shock and disbelief, a sensation which will affect anyone who seeks to examine the American impact on Australian education without first understanding why Australians were behaving, educationally, as they were in the 1950's.

Put very briefly, the Australian decision to centralise the administration of public education (to have only one school authority in each State, although one of them, Western Australia, is as big in area as Texas, New Mexico, Arizona, California, Utah and Nevada combined) was based on the belief that only in this way could a uniform standard of education be provided for the thinly dispersed population in those States. Throughout the greater part of the nineteenth century each State (or Colony, as the name was before Federation in 1901) had experimented with Church control of education, with local control of education, and with a combination of local and central control. By the middle of the century there was no doubt that the Churches could not handle this vast enterprise (even if an increasingly secular society had been disposed to let them), and there was a diminished confidence in the capacity of local authorities to do so.

The truth was that despite the nostalgic attempts of some early governors to impose an English pattern of local government upon the Australian continent, the realities of settlement made such a pattern unsuitable. It must be remembered that most of the settlements were initially (and for some decades) not fragments of English society transplanted to the South Seas, but gaols to house a convict population; and gaols require authoritarian control rather than local democratic institutions. Moreover, when free settlement was belatedly permitted the newcomers found themselves in a poorly-watered, comparatively barren environment which, by the techniques of the time, would support only a scattered population incapable of banding together to provide essential services such as water supply, roads and (later) railways and telegraph. For these services they looked to the central government for provision and, perforce, accepted central government control.

Moreover, whereas in America the presence of the Indian made cohesion between settlers necessary for defence, in Australia the small, primitive aboriginal population scarcely posed a threat; again, whereas in America the heterogeneity of the immigrants produced ethnic and religious sectionalism which expressed itself in local cohesion, in Australia the homogeneity of the immigrants (until very recently almost entirely British) gave them no cause for sectionalism. Even the terrain worked towards the same ends for, in contrast to the rich variety of landscape and climate which makes America the distinctive continent it is, and thereby adds regionalism to sectionalism, the Australian continent is, by comparison, monotonously uniform from coast to coast.

In Australia, therefore, local government never took firm root, and when public education had to be added to the services wanted or needed by the community it, like the others, was provided by the central government. This administrative necessity of the nineteenth century remains, either through inertia or as a matter of administrative convenience, the pattern today; there is a great deal of debate among political scientists, sociologists and educational administrators on the necessity, desirability or feasibility of breaking this pattern but, with the exception of minor administrative experiments in one or two States, the educational pattern, at least, is unchanged.

Little wonder that visiting American educationists were disturbed by what they saw. Thirty years ago Kandel, after his stay in Australia, warned:

In the absence of any agencies for constructive criticism, the administrative machine becomes more solidly entrenched, more self-satisfied, and more complacent . . . the maximum of efficiency is soon reached when there can be no questioning of the desirability of the ends and consequently no change in the means.[2]

Today, the majority of Australian educationists, depressed by the inertia and complacency of many State Education Departments, concede that Kandel's diagnosis of our condition was correct, but they are still loath to concede that the American remedy of decentralisation is the correct one to apply.

In general, they would base their objection to this solution on the grounds that the prevailing trend in public administration is towards further centralisation rather than decentralisation, and they would echo the words of one of their political scientists, A. F. Davies:

There is . . . a natural tilt of the board in Australia against decentralisation. . . . Educationists may well be right in thinking that affluence may bring out behaviour in local communities that poverty and hardship could not. Let us hope that they are. But we should appreciate the fundamental novelty of such participation in Australian political life.[3]

Pressed further, they would justify their rejection of the American solution on at least four other grounds:

1. That the centralised control of educational resources has allowed the Australian States to provide a uniform standard of

education in every corner of their vast territories, no matter how remote the pupil's home and no matter how impoverished his family or his district. Whether this equal distribution of society's resources is to be counted as great a democratic virtue as local control of educational resources is, no doubt, a matter of debate. Butts was content to say:

... I have nothing but praise for your efforts to provide equal educational facilities throughout a State system. To find good buildings and well-prepared and well-paid teachers in the poorest and most remote sections of a State as well as in the wealthiest and most densely populated areas is, I believe, a remarkable achievement. I would not find this same quality in the United States.[4]

2. That centralisation, while failing to give the people a direct and effective part in the running of their schools, has protected the schools, the pupils and the teachers from the uninformed and often dangerous interference of laymen in the determination of the curriculum, text books and teaching methods.

3. That Australia's centralised education systems are big only in terms of the areas they serve and not in terms of the number of pupils they serve. (The school authority of any one of several American cities would deal with a far greater school population than would be found in a small Australian State such as Tasmania.)

4. That the trend in America is towards a reduction in the number of local boards and their consolidation into larger, more efficient units.

In deciding that, on balance, a centralised school system is better suited to the country's needs than a decentralised system, the Australians are, of course, not only rejecting an American solution; they are also rejecting the traditional British solution. Nevertheless, this rejection remains a striking example of Australian resistance to American impact.

When we turn to the American impact on pedagogy—school organisation, curriculum and methodology—we again find Australian resistance, but in this instance offered with less certainty. At least superficially, the primary (or elementary) school in both countries was called into being to serve the same purpose. Without protracting this comparison by citing evidence in detail one can fairly say that both communities were originally concerned to ensure that their children attending the public schools should receive a moral education (both communities having rejected the notion of a specifically religious or denominational education); beyond this both communities, under the pressure of events, called on the schools to perform other functions.

They expected the schools to perform a 'police' function; believing that ignorance was a source of crime they called on the schools to dispel ignorance and thereby create a generation of respectable, respectful, law-abiding citizens, trusting that Adam Smith had been right when he advised them that 'An instructed and intelligent people . . . are always more decent and orderly than an ignorant and stupid one.'[5] Further, they expected the schools to perform a political function by protecting society from the consequences of a widening franchise; the aphorism, 'We must educate our masters', though originally tossed off by an English politician, was echoed again and again in both America and Australia. And finally, under the impact of industrialisation and increased commercial rivalry, both communities expected the schools to provide the universal literacy and numeracy without which a skilled, enterprising, inventive labour force could not be created.

These expectations both communities had in common, but to them the American community added a further expectation which gave a distinctive tone to their elementary schools. In essence, they were much more concerned about the duty of the public school to produce a politically intelligent and responsible citizenry than the Australians were, and this for the very good reason that they, the Americans, were faced with the assimilation of millions of migrants drawn from a score of countries; if the United States of America was to develop a national entity then the school, above all other social agencies, had to provide not only the intellectual but also the emotional basis for national cohesion. As if to underline the urgency and complexity of this task the Civil War tore the frail fabric of the community apart in the tragic years 1861–65, leaving the schools the seemingly impossible task of weaving it together again. This sort of task, not unknown to European schoolmasters such as those of Prussia who had given life and dignity again to the generation that grew up after the humiliation of Jena and the Treaty of Tilsit (1807), is something completely unknown to the Australian schoolmaster; nor, until the last ten years or so, has he had any reason to ask himself how a school can weld together into one nation a dozen or a score of migrant nationalities.

This, to speak only of the elementary school for the moment, is the reason why Americans expected so much more of their schools than the Australians did. In turn, this expectation led American educationists to attempt more, to experiment more than their Australian counterparts did; without the American sense of need and urgency the Australians were content to follow traditional lines, to accept mild change if it were in the British tradition, but to regard much of what the Americans were doing as unnecessary, extravagant and, indeed, unsound.

The American educationists' answer to the problem of migrant assimilation and nation building was Progressivism. Of that movement Lawrence A. Cremin has said:

Actually, progressive education began as part of a vast humanitarian effort to apply the promise of American life . . . to the puzzling new urban-industrial civilization that came into being during the latter half of the nineteenth century . . . First, it meant broadening the program and function of the school to include direct concern for health, vocation, and the quality of family and community life. Second, it meant applying in the classroom the pedagogical principles derived from new scientific research in psychology and the social sciences. Third, it meant tailoring instruction more and more to the different kinds and classes of children who were being brought within the purview of the school . . . Finally, Progressivism implied the radical faith that culture could be democratized without being vulgarized.[6]

This was a response to an American need; it was not an Australian need. In so far as Australians felt a need to revitalise and improve the curriculum and methodology of their elementary schools to-

wards the end of the nineteenth century they found a more acceptable pattern in another movement, the New Education Movement,
which was gathering momentum in England. In a recent study of
this movement an Australian, R. J. W. Selleck, has written a book[7]
which should be put alongside Cremin's study of the Progressive
Movement. Although these two studies make it clear that the two
movements had much in common, they also reveal the gulf that
separated them; the contrast between the scope and intention of
the American movement and the British-derived Australian movement helps to explain this further manifestation of Australian
resistance to American impact.

In Australian secondary education we encounter a clash of
opinion between the two countries at the outset. Leaving aside the
development of private, fee-paying secondary schools and confin-
ing our attention to public secondary schools we find that the
transformation in America of the Jeffersonian concept of political
equality into a belief in equality of opportunity—and specifically a
belief in educational equality of opportunity—was very slow to gain
acceptance in Australia. When it did gain half-hearted acceptance
(in the 1940's) it probably derived more from the English 'equal-
but-different' variety of that faith (as expressed in the English
Education Act of 1944) than from American precedents.

James Bryant Conant, in a memorable attempt to state concisely
the nature of the American high school, declared:

I believe it accurate to state that a high school accommodating all the
youth of a community is typical of American public education. I think
it safe to say that the comprehensive high school is characteristic of our
society and further that it has come into being because of our economic
history and our devotion to the ideals of equality of opportunity and
equality of status.[8]

By way of contrast it could be said that although the Australian
high school came into being because of our economic history, it
owed very little to the ideas of equality of opportunity or equality
of status, and that although these ideals have been invoked in
recent years they have won only partial acceptance and have given

rise to comprehensive high schools in only some of the States.

Almost without exception, high schools in Australia date from the early years of the present century. (Their belated appearance accounts, in part, for the power and prestige of the private schools in Australia.) To the American reader who chanced to read the recommendations of a Royal Commission on Education which sat in Victoria (the second most populous State) between 1899 and 1900, the discussion on secondary education must have seemed ludicrous. Knowing that his own tax-supported high schools could trace their origins back to the 1820's he must have read the Royal Commissioners' words with a mounting sense of incredulity:

The idea formerly entertained that the function of the State in matters educational was merely to provide the most elementary form of instruction has long since given place to a recognition of the duty and responsibility of the Government . . . to afford facilities for the highest intellectual training and development. . . . We are convinced . . . that the need for trained intelligence in every branch of industry must rapidly be recognised by the people of Victoria. . . . The evidence submitted to us by manufacturers and working tradesmen alike clearly shows that the average standard of educational equipment is insufficient to enable lads to enter upon their apprenticeship. . . . This undoubtedly points to the need for a higher degree of primary education than that at present obtainable. The institution of continuation schools would in no way interfere with the existing secondary or public [i.e. private] schools, or encroach upon the province of secondary education as understood in this State. The class of students for whom provision would be made by continuation schools would be largely the children of the working classes, who will ultimately have to support themselves by manual work; and the instruction afforded would differ distinctly from secondary education, which has for its main object the training of young men destined for the professions. . . . Stringent conditions as to entrance to continuation schools should be imposed. . . . We consider that free instruction in the State continuation schools might in the first instance prove detrimental to their success. . . . The charging of a fee . . . would create a feeling that the instruction was worth paying for. . . . Ample provision should also be made for securing the enrolment of bright, clever children, who are likely to benefit most from the higher instruction, by adopting a system of scholarships. . . .[9]

To most Americans, every statement in the Royal Commissioners' report was anathema: the underlying doctrine of élitism, the vocationalism, the selectivity, the charging of fees. His worst fears were confirmed when Victoria finally moved into the field of secondary education for, beginning with a secondary school for the preparation of future elementary school teachers (the Melbourne Continuation School, 1904), it proceeded to develop a bewildering variety of schools allegedly suited to different types of pupils: High Schools, Agricultural High Schools, Junior Technical Schools, Domestic Science Schools, Higher Elementary Schools, Central Schools. By the mid-1940's when Victoria, in the heady post-war atmosphere of social change, legislated to make secondary education compulsory and free for all adolescents it found itself a prisoner in its own defence works. The flood of unselected pupils who now, perforce, presented themselves for secondary education brought with them all the problems of curriculum and methodology with which Americans had been familiar for a century or more, but Victoria, apart from tinkering with the curriculum by adding subjects vaguely derived from American precedents (e.g. Social Studies) could not, or would not, face the challenge of the comprehensive high school. In a last, half-hearted attempt to do so, the State Government, in 1958, appointed a Committee of Enquiry led by the Director of Education. Victorians who rushed to buy copies of the Committee's report, when it was published in 1960, at first believed that a milestone had been passed for there, on p. 102, was a thorough denunciation of the separate-school-for-separate-types theory:

Our conclusion is that, on the basis of expressed interests or of predicted vocations, it is dangerous to attempt to separate children of equal ability at this stage into different courses . . . or into different schools. . . . Our conclusion is that under these circumstances, opportunities to form friendships with the sons and daughters from other kinds of home, to develop a proper appreciation of the full range and significance of occupations, and to broaden perspectives that must necessarily be limited at the present age of transfer, may thereby be restricted.

But the very next page destroyed all hope:

Were we, therefore, considering the organisation of a system *ab initio*, we would consider that there is merit in a system whereby all children should pass from the primary school at about age twelve, into a common secondary school. . . . But we are not initiating a system of education. We have inherited a complex system which satisfies many, and there are strong arguments in favour of continuing the present system rather than scrapping it in favour of a uniform system of comprehensive secondary schools.[10]

In defence of the Victorian educationists who refused to accept the American comprehensive high school solution it must be said that their reluctance to abandon the traditional, specialised form of secondary education to which they were accustomed was being reinforced by the wave of anti-Progressivism and general educational criticism which came out of America in the 1950's. Before Butts published his *Assumptions Underlying Australian Education* in 1955 (and he could be taken to fairly represent the Columbia Teachers' College brand of Progressivism) some Australian educationists were familiar with Albert Lynd's *Quackery in the Public Schools* (1953), Mortimer Smith's *The Diminished Mind* (1954) and Arthur Bestor's *Educational Wastelands* (1954). Butts' book certainly had an immediate and sustained impact on educational thought in Australia (it was printed twice in 1955 and again in 1957, 1961, 1964, 1965 and 1966), but it had to contend with Arthur Bestor's *The Restoration of Learning* (1955), Paul Woodring's *Fourth of a Nation* (1957), Jacques Barzun's *The House of Intellect* (1959), Admiral Rickover's *Education and Freedom* (1960) and Myron Lieberman's *The Future of Public Education* (1960). The Victorian educationist who stood his ground had some powerful allies.

In only one State, but that the most populous (New South Wales), has a secondary school pattern emerged which bears unmistakeable marks of the American impact. In 1953 the Director-General of Education in that State, Dr H. S. Wyndham (significantly a graduate of Stanford as well as Sydney), persuaded the State Government to authorise a sweeping enquiry into secondary education. Wyndham was appointed chairman of the Committee and began a four-year battle with the traditionalists over the future development of secondary education in New South Wales, where the presence of a number of prestigious, selective high schools and eminent private schools provided a hard core of resistance. Wyndham was looking for what Paul Woodring was shortly to call a synthesis of the classic thesis and the pragmatic antithesis, and by October 1957 his Committee was prepared to agree to the following proposals:

On completion of the primary school course and, in general, about the age of twelve years, all pupils should proceed, without examination, to secondary education. . . . The organisation and curriculum of the high school should be such as to provide a satisfactory education for all adolescents and should be designed to cover four years, to the age of about sixteen. . . . On satisfactory completion of the four-year course, a School Certificate should be issued on the basis of the result of an external examination. . . . The curriculum should be designed to provide a core of subjects common to all schools, together with a progressive increase in the proportion of elected subjects. . . .
Under teacher guidance, election of subjects should progressively be made in the light of pupil achievement or potential. . . . Elective courses should . . . be of adequate duration and demand adequate standards. . . . Pupils who wish to proceed beyond the School Certificate level . . . should remain at school to follow . . . courses leading to the Higher School Certificate. . . . The further course of study should be designed to cover two years.[11]

Controversy still surrounds the Wyndham scheme, and as the first intake into the Wyndham schools graduated from high school only at the end of 1967 it is far too early to speak definitely of its success. Nevertheless it is clearly becoming a model for other States to follow and its blend of the new and the old, of comprehensiveness allied to a concern for individual talent and differences may well become the accepted pattern for the whole country.

Meanwhile, here and there, other American solutions to the problem of organising secondary education for all are being examined and experimented with. In Tasmania, for example, a form of senior high school was recently established which will give that State, in effect, a '6-4-2' system (i.e. six years of elementary school, four of junior and two of senior high school); in Victoria, a very ambitious scheme of junior and senior high schools has been prepared but awaits official approval. Over-all the trend is undoubtedly towards the comprehensive school and probably towards a junior-senior high school system. It could be argued that once senior high schools are firmly established they might begin to extend upwards and take on something of the characteristics of the American College. James Bryant Conant, in comparing American and Australian education in 1956, felt sure that the American college was a 'special phenomenon',[12] and could see no indication of Australia departing from the British pattern it had adopted whereby a boy or girl enters a university, by selection, directly from high school at the age of seventeen, eighteen or nineteen and proceeds directly to specialised and professional studies leading, in the first instance, to the appropriate bachelor's degree. In 1968, however, it is not so clear that this will remain the pattern. A nation-wide shortage of university places, increasing affluence, and the desperate need of the teaching profession for more teachers with tertiary education than the universities can supply may well lead Australia to think in terms of colleges not unlike the American model.

Until the beginning of this decade the Australian educationist's response to the American impact was one of resistance or, at most, an ambivalent acceptance-rejection of American models. To some extent this response reflected an Australian distrust of American 'superiority', a feeling of being overwhelmed by a neighbour with vastly greater resources and, only too often, an over-weening confidence in his use of those resources. To some extent this response reflected an Australian preference (both emotional and intellectual) for other models with which he was more familiar. The typical Australian academic and educationist had been taught by Englishmen (if not in Australia, then in England when he undertook postgraduate studies) and having eventually succeeded at Oxford, Cambridge or London and returned to Australia he was thereafter in a position to recommend his best students to those same institutions. It was rare indeed, until a few years ago, to find an Australian preferring to study at an American rather than an English university. There was no tradition of going to America; it was expensive; and his teachers were not in a position to write the letters of introduction they could so easily write to Balliol, the Cavendish or the London School of Economics.

The essential barrier to academic and educational communication between the two countries was the Australians' ignorance of the realities of American academic and educational life. Then came the Fulbright scheme, and at first a trickle, and then a flood of Australia's best young teachers descended on every American State to teach in their schools for a year, to visit their universities, to enjoy the hospitality of American homes and to see, at first hand, how American education worked. They did not come back as starry-eyed converts to everything American, but they came back with a great respect for many things American and, most important of all, they came back with the means of communication: with subscriptions to professional and learned journals they had not heard of before, and with the warm assurance that the Deans, Superintendents and Principals who had urged them to write and 'keep in touch', wanted their association to continue.

The effect of this new relationship can be clearly seen in the new science courses now being introduced in Australia's secondary schools. Of course we have looked to the Nuffield Foundation and other non-American sources for guidance, and we have used our own eclectic inventiveness in designing certain new courses, but the overwhelming impact has come from the new American courses: the Biological Sciences Curriculum Study (BSCS), the Chemical Materials Study (CHEM Study), the Physical Sciences Study Committee (PSSC). Watching Australian committees studying and adapting these courses one quickly becomes aware of the Australians' new familiarity with America, of the number of teachers on these committees who can say: 'I remember working with the teacher who wrote this part of the programme', 'I was at X High School when they ran the pilot programme on this', 'There's an article in such-and-such a journal which raises doubts about this'.

What is true of Fulbright applies with equal force to Carnegie,

Rockefeller, Ford, Eisenhower, Harkness and a score of other benefactions which exist to forge cultural or educational links between America and, amongst others, Australia. What happened to the Australian primary and secondary school teacher, through Fulbright, can be seen happening to academics through the same and similar agencies. The opportunity had first to be created for the Australian academic to study in American institutions; out of this experience, if all went well, came a respect for American scholars with whom he worked and a wish to recommend to them his colleagues and advanced students. By a process of geometrical progression one Australian, so influenced, quickly produced a dozen more.

The American impact on university education is to be found, not so much in the structure and organisation of Australian universities, but in matters of scholarship and methods of instruction. Each month, for example, the University of Melbourne (Victoria) publishes, for limited circulation, the names of examiners for the degree of Doctor of Philosophy. Ten years ago the external examiners would have been appointed, almost without exception, from British universities, and the discerning reader would have appreciated why Professor X in Melbourne had asked Professor Y in Oxford to examine; the scholarly relationship between them would have been apparent. Nowadays, however, one notices that nearly every second thesis is to have at least one American examiner: Microbiology, one notices, has asked for an examiner from the Scripps Clinic and Research Foundation at La Jolla, California; Forestry has turned to the University of California, Berkeley, Biochemistry to Yale, Physiology to Johns Hopkins. Again, the discerning reader can detect the scholarly relationship which has evolved from the initial contact, a few years ago, between an Australian academic and an American colleague or institution.

Of course the process sometimes begins with the visit of an American academic to an Australian university but, in general, the Australian must also be encouraged to see American practices in operation.

For example, in August 1951 Dean Erwin N. Griswold, of the Harvard Law School, visited Australia and participated extensively in the annual conference of the Australasian Universities Law Schools Association. To audiences made up of law teachers trained on traditional British lines he expounded in detail the Socratic and casebook method of teaching law. His audiences were impressed but not totally converted. Dean Griswold then followed up his exposition by arranging for certain staff members to visit the United States; their acceptance of American practices was not uncritical, but they were convinced that change was needed and they began to adapt American practices to Australian circumstances. Today, almost half the senior members of the Law Faculty in the University of Melbourne have taken an advanced law degree at an American university.

Australian culture has always been substantially derivative; it will probably remain so for some time; in the meantime it is clear that in developing his own educational synthesis the Australian is becoming more aware each year of the place of the American element in it.

A. G. Austin

[1] James Bryant Conant, *Education and Liberty* Cambridge, Mass., 1956, p. 2.
[2] I. L. Kandel, *Types of Administration*, Melbourne, 1938, p. 14.
[3] A. F. Davies, 'Problems of Decentralization in State Government in Australia', in E. L. French (ed.), *Melbourne Studies in Education, 1958–9*, Melbourne, 1960, pp. 156–7.
[4] R. Freeman Butts, op.cit., p. 14.
[5] Adam Smith, *An Inquiry into the Nature and Causes of the Wealth of Nations*, Edinburgh, 1859, p. 353. (Original edition 1776.)
[6] Lawrence A. Cremin, *The Transformation of the School: Progressivism in American Education, 1876–1957* New York, 1961, pp. viii, ix.
[7] R. J. W. Selleck, *The New Education: The English Background, 1870–1914*, Melbourne, 1968.
[8] James Bryant Conant, *The American High School Today*, New York, 1959, p. 8.
[9] *Victoria: Royal Commission on Technical Education 1899–1900*, (Final Report), Melbourne, Government Printer, 1901, pp. 9–25.
[10] *Report of the Committee on State Education in Victoria*, Melbourne, Government Printer, 1960, pp. 102–03.
[11] *Report of the Committee appointed to survey Secondary Education in New South Wales* Sydney, Government Printer, 1958, pp. 103–08.
[12] *Education and Liberty*, op.cit. p. 31.

6 The American Impact on Australian Business

Much has been written of the role played by American capital in the development of the Australian economy. Just as important, but perhaps not so openly acknowledged, has been the American impact on various aspects of Australian business. Although rather difficult to substantiate with cut and dried facts and figures, this latter influence is, nevertheless, much too real to be denied.

The Shape of America's Impact. One of the reasons for an apparently strong American influence in the Australian business community is surely the extent to which the Americans control the direct investments they make in this country. It seems to be an American trait to purchase equity capital in Australian concerns, with the purpose of gaining the right to have at least a partial say in the running of the companies in which they acquire financial interests.

United States businessmen have become skilled in oversea operations. Along with the developing pattern of international business has evolved the concept of the 'global corporation'. Rapidly advancing technology means that the economies of scale in an increasing range of products are outstripping the size and growth of individual markets. In keeping with this trend, growing numbers of big American firms are extending their operations beyond their national boundaries. The number of United States corporations

The author wishes to acknowledge the assistance received from Mrs E. M. Duncan, B.A., Research Officer, Australia and New Zealand Bank Limited, Melbourne, in preparing this Chapter.

earning more than half their revenue outside the United States topped twenty several years ago, and the United States Department of Commerce calculated that one-fifth of all capital expenditure in 1966 was outside America. The bulk of direct United States investment in foreign countries is destined for Canada (31 per cent of the total in 1966), and, in recent years, Western Europe has been absorbing a great deal under the impetus of the protective policies of the EEC countries. But the quantity flowing to Australia is increasing rapidly, with growing significance to this country.

Many United States investors are finding Australia a worthwhile target for the extension of their foreign activities. Politically she has enviable stability, economically prospects for continued growth are excellent, and there are no language barriers. Taxation on company income is not heavy, and at present there are no restrictions on remittance of profits or repatriation of capital. One further, and considerable, asset is the fact that there is no requirement that oversea businesses should operate in Australia in association with local interests.

This last aspect carries considerable weight with American entrepreneurs, who seem traditionally to favour whole ownership. A Department of Trade and Industry Survey revealed that, in 1966, of a total 255 Australian manufacturing firms with equity share interest owned in America:

18 had less than 25 per cent United States equity,
23 had between 25 per cent and 50 per cent,
13 had between 75 per cent and 100 per cent,
and 143 (or 56·1 per cent) were 100 per cent American owned.[1]

The method of approach of most American concerns operating outside the United States appears to be to endeavour to maximise the return on their investment, and then plough back accrued profits to promote growth of the business. The preference for wholly-owned subsidiaries is understandable in this light, as it enables the parent company to concentrate on growth, rather than on dividends, in a way that would be difficult if the interests of a high proportion of local ownership had to be considered. Unified ownership is also, presumably, thought to be in the best interests of co-ordinated control, which, in turn, should result in improved business efficiency and decision-making based on sound business principles.

American businessmen are renowned for the great enthusiasm and vigour with which they pursue their goals. That something of this American keenness has been transmitted to the Australian business climate must surely be considered an advantage.

Technical Benefits. American influence in Australia has been manifest, perhaps most conspicuously, in a great infusion of 'know-how'—both in relation to technical abilities and managerial skills. It has been responsible for the introduction of new products, new processes, new marketing techniques, new markets, new ideas on organisation and training, new attitudes towards planning, and new concepts of performance and so on. It can fairly be said that innovations, largely attributable to America, have gone a long way towards revolutionising Australian industrial development and business practices.

Australia is heavily dependent upon the fruits of American scientific research, and one of the most important benefits of American investment in this country is the gain in technical and scientific know-how as it is transferred by parent companies to their affiliates.

The rest of the world appears to have lagged seriously behind the United States in all the major technological innovations of the last twenty years or so (see table below). Even in some fields where the technical lead may have been taken from it, an American company can have built up, in the meantime, such a commercial start, in its particular sphere of operation, that its position is difficult to challenge.

Origin of 140 major developments of the last twenty years,[2] (expressed in percentage).

United States	60
Great Britain	15
Germany	10

Switzerland	4
Sweden	3·5
Other	7·5

Fortunately for Australia, as with the rest of the world, American businesses have been exceptionally generous with technical information, and their discoveries have not remained within the bounds of that country. In fact, the speed with which American-based technology has spread round the world is one of the most notable industrial phenomena of the last decade.

It would appear that American business participation in Australia has not necessarily discouraged local industry, but, frequently, has moved into a void and opened up new fields.

International comparisons illustrate that Australian businesses have lagged behind their counterparts in many other countries in the application of resources to research and development. Very few private businesses are willing to put money into these activities, and about 80 per cent of the research and development in Australia is financed and carried out by Governments and Universities. This is in contrast to the United States, where the bulk of such work is carried out by the private sector, even though a large proportion (about 60 per cent) is paid for by the Government.

A serious difficulty for Australian industry is that comparatively few Australian firms are large enough to be able to finance meaningful or fruitful research projects. A most important feature of the growth in American business associations in Australia is that local businesses have been able to benefit from the research discoveries of their American affiliates. Many subsidiaries of American companies in Australia have the advantage of being able to draw on the research and development resources of their parent or, when this is not the case, can benefit from the reputation of the parent company in assisting them to raise finance locally. These firms often have an added advantage over an Australian-financed company in that they are able, when conducting research or when commencing new operations, to do so on a substantially larger scale, thereby securing significant economies of scale. This is an important point, as American experience seems to prove that money concentrated in large sums on relatively few, big projects bears more fruit than does capital fragmented over a series of small research concerns. OECD research supports this fact: 'there are certain minimum threshold levels below which innovative efforts are likely to be largely unproductive'.[3]

Australia has compensated for her comparative lack of indigenous technological developments by attracting and welcoming American investment and by using licensing agreements and similar arrangements from the United States. In some affiliated companies, Americans have acquired part of their Australian shareholding in return for technical know-how, rather than in return for cash. It has been estimated that about one-third of the American firms which have commenced manufacturing in this country since the end of World War II have done so with the specific purpose of introducing a new production process.

Dr Donald Brash, in his recent survey of American investment in Australian industry, conducted while he was at the Australian National University, was convinced that American affiliated firms operating in Australia believed their access to American technology to be of vital importance to their continued growth and success in the Australian market. Most parent companies maintain a steady flow of technical information to their affiliates, thus giving them the benefit of their own experiences. The flow of information is maintained in a variety of ways. Some companies issue regular monthly bulletins to their subsidiaries, others hold world-wide symposiums of the staffs of their associated companies, and many conduct company schools to keep their staff up to date. It is becoming common practice for employees from Australia to travel to the United States to familiarise themselves with processes operating in the parent plant or, vice versa, for an expert from the parent plant in the United States to visit the subsidiary in Australia and instruct its operators in the new methods.

It is probably fair to conclude that, on the whole, Australia benefits more from American product development than she does from process research. Many of the methods evolved in the United States are not entirely suited to Australian operations, which tend to be considerably smaller than American ventures in similar fields. In fact much of the development work which is done in Australia is concentrated on the adaptation and modification of oversea designs and formulae to suit local conditions.

Some original design and product development work is done in Australia by American affiliated firms, particularly in the vehicle, chemical and food industries. Some such companies operate in fields untouched by their American parent, while some have been known to develop products superior to the parent equivalent, which have subsequently been adopted by the parent company itself. One Australian-based firm lays claim to a production method, entirely designed in Australia, which has been copied by its parent company.

Licensing. Although most American companies investing in Australia have brought in their technology along with their dollars, not all American influence has been prompted by a capital inflow. Some firms have contributed to the development of Australian industry, particularly manufacturing industry, by licence or similar arrangement.

A company's decision to expand into oversea operations is affected by a combination of economic and human motives. Different types of operations are effective in different types of industries and, although no clear-cut pattern is obvious, a recent survey of American production abroad[4] concluded that, in general, the more advanced the technological developments in a line of production, the greater the probability that a firm would undertake oversea production. Among smaller firms, financial limitations are a greater constraint on the extent of foreign investment, and are one of the major reasons why many of these firms rely on licensing to earn, with a minimum of effort, representation in an oversea market and a reasonable financial return.

Foreign companies in Australia are subject to a minimum of control by the Australian Government in the licensing of patents, technology and know-how to Australian subsidiaries, joint ventures and also to otherwise unrelated firms. There is little official data available on the number of licensing agreements between Australia and oversea firms. However, in 1963, the United States

Chamber of Commerce in Australia estimated that there were in existence more than 800 such agreements between United States and Australian companies. The total today is thought to exceed 1,000.[5]

In keeping with the general pattern, cases of pure licensing are usually between the smaller and medium-sized American firms and independent Australian companies. It is interesting to note that in the past, some such agreements have been known to result in joint ventures, the American firm taking an equity in the business of its Australian licensee, or even making a direct acquisition of the local firm.

The Australian Government recognises the benefits gained by local business, and has not, as yet, intervened in the licensing field. However, it has, on occasions, voiced its displeasure at clauses within licensing agreements, which act to limit the Australian licensee in his access to overseas markets. It has been a criticism of American licensors that many are guilty of applying such restrictions. The proportion of United States contracts containing 'restrictive export franchise' clauses is thought to have changed little since 1959, when it stood at about 40 per cent[6]. The Government's principal objection to these conditional agreements is that they hinder Australia's endeavour to increase export earnings and achieve a better balance in overseas trade by diversifying sources of exports and increasing the proportion of export income obtained from manufactured, as distinct from rural and primary, products.

Spheres of Influence. North American capital has been prominent in the post-war development of Australia, and American affiliated companies have played, or are playing, a crucial role in the establishment of new, large-scale industries and in the development of some of Australia's key economic sectors. In this respect, American firms are in a position significantly to affect the economy as a whole. Although the importance of American capital in the development of Australia's mineral and petroleum industries is rising spectacularly, the biggest single category of American investment is still in the manufacturing sector.

By far the largest of these investments in Australian manufacturing is in the motor industry which, since its inception, has been dominated by American influence. Of the five automotive industries listed among Australia's top fifty companies, four are wholly owned by American parent companies.

American influence in Australian industry is not only substantial, but also diverse: electrical products, metals, food and drink, chemicals, pharmaceuticals, toiletries, cosmetics, oil products and computers, some engineering fields and rubber and plastic products. The spread of American interest is reflected in the increasing number of agreements between United States and Australian organisations and in the widening range of industries affected by American participation.

In recent months a great deal of attention has been focused on special American methods being used in oil and mineral exploration in Australia. Some of the more notable examples are the development of the iron ore deposits at Savage River in Tasmania which entails the piping of low grade (38 per cent Fe) ore a distance of fifty-three miles in slurry form, and the upgrading of the low iron content ore into pellets of 67·5 per cent Fe. Much of the technical knowledge, the construction techniques and the necessary equipment for off-shore oil exploration, as it is being carried out in the Gippsland basin, are being supplied from the United States. A large floating barge with a 500-ton crane, supply boats, tugs and equipment barges, all from America, are assisting in the operation. There have been recent American innovations in the field of off-shore seismic work, and off-shore pipeline laying techniques are helping in oil exploration as well. Again, two American-based companies have undertaken to supervise the conversion of all domestic and industrial gas burning appliances to cater for the imminent introduction of natural gas to Australian markets. A core of experienced American personnel is training Australian technicians to handle such change-overs. Another American firm is hiring out its specialised knowledge in the techniques of oil well reservoir assessment. With the use of computers, it is able to assess both the quantity and expected production life of oil occurrences.

Although these developments have taken place recently in some of Australia's most rapidly growing and most glamorous new industries, American influence has been felt in Australian manufacturing industry for a long time. This influence has probably been most far reaching in the durable consumer goods areas, covering the whole range from motor-cars to outboard marine motors, and from household refrigerators to washing machines.

As has already been mentioned, the Australian motor manufacturing industry is indebted to United States automobile manufacturers for its first move into local manufacture, which was taken by General Motors in the early years after World War II, and for the development of local production which now covers some 70 per cent of Australian motor-car registrations.

The techniques and capabilities of the plants established in Australia by United States companies have profoundly influenced the whole range of local manufacture of the goods concerned, and have also greatly influenced the markets for those goods.

The rapid rate of growth of the Australian economy in the two decades and more since 1945, has coincided with a marked rise in the affluence of the Australian consumer market. It is probably both fortunate and to be expected, that American technical knowledge and know-how would be made available to provide for the rapidly growing demands of the market in volume and range of products. Australia, probably as much as any other country, has absorbed American assistance in capital, know-how and business techniques in the rapidly expanding, affluent society of the mid-twentieth century.

An important feature in the significant influence of American technological developments, industrial designs and methods on Australian business has undoubtedly been the broadly similar basic circumstances of the two countries. Not only is the absence of any language barrier of great significance, but also the similarity in size of the two countries has been most important in the introduction of American methods and equipment for Australian activities and enterprises. The vast scale of distances to be travelled and volumes of material to be moved are far more comparable between Australia and the United States than between United States and any

European country or even, in some respects, between United States and Europe as a whole. In these circumstances the design of American equipment, although not always ideal, will often be more suitable than any other foreign type for Australian requirements. It is, therefore, not surprising that, so frequently, American equipment and methods are employed.

The Australian Government is aware of the impact American ventures are having on the country's development. It is also aware of the need to attract qualified men to fill the gaps in Australia's business structure, so that development can proceed unhindered. The Visiting Expert Agreement is designed to do just this.

Under this agreement, American experts, technical or otherwise, who contribute skills not readily available in Australia, are able to live in this country for a period of up to four years, in which time they are eligible for considerable income tax concessions.[7] Their income tax is levied at the Federal rate current in the United States which, in most cases, is substantially lower than the Australian tax on an equivalent income. This concession is automatic in the first year but subject to review in the subsequent three years, when an authorised person (e.g. Secretary to the Department of Trade) must certify that the visitor's contribution is assisting in the development of Australian industry.

Impact on Australian Suppliers. Great weight attaches to the importance of the American impact as it has been felt through the Australian suppliers to American subsidiaries. Their considerable purchases of goods and services have been, in fact, one of the most effective means for American companies of making their presence felt in the Australian market.

Australian firms supplying American affiliates with materials and parts have benefited from the operations of their American-owned customers in much the same way as these customers have gained advantage from the operations of their American parent companies.

American affiliates seem to have had the greatest impact on their supplier firms in the years immediately after their establishment in this country, when they had to educate their suppliers to meet their demands and specifications. The ancillary firms, in the face of competition from imported components, accordingly set about revising their procedures. Benefits were for the mutual advantage of 'pupil' and 'teacher', and for Australian manufacturers generally, as they found themselves served by an increasing number of efficient sub-contractors.

The most outstanding example of the impact of American subsidiaries on their Australian suppliers can be seen in the motor vehicle industry. Dr Donald Brash concluded that, 'the contribution which General Motors-Holden's (GMH) has made to the efficiency of Australian industry over the past twenty years, must undoubtedly be rated among the greatest benefits which Australia has received from American investment'.

The interdependence of GMH and its suppliers is clearly illustrated by the fact that payments by GMH to suppliers exceeded 55 per cent of all proceeds from the sale of its products in 1967.[8] Not infrequently, GMH, and other motor vehicle companies, have paid to Australian suppliers a considerable premium above the price of equivalent imports to encourage local production and to build up local firms to the point where they could produce on a larger, more economic scale. Suppliers to the automotive industry have benefited considerably from its rapid growth and can now produce the full range of parts needed for the modern motor vehicle.

American subsidiaries were particularly interested in the quality control and scheduling systems of their suppliers. However, in the process of revolutionising these, the American affiliates provided technical information and managerial know-how which led to improvements in all sorts of procedures: manufacturing methods, machinery design, materials formulae, inspection techniques, forecasting systems, finance methods, selling and purchasing procedures, market research and personnel training. Many of the changes involved computers, the increasing use of which has had far-reaching implications for the business world.

The comparatively more demanding American business procedures have, as mentioned, influenced the financial aspects of their

Australian business associates. Some local firms, which admitted to infrequent and relatively ineffectual budgeting, now, largely as a result of their contracts with American companies, compile comprehensive monthly accounts and engage in detailed budgetary planning.

Long-range planning is becoming a feature of increasing impor- tance in Australian business operations, again largely as the result of American experience, example and demands. Objectives are set, and plans drawn up for their achievement. Figures are analysed extensively and past results are compared with predetermined targets. When necessary, forecasts are revised for greater accuracy.

Managerial Expertise. It has not been purely technological skill which has kept America ahead of the rest of the world in this advanced age, but, to a large extent, the efficient management of scientific innovations. The Americans themselves acknowledge that educated management is probably the greatest single reason for their success, and the asset which probably receives greatest care and attention in planning for the future.

From reports of the recent meeting of members of the OECD to investigate the so-called 'technological gap', it would appear that rapid technological innovation requires a certain state of mind in industry which, judging by American experience, is due to broad, higher education for business. There appears to be a definite correlation between the level of general education and the rate of innovation in a country. For instance, the United States has a greater number of graduates (i.e. seventy-six) per 1,000 of total working population than has any other country, and also has the fastest rate of innovation.

As has been the case with technological break-throughs, advanc- ed management techniques are spreading rapidly throughout the industrialised world, and many of these are fully recognised as having originated in the United States. Because of the apparent success of these methods and their wide dissemination, many pro- gressive firms in Australia are using American methods, whether their companies happen to have American affiliations or not. Australian businessmen have learned to respect the business acumen of their American counterparts and are rapidly becoming more eager to learn their basic skills. Some evidence of this is seen, for instance, in the increasing numbers of Australian firms which, along the lines of American practice, are seeking the services of management consultants.

Many Australian executives have become versed in American managerial methods by direct example and training. The expansion of United States firms into international business seems to depend rather heavily upon the availability of people who have the skills needed to oversee such operations. Many American companies appear to relate their rate of expansion abroad to the speed of recruiting and training of American management personnel, or to the evolution of international managerial skills.

In Australia's experience, the usual practice has been for American companies to make use of American managers and technicians in the formative years of an affiliated firm's life. Once the operation becomes established, however, these experts are normally repatriated, leaving qualified local executives to take over the running. In some cases, where there is simply an insufficiency of Australians with the necessary qualifications, or in others, where a pioneering firm finds that it has created a demand for a new type of skilled labour, the Americans take it upon themselves to provide the necessary training and experience.

Some corporations like to retain Americans in the top executive positions of their Australian affiliates, but, on the whole, the number of Americans employed in direct investment enterprises in this country is small. A survey prepared by the American Consulate General of all the American firms having subsidiaries, affiliates and branch offices with headquarters in Victoria and Tasmania, revealed that, of the 166 companies listed in this area in January 1967, as few as forty-eight had United States managers. Current training methods of most American companies operating in Australia, either through a subsidiary or through an affiliate, ensure an increasing supply of Australians with the ability to qualify them for top management positions.

Training. Mention has occurred already of the great stress placed on training by American corporations. The greater mobility of labour, which has evolved hand in hand with the philosophy of the 'global corporation', is speeding this process and the Australian business community is seeing the need to place similar emphasis on the education of staff. Training is not confined to a few specific areas, but is expected to encompass all facets of business life. As the flow of technical information is maintained between parent companies and their associates, so other information, perhaps most importantly new management ideas, are conveyed between the member companies of a world-affiliated group.

Americans have been as generous with their managerial developments as they have been with their technical know-how. United States business schools have been accepting growing numbers of Australian post-graduates each year, there is a plentiful supply of American literature for the management student and, now that travel is easier, more and more Australians are going abroad with the prime purpose of looking and learning. United States company consulting teams visit subsidiaries and advise on procedures and, with the growing trend towards rotation of staff, more Australians are sent to the United States to participate in comprehensive training in American production techniques and business methods. There even appears to be an increasing tendency to use Australian personnel in the higher echelons of the American parent company itself.

Conditions in the business world are changing continually as advances in all fields take place at an almost alarming rate. Successful American companies are vitally aware of the need to adapt their management, and to condition their executives to be receptive and responsive to new ideas. It is with this end in view that they engage in extensive retraining programmes. Not only do they train their personnel in various aspects of the firm as they move through the ranks, but they familiarise them with new procedures whenever the need arises. They feel that it is important for the higher management to be included in these refresher courses, a fact which more Australian companies are also accepting. American business leaders feel that it is important for top executives to move with the times, if for no other reason than to appreciate the capabilities of their younger staff, so that they will make full use of their training and their talents.

D. H. Merry

[1] *Directory of Overseas Investment in Australian Manufacturing Industry*, Department of Trade and Industry, Canberra, 1966, p. x, Table 3.
[2] *The Economist*, 16 March 1968.
[3] Ibid.
[4] *U.S. Production Abroad and the Balance of Payments*, a study by The National Industrial Conference Board.
[5] *Business International Australian Round Table* (New York) Briefing Paper, 29 Oct.-3 Nov. 1967, p. 24.
[6] Ibid.
[7] See Income Tax Assessment Act 1936-1967, Section 23c, vii.
[8] GMH *Annual Report* 1967.

7 American Culture in Australia

LITERATURE *Grahame Johnston*

When Mr Pierre Salinger was in Australia a couple of years ago, he was rather puzzled by one question that reporters kept putting to him wherever he went. After asking about his experiences as President Kennedy's press secretary and the reason for his trip to Australia—as an airline executive—they would often add, 'And when can we expect to read your next book?' After a time it became clear to him that if the name Salinger was one to conjure with in Australia it was mostly because of the wide, if not informed, readership enjoyed here by J. D. Salinger, author of *The Catcher in the Rye* and of the chronicles of that strange family which someone has rather unkindly called the Glass menagerie.

In a sense this anecdote characterises the way American literature has been received in Australia: with widespread enjoyment and interest, and yet selectively, sporadically and in some confusion. The enjoyment and the interest are undoubted: one has only, for instance, to compare the range of American books and magazines available in Australian bookshops and circulating libraries with that current in New Zealand to see how much easier it is for the Australian reader to obtain American writing. But, comparing the total range of American literature with the knowledge of it that literate Australians reveal in conversation and writing, one is rather struck by the extent to which chance, commerce and censorship have affected their access to it and judgment of it.

Chance and commerce go hand in hand in hand. Whether an American writer is well known in Australia or not often depends on a decision made years ago in some London publishing house: the intricacies of copyright have often meant that Australian readers can neither get the American edition of a book easily nor obtain the English edition, which may have gone out of print. Again, writers easily available in paperback editions are much better known than those only in hard cover. The combination of these effects has somewhat distorted Australians' ideas of the nature and worth of American writing.

To take one marked instance. Among some Australians, especially older people, there is a persistent equation of American writing with themes of sex, war and violence; with massive, turgid novels of tempestuous, often illicit, relationships; and with a use of language which is energetic rather than skilful. For them American literature is *The Naked and the Dead, From Here To Eternity, Sanctuary* and *Gone With The Wind*. And this is largely, of course, because advertising, the cult of the best-seller, and the paperback with the lurid cover have thrust such novels to their attention.

Conversely, many American writers of high skill are virtually unknown in Australia because they have not been reprinted in England. Ask well-read Australians about Jean Stafford, Peter Taylor, Ralph Ellison and (to take earlier writers) Ellen Glasgow, Glenway Wescott, and Edith Wharton, and you will more often than not find that these novelists—far superior in skill to Mailer, Jones and Margaret Mitchell if not to Faulkner—are hardly known at all, or if known, then because of one or two publishing decisions: Penguin Books reprinting Ellison's *Invisible Man* as a modern classic, Constable bringing out their fine new edition of Edith Wharton.

It is frustrating for an Australian to have to wait for an English publisher to adopt an American writer before he can easily and without undue expense read him. But a critical point of some force is that much misunderstanding of not only American literature (which is serious enough) but of America itself results from the remaining restrictions on the flow of American writing into

Australia. Many elements of the American experience, and its general balance of vigour and restraint, mind and heart, civility and energy, are misunderstood in Australia because the representation of American life given to Australians in books (as well as in films and on television) is inaccurate.

When many people think of restrictions, however, they mean censorship, and no consideration of the reception of American writing in Australia which failed to take account of Australian customs regulations would be complete. And yet to my mind the most damaging effects are not the inability of Australians to read William Burroughs or (for a time) Nabokov, but the way in which the publicity given to banned books again distorts the average Australian's picture of American writing.

To take an instance which sharply indicates the effects of censorship: of the three Negro novelists that critics commonly single out as the most significant, Wright, Ellison and James Baldwin, the only one most Australians will have read or even heard of is Baldwin, because *Another Country* was banned. When one considers how important to an understanding of contemporary America is an insight into the complexities of race relationships and a knowledge of the wide spectrum of Negro viewpoints—as Robert Penn Warren showed in *Who Speaks For The Negro?*, a book hardly known in Australia—it is sobering to reflect that censorship in Australia has focused attention on *Another Country* rather than Baldwin's other books, and on Baldwin rather than Ellison or Wright.

Any pressures, official or commercial, which impede the accessibility of American literature to Australians are unfortunate and deserve to be isolated and corrected. But of course the positive side is much the more obvious, and the evidence of it lies all about us.

Mr Pierre Salinger's difficulties with the reporters arose from the fact that adolescent Australians—and not only adolescent ones— have taken *The Catcher in the Rye* to their hearts just as Americans did, and 'that goddam book', as Holden would no doubt have called it, can be found on paperback racks not only in Seattle but in Sydney, where, indeed, it figures in the university entrance syllabus alongside *Huckleberry Finn* and *Of Mice and Men.* Salinger's saga of the Glass family has not achieved the same fame in Australia, despite their connections with this country—about 1922 Les and Bessie Glass, we are told, spent a couple of years in vaudeville in Australia, from which Les has retained some traces of the 'flat Australian accent' and an exit routine taught him by Will Mahoney!

Instances of the enjoyment and interest of Australians in American fiction and drama can be multiplied. In poetry alone are the contacts few and uncertain: as a university teacher, I find that Australian students have no great appetite for American verse, and the major names, with the exception of Robert Frost and (if one counts them) T. S. Eliot and W. H. Auden, make little impact. Whitman they find turgid and formless, Emily Dickinson puzzling, Pound impenetrable, Stevens impressive but too cerebral. Among contemporary poets, Robert Lowell enjoys a vogue in some circles, often rather for political than poetic reasons, and other writers of verse—John Berryman, W. D. Snodgrass, the frequenters of the American quarterlies—are admired by the younger Australian poets for their craftsmanship.

Contact between American poetry and Australian does in fact exist, because some Australian poets who are academics—James McAuley, A. D. Hope, Evan Jones and Chris Wallace-Crabbe, for instance—have visited or studied in the United States. There is little overt evidence of their sojourns there, although one remembers that Hope's magnificent *Ode on the Death of Pope Pius XII* begins with an evocative image of the russet glories of Amherst in the fall, and Wallace-Crabbe's recent collection, *The Rebel General*, bears signs of his time at Yale. What are more important, no doubt, are the hidden influences, such as the example and teaching of Yvor Winters at Stanford, where several young Australian writers, notably Evan Jones, have studied on a creative writing scholarship.

Another influence, if not hidden, then at least insufficiently noticed, has been the impact on Australian teaching of the teaching of poetry in the United States. The critical books, and especially the annotated anthologies, of Cleanth Brooks and Robert Penn

Warren have had an impact in Australia which is considerable, not least because their form of 'New Criticism' (to use the handy but misleading lable) joined forces with the approach of the *Scrutiny* critics to encourage close reading, rhetorical analysis and a preference for compressed wit in verse. One has only to compare Australian university and school syllabuses in English, especially in poetry, as now prescribed and taught with those in force before World War II to see that the whole emphasis has swung away from literary history of the older kind to the sort of reading advocated by the 'New Critics'. In Australia, however, unlike the United States, the revolution has been, if not bloodless, then at least quiet —Australia did not see the Battle of the Books which took place in America.

In drama it has become normal for Broadway and off-Broadway successes to appear on Australian stages not long after their first appearance in America, but mostly in repertory theatres rather than professional. The revival of Eugene O'Neill's plays had much the same currency in the two countries, but the Australian representation of Arthur Miller and Tennessee Williams has been somewhat selective. Of Miller's plays, *The Crucible* seems to me to be the best known, partly because some Australian readers and audiences appear to value it above *Death of a Salesman* or *All My Sons*, partly because others read it as a tract for the times and play it for its topicality. Williams is known chiefly for *Streetcar*, and associated with the moonlight-and-magnolias image of the Old South; the parts of his work which deal with violence and perversion—that is, his later plays in general—have not been much played in Australia, but are known in their film versions.

Of more recent playwrights, easily the best known and most discussed is Edward Albee. *Who's Afraid of Virginia Woolf?* appears to have joined the repertoire of amateur companies and jolted some Australian audiences even before the film of it harrowed others. On the other hand, William Inge, Jack Richardson and Murray Schisgal have rarely been produced. In general, one's impression of the impact of American drama in Australia since the war is that it reached its height about 1950, when the best plays of Miller and Williams were new, and has since tapered off.

The irruption of Albee on the scene may spark a new interest. When most Australians think of American literature, it is in terms of fiction, and especially of the novel, since the allusive, elliptical quality of the modern American short story often puzzles rather than attracts. This tendency, though undoubted, is not always fortunate: an illustration of it is the lack of attention paid to Katharine Anne Porter until she produced a novel, *Ship of Fools*. Miss Porter not only practised a lesser-known form, the short story, but her work was difficult to find any purchase in Australia, so that when *Ship of Fools* appeared it had an impact like that of a writer just beginning to be known instead of an established one. (In the United States itself Katharine Anne Porter, though an honoured name to readers of the quarterlies, only achieved a popular reputation with *Ship of Fools*, so that the Australian situation is similar.) The preference for the novel likewise means that Malamud's novels are more read than his stories, and Bellow's novels more than Malamud's work in general.

These last three names—Porter, Bellow, Malamud—remind one that the popularity or appeal of American writers depends a good deal on the universality of their concerns. Miss Porter, in so far as she is a Southern writer, gains in understanding from Faulkner's achievement in making the South a country of the mind for readers all over the world, and writers like Truman Capote, Carson McCullers and Robert Penn Warren would be other beneficiaries: whether readers abroad 'really' know the South or not, they believe they do, which is to them all that matters.

It is doubtful whether many of the modern American writers of Jewish descent, especially if their concerns are markedly Jewish, find as large an audience in Australia as they do at home. On the popular level, Herman Wouk's *The Caine Mutiny* was (I think) more read and enjoyed than *Marjorie Morningstar*, although the latter was serialised in Australia's biggest weekly for women. And Bellow's *Herzog*, though much acclaimed by the reviewers in Australia as in the United States, was essentially a *succès d'estime*.

If these impressions are correct—and any account of these matters can only be impressionistic—what we encounter here is a difference of reading taste based on the very different ethnic composition of Australia as compared with the United States. The two countries share so much common experience—especially the English, Scottish and Irish heritage—that one occasionally forgets how much that is American is not Australian. In this regard the recent influx of migrants into Australia has a special significance: to many of us it has brought home the sheer magnitude and importance in American history and literature of the vast immigration to the United States in the nineteenth and early twentieth century. The Australian immigration programme, so much smaller as it is, has affected so markedly the quality of life here since World War II that one begins to understand anew the profound changes the larger American settlement produced. There are several Australians teaching English to migrants whose love for Leo Rosten's H*y*m*a*n K*a*p*l*a*n was such that they welcomed his return most joyously.

The American writers of fiction who are most read in Australia are, with the qualifications already specified, mostly those who figure largest on the American scene. The great nineteenth century novelists continue to be read, and accepted as classics of the English tongue: one expects people to have read *The Scarlet Letter* and *Huckleberry Finn* as they would have read *Pride and Prejudice* or *Oliver Twist*. But the Australian lack of interest in Whitman—although Geoffrey Dutton has written a monograph on him—seems to be paralleled by a rather diminished appreciation of Melville: I doubt if *Moby Dick* finds the audience in Australia that it does in the United States. This may largely reflect the different school and university curricula, but in some way, perhaps, also attests a certain lack of appeal in the 'barbaric yawp' of some American writing, witnessed to again in the absence of Australian interest in Jack Kerouac, the Beats and Allen Ginsberg. It is often interesting, and may be significant, to see which parts of the American experience either do not travel or are rejected by the Australian reading public.

The mention of schools and universities is very much to the point, however. To a large extent what Australians (or any other people) read as adults depends on the kind of literary education they have had as children and under-graduates. Here one can, indeed, point to a growing appreciation of American literature in Australia since World War II. At the school level there is no systematic introduction to American writing, but individual poems or novels find their way into the curricula. These are mostly the ones thought likely to appeal to children—hence *The Catcher in the Rye* and *Huckleberry Finn*—and otherwise present no coherent pattern, so that the representation of the different authors would no doubt appear arbitrary to an American. This phenomenon is, of course, not unusual: one thinks of German students solemnly writing theses on the *Weltanschauung* of Somerset Maugham or the *mythos* of Beatrix Potter.

In the Australian universities the study of American literature has been making its way gradually. At Sydney it has long been available as an option for honours students of English literature; in most other universities American authors figure, often prominently, in English literature courses (alongside Australian authors, who are usually treated in the same subsidiary fashion); in one or two, notably Monash and the Australian National University, a full or half course in American literature is generally available to humanities students. The extension of these studies depends a great deal on the provision of books and staff, and to date these have not been forthcoming in any great numbers, although the great American Foundations have assisted many libraries and scholars.

In this connection small beginnings can produce remarkable results. Some years ago, several universities received a gift of a few hundred well-chosen American books from the Carnegie Foundation. These books are now much worn and in some cases battered from repeated use, but they formed the nucleus of American literature collections, on which both university and extension teaching has been based. The value of such gifts is out of all proportion to their monetary worth, and there must be many Australian students and scholars who have reason to think gratefully of such benefactors.

And not only students and scholars. The impact of America and American writing specifically on Australian writers must be a matter of impressions, but it does seem to have been surprisingly small. Poetry I have already dealt with; in drama one might perhaps point to American examples for the realism of the Australian plays like *The Summer of the Seventeenth Doll* and *The Shifting Heart*. Such a connection might be hard to substantiate, but if one thinks of English drama having a meaning to Australian play-wrights bounded by Shakespeare, Shaw and modern drawing-room comedy (before the advent of Pinter, Osborne, Wesker and their ilk) then the parallels to Beynon's slum-dwellers and Lawler's canecutters are to be found in O'Neill and Maxwell Anderson instead. Generalisation at all is risky.

In Australian fiction the following of American examples is clearest at the pulp level: some local publishers and writers have not been slow to duplicate the appeal to a certain audience of Mickey Spillane and *Playboy*. Above that, in certain specialised kinds of fiction (such as war stories) similarities, probably dependency, are again clear: Australian writers on war know their Hemingway and probably their Mailer pretty well.

But otherwise American fiction has no large-scale general effect on the writing of Australian fiction. What there is—social documentation of the Steinbeck kind—points to the explanation of this lack of influence. Many Australian novelists, although probably to a greater extent between the world wars than recently, have (for either political or artistic reasons) concentrated on the underdog, the 'battler' to use the Australian term. To many of these writers, the lodestar was not Washington but Moscow; and even to those to whom it was not, America made no appeal.

One has to recognise that in some Australians, and more in 'intellectual' circles than elsewhere, antagonism to the United States is ingrained, and their reading of American literature as of American politics is highly selective. The high proportion of Australian writers of left-wing views seems to me to account sufficiently for the lack of American literary influence and for its heavy stress on protest, realism and even naturalism where it does exist, so that apart from Steinbeck the accredited names are those of Richard Wright, James Farrell and Erskine Caldwell.

The literary traffic between Australia and the United States has of course not been all one way, though the literary balance is just as lopsided as that in trade. As well as reading American authors in great numbers, and publishing them in Australia in some instances—both in editions and in periodicals of international scope like *Meanjin Quarterly*—Australians have lately begun to make their mark on the American literary scene. The poet A. D. Hope has achieved a considerable audience and attention in the United States; Shirley Hazzard and James Aldridge, of Australian birth although living and writing in America, have each made a reputation in fiction; and Patrick White's fame probably owes as much to his reception in New York as it does to London, because *The Tree of Man* (his first major success) appeared in North America before it was published in England. White's status as a prophet without honour in Australia until first the American critics and then the English acclaimed him is interestingly similar to the rise in the reputation of Christina Stead, who seems to have been largely forgotten in Australia after her departure for America until Randall Jarrell and Elizabeth Hardwick 'discovered' her. Now she is being reprinted in an Australia glad to claim her as its own.

The literary relations of the United States and Australia cannot be summed up in a simple formula. Like the two versions of the English language in which they are written, American literature and Australian literature are in some respects similar, in others widely divergent. There is (if one likes) an identifiable 'Negro novel'; there is no 'Aboriginal novel'. If there were Australian Beats on the road, they did not become very apparent. On the other hand, the reader of Louis Auchincloss would be at home with Martin Boyd as he would be with the Welshman Anthony Powell; Allen Tate and James McAuley are very much alike, especially as critics, while there are similarities between Robert Frost and R. D. FitzGerald.

What all this means is that we are dealing with two varieties of colonial experience, if both Americans and Australians can ignore the dyslogistic implications of the adjective. To America in the seventeenth century as to Australia in the eighteenth came Englishmen, Scotsmen and Irishmen bearing the flag, the rifle and the Bible. What they began has turned out very differently in the two continents separated by the Pacific, but (as the two literatures testify) it is all part of the one movement of history. What Scott Fizgerald wrote of even earlier visitors to America, that for the Dutch sailors the 'fresh green breast of the new world' flowered for their eyes, is something that Australians can understand; and his speculation about their emotions on first sight of America is, historically, even truer of the first settlers in Australia: 'for a transitory and enchanted moment man must have held his breath in the presence of this continent, compelled into an aesthetic contemplation he neither understood nor desired, face to face for the last time in history with something commensurate to his capacity for wonder'.

THEATRE *Wal Cherry*

In the early years of this century one of Australia's most famous Americans paused briefly in Adelaide and had this message for the new Australian Federation. He said in the course of a press interview, reported in a Melbourne newspaper:

By the time I get back to Sydney I will have been away six months. I went first to San Francisco, where I spent a week. After a week in Chicago I proceeded to New York, but had several stops en route. I had a fortnight at New York, but from the time I landed at San Francisco till I reached New York I was always on the go. I saw seven or eight performances every week all across the Continent, and in New York I saw the leading stars and the principal plays being produced. I selected those I thought best suited for the Australian market, and arranged for their production, and completed arrangements with Mr Frohman whereby I have the Australian rights of all pieces produced under his management in America. He will also send out his leading stars from time to time.

This man was J. C. Williamson. He organised and ran one of the most successful commercial theatre combines in the twentieth century. He gradually put most of his competitors out of business in the latter part of the nineteenth and the early years of the twentieth century and his organisation to this day stands unchallenged as the arbiter of Australian theatrical taste. The Williamson empire has spanned every Australian State and determines what is seen by those relatively few Australians who go to the theatre. Williamsons have brought to Australia a variety of plays and musicals but the Firm's greatest single contribution to the Australian theatre has been the entrenchment of the American musical.

In Sydney, in Melbourne, in Adelaide, and in most Australian capital cities, it is possible to see the newest American musical play often before it is shown in England and very soon after its Broadway production. The policy which Mr Williamson outlined to the press in his statement in Adelaide is still applicable to the policy of Australia's leading entrepreneur these sixty odd years later.

Australia is a mimic's country. What we have of our own, what makes us distinctive, has been given to us by nature. The tangible symbols of our nationality—our landscape, our beaches, our harbours, our vegetation, and our animals, our aborigines and their complex culture—all of them were here when the Australian people arrived. It is still possible to say this in Australia even though the country is nearly two hundred years old. We are very new here. The Australian theatre is a theatre of mimicry which helps us to link up with the outside world. We import or we copy: very rarely do we search for our own style or our own statement. The two countries we like most to copy are England and America. We still judge Australian actors, dramatists and sportsmen by whether they would be successful in England or America if they left their own country. We suspect as inferior the man who never leaves. (One of the few exceptions to this rule is the Australian Rules footballer. No one else plays the game.) We judge our plays by whether they echo the standards and the aims of overseas playwrights. We still value our contribution to the theatrical world by whether the rest of the world notices it enough, not by whether the world is influenced by it.

Louis Esson wrote feelingly on this subject in the year 1912:

> To hold, as 'twere, the mirror up to nature
> (Said Hamlet) was the Drama's leading feature.

But now, it seems, when sundry shows we scan,
We hold the mirror to the booking plan.
Give people what they want, and leave the rest;
The play that runs the longest is the best.
Choice Melodrama, Farce and Pantomime,
Stockbrokers' Music, Picture shows sublime,
Shakespeare or Cibber played at distant years,
Shaw for the suburbs, Ibsen without tears—
Such is our Drama. In this busy age
Plain business men control the modern stage.
'London Success!'—Thus all the legends run
And local drama we have but begun.
Bad may our plays be, futile, dull, perverse
But than the rest they surely can't be worse.
What worse than THAT! Then drop the curtain down,
Someday a Marlowe will amaze the town.

Someday a Marlowe, but certainly not yet.

There are attempts from time to time to break out of this national, self-imposed frustration. This paragraph, for example leaps out of the pages of *Evening Sun* of Melbourne in the year 1923:

The productions of the Pioneer Players are, as a rule, confined to Australian plays. An exception was made last night to give their supporters an opportunity of hearing Anna Christie, a four-act play by Eugene O'Neill, the American Dramatist.

The Pioneer Players were a brave and resourceful group of writers who were mostly professionals (Vance and Nettie Palmer, Louis Esson), and actors and directors who were mostly amateurs. They were anxious to establish a drama which held the same place in the lives of the Australians as Sean O'Casey and Synge and the Abbey Theatre held in the lives of the Irish. They were not and could not be successful. They had no proper theatrical facilities and no proper mechanism by which they could make their work known to the public, and no profession which could become interested in them.

The theatrical profession was geared to the Williamson machine. It still is.

At the present time we have attempts to establish the native Australian drama and I have no wish to minimise these. We have a number of writers such as Seymour and Lawler who attempt in their various ways to examine the world through local eyes. But these sporadic attempts and the efforts of directors and actors and managements, such as the Australian Elizabethan Theatre Trust, do not add up to any kind of 'Movement' in the Australian Drama.

There are influences on Australian dramatists which do not derive from specific English or American origins. The first of these is what could be called 'Steele Ruddism' or the 'Dad and Dave' complex. The attitudes inherent in this point of view are reflected in the plays of Alan Hopgood: *And the Big Men Fly, The Golden Legion of Cleaning Women, Private Yuk Objects*. A more recent example has been a play presented at the 1968 Adelaide Festival of Arts—*The Lotus Eaters* by Patricia Hooker. In this kind of writing caricature replaces characterisation, easy laughs are gained by incongruities of language. An example of up-to-date 'Dad and Dave' farce is a recent film made in Australia, and very proudly at that, called *They're a Weird Mob*. This title contains the essence of the genre. In these works the Australian is exhibited as an easy going, farcical person who is warm hearted and likes to see the other chap get what is called a 'fair go'. Everyone admits that such characterisations are farcical. But the success of the film *They're a Weird Mob* indicates with some clarity that although the Australian would be unlikely to recognise himself in such a film he does recognise aspects of Australian society which he considers to be lovable and which make him distinct from the rest of the world. Perhaps a case could be made for saying that this kind of Australian drama reflects not so much a *desire* to find out what we are like, but rather a *fear* of discovering what we are like. This view is supported by the continuous use of set patterns of behaviour in plays and films which are supposed to depict Australian characteristics. The scene in *They're a Weird Mob* where the men are sitting on the couch with, of course, hearts of gold, unable to cope with a cup of tea and some meringues, reflects a series of recurrent attitudes. We are an easy, informal people who like beer rather than tea. Get to knows us mate, we are worth it.

The second characteristic of Australian drama, which is not specifically American, is the attempt by a group of modern Australian writers to imitate the techniques of the theatre of the absurd. It seems as though the kind of absurdity inherent in Steele Ruddism is no longer adequate for the young Australian of intellect and he requires a different sort of absurdity more in keeping with the times. Playwrights like Tony Morphett and some of his younger contemporaries tend to mimic the manner of Ionesco and Beckett without any of the matter.

The current cult of the obscure in art is sprinkled through with practitioners who are clearly important contributors to our theatrical traditions. But obscurity can often be no more than an effort to hide a lack of insight into the facts and deliberate obscurantism for poetic and theatrical effects often degenerates into a kind of feeble 'in-joke'. The 'little theatre' in Australia has been influenced by the art theatre of the mid-1950's in Paris and we have been subject to a wave of 'intellectual' drama. Within the context of European post-war disillusionment this material often makes a good deal of sense. It makes no sense in Australia unless it can be made to refer to our own sense of humour, incongruity, despair. Our writers and directors, had mimicked the influence, not absorbed it.

I have raised these two characteristics of Australian drama because I believe that they show a tendency which is clearly compatible with our desire to mimic. The tendency is to avoid observing the immediate environment. I suspect that underlying this avoidance is a fear that we are not basically a very interesting people.

I believe that these two factors plus the influences of American and English drama constitute the major discernible characteristics of Australian drama at the present day.

It is impossible to separate theatrical influences from the general forces which are at work in society. The influence of American society on Australian is profound and far-reaching. The influences on Australian theatre are not simply theatrical influences. Which of those influences can be isolated and which directly affect the Australian drama? At the risk of spelling things out a little too clearly I would like to list the possible sources of influence.

The first is the American playwright. His works are performed throughout Australia and have been performed extensively since 1945. There are few American works of importance which have not been seen in Australia since World War II. Some of these have been performed by amateur companies but a large number have been produced by smaller professional theatres and a few by J. C. Williamson and the less virulent Australian commercial organisations, such as that of Garnet H. Carroll. The repertoire of theatres like the Melbourne Theatre Company (formerly Union Theatre Repertory Company) and St Martins Theatre in Melbourne, the Old Tote, Independent and Ensemble theatres in Sydney, is largely composed of plays by American dramatists. Since its inception in 1954, the Union Theatre Repertory Company has produced the following representative American plays: *The Gentle People, The Time of Your Life, Bus Stop* and *Picnic, Death of a Salesman, Cat on a Hot Tin Roof, A Street car Named Desire, Orpheus Descending, View from the Bridge, After the Fall, Incident at Vichy, Summer and Smoke, The Matchmaker, The Troublemakers, Hatful of Rain, Our Town, Tiny Alice, Who's Afraid of Virginia Woolf?*, and many more. American plays are performed in Australia and performed extensively.

The next influences on Australian drama is the American musical theatre. In Australia's reaction to this entirely American phenomenon we have the story of Australian drama writ large. The J. C. Williamson management by pursuing the policy set out so clearly by Mr Williamson himself and reinforced by his oft-quoted maxim 'Australians will not have Australians', has created a quite unique situation in Australia. A home-grown musical is almost unknown. There have been one or two attempts since the war but they have been minor. Among these we could number *The Sentimental Bloke*, that red herring of Australian culture, *Lola Montez, Reedy River, The Ballad of Angel's Alley*, and more recently *A Bunch of Ratbags*. All of these works have shown a marked American influence both in musical content and the approach to style in presentation. But these were not a contribution to the Australian theatre which can compare in magnitude or importance with the revamped versions of American musicals such as *Damn Yankees, Oklahoma, The Pajama Game, The Most Happy Fella, South Pacific, West Side Story, My Fair Lady, Kismet, How to Succeed in Business etc., A Funny Thing Happened etc., Finian's Rainbow, Carousel, Can Can, Sweet Charity, Kiss me Kate, Paint your Wagon, The Sound of Music, Fiddler on the Roof, Hello Dolly!, The Music Man,* and so on. And on. All this since 1945. It does not need much calculation to realise how time is consumed in Australia's largest theatres by the presentation of American musicals.

But how are they presented? Australian audiences see a production, quite often directed by somebody who was associated with the original American production, presented with Australian actors, dancers and singers in minor roles, although occasionally this rule is broken, and with American leading players, working in front of copies of the original sets, and dancing copied choreography. We have been fortunate enough to see the choreography of Jerome Robbins and Agnes de Mille without these good people ever having set foot in the country. The imported players are seldom those who performed the work in its original production.

The Australian theatre has developed a degree of expertise in the presentation of American musicals which is astounding. A race of imitative choreographers, musical directors, dancers and actors has been developed to cope with those works. And they cope with them extremely well. The Australian performer who has worked in one of these musicals, and some of them can run for years, has been so influenced by his effort at imitation that he is scarcely discernible from the real thing. This is the ultimate in influence.

The third major influence on Australian drama has been the American film. All Australian actors and directors, writers and audiences, designers and musicians have been directly or indirectly exposed to Hollywood.

In the year 1965, 1,162 films comprising 4,500,000 feet were imported for exhibition in motion picture theatres. 351 of these films originated in the United States of America and 349 in the United Kingdom. Included in these imports were 435 full-length feature films. Of these, 144 came from the United States and 78 from the United Kingdom. During this period Australian film censors viewed 184, 729 feet of Australian produced 35mm film. These films were mainly newsreels and documentaries. The potential American influence is obvious.

The fourth major influence is television. For the mimic, television is a boon. Australians can now be even more authentic in representing Englishmen and particularly Americans upon the stage. At least the mimic is not deprived of the opportunity to study. In the year 1965, 11,129 films, predominantly 16mm, amounting to 14,500,000 feet, were imported into Australia for presentation on television. This represents 6,753 hours of screening time. On a footage basis the United States supplied 79 per cent of the total imports and the United Kingdom 16 per cent. In 1965 there was one television set for every five people in Australia and a density of one television set to every 1·5 dwellings. The potential television audience is enormous.

Any attempt to separate cause from effect in the jumble of modern culture can be little more than informed guess-work. My guess is that the cumulative effect of so much American influence on Australian drama has been, firstly, confusion in style and, secondly, an almost complete identification of drama with 'Show Business' both in the public mind and within the various dramatic professions themselves. For the great mass media have not only brought direct theatrical influences, they have also brought the publicity and over-statement which is forever associated with Hollywood and Broadway. The Australian believes in the theatrical pie in the sky. He believes it because he has been told on good authority that it exists. He has never been there to find out that it does not. The theatre in Australia is a tawdry and tiny spectacle in comparison with what our newspapers and television sets tell us about its American counterpart. The young Australian who is interested in the drama has stars in his eyes but these stars are not Australian stars. For all his pious yearnings for an Australian drama he will take himself overseas at the first opportunity in search of that well-publicised fame and fortune which lies at the end of the rainbow, American Style. But here his confusion is amply illustrated: he does not go to America, he goes to England. Why? Because it is traditional; it is the well-worn track of Australian actors. It is Overseas.

And this confusion manifests itself in the problem of style. The Australian actor is a mimic; he mimics behaviour and his mimicry is based on theatrical models. He mimics films, he mimics television plays and television programmes. The Australian performer admires the easy naturalism of the American. The Australian dramatist admires the selective realism of his American counterparts. Ray Lawler, for example, the author of *Summer of the Seventeenth Doll* had a great admiration for Tennessee Williams. I probably reflect just this set of influences when I say that the title *Summer of the Seventeenth Doll* sounds to me like a Williams title. But realism to most Australians does not mean a way of approaching the raw materials of drama. To them it means a copied style, if it means anything at all. Realism must describe an attitude of mind. Realism is no more than the desire to discover and portray what is happening in the world around.

There is no doubt that when Ray Lawler wrote *Summer of the Seventeenth Doll* this desire exhibited itself in his work. There is an attempt to examine the problem of the inarticulate man faced with frustrations and fears which he cannot incorporate into the pattern of his life. His inarticulateness must turn to violence. Lawler examines this problem and examines it beautifully within the terms of the characters and situation he has chosen. He is the only Australian dramatist who has successfully combined idiomatic speech of the 1940's and 1930's with an attempt by characters who are growing old to express themselves in a new situation. The success of *Summer of the Seventeenth Doll* as an expression of Australian idiom lies in just this. The characters belong to the past but they have validity in the present. So much Australian writing makes people talk as though the idiom of the 'thirties was still the way in which Australians converse. In Lawler's later play *The Piccadilly Bushman* his language is not nearly as successful because he has not been able to make a fusion between the attempt of the characters to express themselves in a particular situation and the language which they use. Although *Summer of the Seventeenth Doll* is in many ways a bitter play it is tinged with the kind of romanticism which Tennessee Williams possesses.

PEARL (*winding wool, unaware of the havoc she is to create*). Well, it was in the early part, when she first started to tell me about you two. We'd been talkin' one morning, she was trying to describe how she felt about youse comin' down every year, when in walks this fat feller. Real ear-basher he is, always on for a yap. This particular time he get gassing about birds, sayin' how some of them fly all over the place, spend a season here and a season there, sort of thing. Well, me, I couldn't have cared less what they did, but Olly got real wrapped up in it. After a while she turned to me and said . . .

OLIVE (*interrupting*). It was when he'd gone, I didn't say it in front of him.

PEARL. When he'd gone, then, she turned to me and said— (*Pauses enjoyably.*) What was it? Oh yes—that's what they remind me of, she sez, two eagles flyin' down out of the sun and coming south every year for the mating season. (*She goes off into a smother of mirth and resumes winding wool. The other three are not amused.*)

The problem of inarticulateness and the pioneer growing old are the stuff of Ray Lawler's play. It is the most popular play that has been produced locally in this country. It deals with areas which the Australian has not previously seen exhibited with such care on the stage. We hope that this is not the end of such honesty. But although the 'Doll' is the best Australian play produced to the present time, it is a curiously dated work in the 1960's and has little to do with a country trying to find its place in an Asian community and desperately anxious to hold on to its European ties. The problems of Australia are no longer the problems of being inarticulate but rather the problems of what to be articulate about.

The structure of *Summer of the Seventeenth Doll* owes more to English well-made play traditions that it does to American influences. The Three Act form and the convention 'curtains' put it at a distance from the work of either Miller or Williams and place Lawler firmly in the area of taste of the country he now seems to have adopted. Unfortunately, the English theatre now seems to have adopted new tastes.

The English drama has an appeal to Australians almost equal to the American. What distinguishes the English theatre for the Australian actor is not its easy naturalism, but its formality. The beautiful voice of Gielgud is reproduced nightly in many an Australian theatre. Again it is not English method which interests the Australian actor it is English style. And the same thing can be said of Australian audiences. I remember there used to be an axiom printed on the back of Melbourne tram tickets: 'We become like those we habitually admire.' This axiom could well be the motto of the Australian theatre. Unfortunately as a practical method of providing a community with drama, it simply does not work at all.

There was a memorable year in the mid-'fifties when Australia's commercial theatres were in a Play Phase. In one Melbourne theatre the Carroll management was presenting *Tea and Sympathy*, an American play produced and staged by locals. In the cast, however, was Dulcie Gray, an English actress. The performance was an extraordinary mixture of styles which, like some buildings, ought to have been preserved for that and for that alone. It was a curiosity. Across the way Williamsons were presenting *The Reluctant Debutante*. Here the formula of Williamson's success was repeated as usual, in the leading roles were Roger Livesey and Ursula Jeans, Complete and from the Old Country. They were supported by an Australian cast. Here the style problem was solved by what is called in the theatrical profession 'cod'. 'Cod' means a successful pretense of that which you do not possess. In the Australian theatre it can also mean cash on delivery.

Australians can learn a great deal from American drama and some have already done so. Watching American actors on the stage, on television and on films, observing the methods of American playwrights, directors and scene designers, listening to the idiom of the language and how it is used in the theatre—all this can teach Australians a great deal about the nature of the vital, energetic and highly observant realism which is the hallmark of the American drama. It is a condition of realism that it puts its roots down solidly into the society in which it exists as a style. The word does not describe a way of doing plays so that audiences will believe in them. The word describes a way of approaching the raw material of life so that it can be wrought in theatrical terms. Australians can learn that their drama exists in an age of science and technology. They can learn about professionalism and the capacity for taking pains. The techniques of realism are the five finger exercises of modern drama and if some of us believe the Americans have continued to play five finger exercises when men like Brecht have played symphonies this does not lessen the value of the exercises to Australians.

There is for Australians, however, very little value in slavish imitations of anybody because modern communication has made the real thing so easily accessible.

Drama has always been a regional activity. This is the paradox. When it tries to exist without roots in its nearby audience, when it cannot speak directly to its own community, it cannot speak to the world, no matter how much it yearns after recognition or tries to imitate its elders and betters.

Let an American dramatist have the last word. In the preface to his *Collected Plays*, Arthur Miller says: 'A play ought to make sense to commonsense people. . . . The only challenge worth the effort . . . is the people themselves.'

MASS COMMUNICATIONS *Robin Boyd*

How pleasant the world might be if the familiar term 'mass communication' meant mass communicating with mass—that is, the American people in mass communicating with Australian people in mass, and vice versa. But we know that that does not and cannot happen and we understand the term to describe the action of one person or organisation on one side communicating with the mass on the other side. Furthermore we know that there is no vice versa in the present context: communication is virtually one way along the Pacific axis. The ocean acts as a valve which lets communications flow freely from the higher pressure to the lower pressure area but makes reciprocal action almost impossible. The term therefore boils down to meaning the communications received by the Australian people from relatively very few sources in the United States.

Australians absorb a great volume of such communications, but from a narrow band on the spectrum of domestic mass communications within America. The Australian people never see an American daily newspaper, or a magazine of comment, virtually never see an American television newscast or hear an American television discussion or see American sport, or American art. They never hear American radio. Australia is still remote and separated from the day-to-day emotions, the drive and the braking forces, the flow of life in America—almost as remote as she was when the only medium of communication was a clipper. What Australia sees and knows of America comes almost exclusively through the self-conscious and self-satisfied and anti-esoteric media, the mesmeric media which justify the most extreme McLuhanism since they are so clearly more delightful and important than anything they communicate.

On the one hand, clam chowder, a ginger-glazed crown roast of pork, prune whip and lemon meringue pie served on pink cast-iron furniture by the pool, a repeated grape-motif reflecting the chandeliers; on the other hand, Batman, T.H.E. Cat, Hawk and all the other hypnotists of Hollywood's last season but one. Australia sees these two dream visions of America in the two media in which she herself is least proficient: the film (for television or cinema) and the colour magazine. Those are expensive media demanding big populations to feed upon, far bigger than Australia will have for many years at the present rate of development. Nevertheless, a little reciprocation is the only thing that could eventually make the American communications invasion acceptable to chauvinistic Australians, so it may be worth a moment's thought to consider the likelihood of reciprocation ever happening.

Australia's own internal mass communications are limited to the comparatively economical media: daily and weekly newspapers, radio, live television, books, and in all of them she is thoroughly competent if no more outstanding than might be expected of one her size. These domestic communications are not of course intended to travel, and never do. If there is ever to be any reciprocal action to the magnificent American communications which flood Australia, however proportionately small, it must be in the expensive super-media—the full production film and the full colour magazine—the only media which could safely fly the Pacific. Many Australians deplore the absence of both in Australia, especially the absence of a film industry. They call for the government to sponsor or support film production and they muse about a day when Australia might compete with the world at Cannes. They are dismayed at the uncouth image of Australia seen from abroad and imagine wide screen colour depictions of sophisticated life in Sydney and Melbourne as background to sensitive cinematic drama. They envy greatly the aura of America which her expensive media exude.

The image of America in her export communications is indeed so consistent and at the same time so misleading that naive antagonists might suspect a conspiracy. Of course there is no conspiracy or need for one. The big mass communications naturally follow with only minor deviations a formula which has proved successful over many years of intense competition. On the principle that the nicest communication which anyone can receive is a congratulation, they conduct every issue or episode as a special message of congratulations to every reader or watcher for being American, and they offer him first prize in the lottery of life: a cloudless prospect of the greatest nation on earth perpetually lunching on the pink cast-iron by a pool terrace.

The presentation of this prize is remarkably formal and almost ceremonious. America's export-quality mass communications share a common language which is basically dynamic, direct and hard, but has carefully proportioned additives of sensitivity and humour. It is not the language of the American street or the American livingroom, but is a second level communications style into which any successful man should be capable of slipping, with no more effort than an automatic car changing gear, when he is communicating under any pressure. This jargon is kept continuously fresh on the surface by the addition of revived or hybrid words and phrases which fill gaps in English not previously noticed. Words like pragmatic, periphery, proliferation, psychedelic—just to take four of the comparatively recent p's—make up a new slang which is enriched continuously only from America and is taken up in Australia only after a time lag of some eight months. No matter how proficient Australian mass communications might become in the next generation, they are unlikely to fly the Pacific on stale slang. A little local inventiveness in language may have to be revived from the 'dinkum' era of a century ago.

On the visual side the Australian domestic magazines are so backward that there does not appear to be any likelihood of their reaching the international level in the forseeable future. Typography is not one of Australia's native talents, as singing or tennis are. It is one of those near-effete refinements which Diggerism shuns. Since the appearance of *The Australian* the better daily newspapers have paid some attention to design, but none employs a full-time, trained typographical designer. If some are looking more presentable than they used to, it is only because of the better taste of younger editors or younger publishers who now know better which London papers to copy. Typography, like most of the thinner branches of design, is no more than an amateur interest in Australia. It cannot be an accident that the most phenomenally successful of domestic mass communications, the *Australian Women's Weekly*, has most of its pages laid out in the Australian style. This style is notable for a dull abandon of all typographical niceties, a heedless jig-saw of old-fashioned type faces and printers' decorative dividers. The better pages are copied peccably from American magazines. The Australian public must approve all this, since it supports its *Women's Weekly* and gives small satisfaction to other rather better looking, if thinner, journals for ladies' homes.

There does not seem to be the least prospect of Australian coloured journalism growing up eventually to a stage at which it might attempt a Pacific trip. On the contrary, the promise of the late 1960's is for a full-scale land invasion of Australia by the American magazines. *Time* magazine was the first to expand its territory by means of foreign editions which packed local advertising in a cottonwool of American communication. *Vogue Australia*, of English parentage, was a similar enterprise, except that it carried more Australian copy. A more recent project called *Vogue's Guide to Living* incorporates a token showing of black and white Australian material amid a rainbow of colour pages borrowed from its overseas' cousins. However, it is *Life Australia*, which began early in 1967, that seems to be the most prophetic of these proxy Australian magazines. It suggests a pattern which more American journals and in due course newspapers and other media may well adopt. *Life Australia* slips a few items of Australian origin in among its American stories and packs all this around a great quantity of Australian advertising. The Australian advertisers are obviously grateful for the good printing and the prestige of the American association. The Australian edition of *Readers Digest* has an editorial office in Sydney which attempts to give an Australian slant to some articles by substituting an Australian quotation or reference for an American one. But *Life Australia* adopts the more direct and efficient technique of running little more than a one-man bureau in Sydney and keeping its editor in a small office in the Time-Life building at Rockefeller Centre, New York.

Is there more hope for Australian export communication in the other kind of expensive mass communicator, the film? Film-making commands a unique position in the Australian heart and the Australian culture. As an art form that belongs to the twentieth century, film attracts the new patriots, who also feel a certain proprietary interest in it. The stirring story of cinematic pioneering around the turn of the century is cafe folk lore. You must have heard that in 1902 an enterprise that has become known as 'the world's first screen drama' was produced in a Melbourne suburb. It was *Soldiers of the Cross*, made on a tennis court by a Salvation Army officer and screened with an interlacing of live action. It was followed by the legendary 'world's first feature film', *The Kelly*

Gang, of five reels. In the second decade of the century no fewer than eighty-eight features were made in Australia. That was the peak. Soon the competition from Hollywood was too intense, and production ran down a steady decline: in the 1920's only sixty-one features, in the 1930's fifty-two, in the 1940's twenty, in the 1950's about fifteen. In the 1960's films that might be called features appeared at an average rate of only about one a year, and there was room for doubt about the justification of many of them to claim feature rank. Most were made by semi-amateur enthusiasts, their only cost being that of the film stock.

However, there was one fully professional film, made in colour for a wide screen. It was *They're a Weird Mob*, and although its commercial success disproved an earlier conviction that no modern film could pay for itself from the limited local market, it was essentially merely one more overseas film made on location in Australia. Indeed it hinted, as did *Life Australia* in the magazine field, at the end of Australian production rather than a new beginning. Australia, it suggested, will continue to be a novel location for occasional use by film companies of the northern hemisphere. In 1967 Mr Eddie Davis, a television film director from Hollywood, visiting Sydney to make the pilot episode for a hopeful series, said he knew plenty of people in America who would put money into an Australian film. 'Of course,' he added, 'it would mean bringing out a name star and a couple of top directors to do it.'

There is in fact no hope at all of a revival of vital commercial film making in Australia. Little films by enthusiasts will continue to give pleasure to all who participate in them for many years yet, but the days of film manufacture in Australia are gone; left behind in another, slower, emptier, silent world. Making films and magazines belonged to a time when Australia also was making her own language and her own legend.

For a few more years there may be opportunities for quite a lively little industry in the making of television films, but none of these is likely to be given the opportunity to communicate to a very large mass of Americans. Gradually Australian production in television will follow the pattern of production in films and magazines. That is, Australian television will not disappear altogether, but an exact measure of Australian content will be edited in at headquarters in Hollywood.

The year 1967 may turn out to be significant in Australia's cultural development, for it saw the beginning of satellite television broadcasts from America to Australia. The sharp, brilliant pictures heralded a coming era when all entertainment other than local news, weather and time reports will bounce across the Pacific, and then no doubt will continue round the rest of the world to be picked up anywhere. Audiences for any show will be measured in thousands of millions. Production will be formulated, computerised and impeccably sophisticated. The entertainment factories of the United States will be centralised and concentrated to an extent that will make the Hollywood machine of today seem as feeble as Amateur Night popcorn. In America, as in Australia, theatre and cinema will become esoteric little interests for odd and arty clubs and the electronic home device will grow even more elaborate and proficient. After the theatre and the cinema die, music-making will be hard pressed, and finally even spectator sports will go. The world's very best drama and music will come to all, Americans and Australians alike, directly as they are performed in New York, faultlessly reproduced. And the Army-Navy gridiron game will eventually supplant the Geelong—St Kilda League final even in Melbourne livingrooms. That might seem unbelievable now but it is inevitable, for all spectator sport is only as successful as the number of spectators it draws, and a game with a billion spectators will eventually swamp out even the attractions to Melburnians of Australian Rules.

Thus the technological advances in mass communications that lie ahead, some still unimaginable, promise to result in rather less than more communicating from Australia to America. Yet simultaneously other technological advances may be doing something to counteract this tendency. The more effective human-mass communication of the future may be by personal contact. We all know that a new era of travel is about to open with the giant air buses and supersonic planes promised for the 1970's. These will make it possible for more tourists than ever to move in either direction across the Pacific, and Australians undoubtedly will welcome the opportunity in ever-increasing numbers. Many Australians, including some in government, seem to be confident that ever-increasing floods of American tourists will pass the departing Australians somewhere over the Pacific, heading for Australia with handfuls of lovely green dollars. Confident Australians argue that there is only one reason that American tourists are not already flooding the country: it is that the Americans have never heard of Australia. Thus advertising for tourists in America is all that is required. And so advertising of Australia is bound to get more intense. Undoubtedly many of the more adventurous kinds of American will respond, and will find much to enjoy in Australia. Yet there are many things—including awful service, brown martinis, imitation orange juice, flies—and some rather ugly hotel rooms, that hinder Australia from being a tourists' paradise, and some of the first jumbo-jet loads of Americans just might notice these things and report adversely to their tourist bureaux when they return home.

Nevertheless, face to face communication is certain to increase and this will expose Americans as never before to basic communication with Australians: voice to voice, face in fact to face. Most American visitors to Australia have an amused tolerance of the accent, but would not claim it to be the thing about Australia that they love the most. On the contrary, the American, like the West-Ender, usually thinks the Australian accent is no more than a low-class corruption of English, close to the Cockney that came with the convicts and hardly more distinguished than Pidgin. Australians naturally resent the Cockney convict association and like to pretend that they think the accent is just another regional branch of the mother tongue as valid as the American. Yet in truth they are not proud of it, otherwise Australians who live abroad would not so quickly shed their accents in favour of English or American, according to their whereabouts.

Whereas no American ever loses his original accent and adopts an Australian one no matter how long he lives in Australia, every Australian who goes to live in America straightens out his vowels, curls his R's and shortens his A's as a matter of course, usually in the first few months. Consider the reciprocal actions of the actor Rod Taylor, an Australian in America, and the showman Bob Dyer, an American in Australia. Taylor's accent turned completely American in a short time, after which his American fans described it as 'the nicest Australian accent' they had ever heard. Dyer, after nearly three long decades in Australia, retains his American accent intact as a badge of authority. No doubt the Australian accent will eventually go the way of the Australian film and the Australian magazine and the Australian figures of speech.

It must be admitted nevertheless, that accent is only a dressing on speech, and that there are other elements which have made the Australian communication unique. There was, for instance, that curious debunking sense of humour, overlaid with a stream of unconscious obscenities that proved the speaker was no cissie. Moreover, there was the overall inarticulateness. Even without the accent and the obscenities a television discussion between Australian politicians of the second rank (one must exclude the leaders, who are not on top by chance) would still be immediately distinguishable from a similar debate between American politicians of equivalent rank simply on the basis of rate of production of thoughts. The reasons for the Australian ponderousness in public communication are deep seated in the colonial background and Digger mateship. Australia has not yet moved far enough from the outback into the city life she has chosen to forget the rules of masculine conversation. No real man is permitted, under these laws of the ancient Diggerdom, to depart in conversation from practical, material, subjective things. Anything suggestive of an abstract idea or a tender feeling is taboo, and to emphasise masculinity every third word has to be the one which refers to an activity requiring a certain amount of female cooperation. Under the tribal rules, however, this word cannot be said in front of females and, thus deprived of every third word in mixed company, the Australian male's technique of communicating disintegrates into a jagged series of hesitant, repetitive, tentative stabs at thoughts. This does not mean that the Australian necessarily has fewer thoughts than the American or even that he could not overcome this embarrassment and free his tongue if he were stung into a necessity to communicate. But at heart he still feels that unnecessary and an invasion of his privacy.

Why should he be forced to say out loud what he thinks? In the past that was not necessary. In a land of few people with similar origins, backgrounds and circumstances—practically everyone who mattered being of the one British blood—the fundamental beliefs of life could be taken for granted. Yet privacy of thoughts was precious. It indicated that one might have individual thoughts within the creed and it relieved one of the trouble of deciding specifically what these thoughts might be. Privacy of the mind made for a quieter life, freer for physical pursuits. Privacy became a prized quality of the Australian way of life, and it is no wonder mass communicating is not a part of that way.

It is worth noting that by far the greatest gift that Australia ever gave America, or is ever now likely to give her, was the secret vote —the Australian ballot, as Americans still call it. It is essentially uncharacteristic of America's open methods, of the 'stand up and be counted' challenge.

Australian leaders, as I have noted, escape the most primitive ties on the tongue, as do her journalists, public-relations men, and all others who have to communicate to the mass. Yet to escape the ties they have to shed most of the qualities that make Australian street speech Australian. Thus even if an all-Australian international mass communication medium were feasible economically, it would not speak Australian except in self-conscious asides and in little touches of local colour dropped in as fillers. A communication does not have to be produced in Australia to achieve such a token degree of Australianism. *Life Australia* can do all that is necessary perfectly well from its little office in Rockefeller Centre. It does not and should not matter to Australians whether that kind of communication comes from Time-Life or Consolidated Press.

In short, it is not at all important or very regrettable that Australia can never mass communicate to America, or even in the long run to herself. Ordinary Americans as well as Australians face a future of fewer and fewer, bigger and bigger, more and more generalised, unfocused mass communications. Ultimately there may be just a single weekly magazine, produced in New York with superb colour, three-dimensions, motion, talking pages—and regional inserts. Yet that one unapproachable mass communicator need not disqualify local and specialised communication by way of critical, creative journalism, live television, folk cinema, radio, and other as yet uninvented media on the sub-mass scale. Indeed it is just possible that ultimately the specialised or localised communications may begin to mean to almost everyone so much more than the marvellous mass communications that the sub-mass media may swing into ascendency. The very perfection, smoothness, sophistication of the technique used by the formulated mass communicators might ever so slowly suffocate even the last of them, so that the mightiest finally might be piled on the junk-heap with the super-streamlined, chromium-plated, dollar-grin-ning, rusting automobiles of the 1950's to which they were so closely related.

ARCHITECTURE *John Buchan*

Irrespective of the 'internationalisation' of so much human creative activity, there are obvious environmental and social factors which must lead not only to a logical resemblance between the many types of Australian and American architecture, but to continuing and probably increasing links between them.

With the ever-increasing expansion of American interests across the Pacific, it is perhaps natural that since World War II some cries of concern have been raised of 'big brother', especially in the light of so many take-overs and mergers. Outbursts have been made by some writers coining catch phrases such as 'Austericans' to describe an inevitable acceptance by us of much of the American way of life, whether it be motels, supermarkets, high-powered cars or television films.

There have been uninformed suggestions that Australian archi-tects have become mesmerised by design trends in the United States, particularly in commercial buildings.

But before World War II, Australian architects were well aware of the great research into hospitals and health facilities in the United States, and had drawn heavily on that knowledge to assist in developing here what is now—perhaps with the exception of Sweden—the finest standard of hospital architecture in the world.

Then, too, Australia's industrialisation really got under way with American capital and know-how heavily invested in all types of industry. It was the prototypes of auto plants—lifted almost holus-bolus from around Detroit—which gave us our big new opportunity to produce industrial architecture and engineering for industry on the really grand scale. Of course, it was inevitable that there would be American influence—sound and logical planning—on the design and lay-out of many of our new plants.

There are geopolitical points of common interest and physical links which have inevitably brought much from the United States across our path; indeed, right into our front door. Our two countries are roughly the same area and the conquest of distance was essential to both groups of early pioneers. It had to be railways and roads which extended their frontiers and ours, and the automobile, largely developed and marketed through their great industrial power, became our own rugged work-horse. The two huge continents, criss-crossed by roads carrying cars and trucks, had to be serviced by oil, marketed in the main through American outlets. And, later, our affluent society of the 1950's adopted for our travelling public the American motel.

Pausing for a glimpse into the distant past, records in the latter part of the nineteenth century are sketchy as to what part Americans had in the planning and development of our towns and cities, or what buildings may have been influenced by American architecture. But one point is clear, clipper ships brought many seeking gold across the Pacific from California to the Australian goldfields. And the famous Cobb & Co. Coaches, tried and tested in the United States, made their impact on rough roads and tracks in opening up our outback. This was a revolution in our transport through the leather-suspended Concord coach.

The wealth created by the new riches beneath the earth produced for us the wherewithal to pay for some large and handsome buildings. The imposing facades of some great city buildings gave to Melbourne and Sydney their first air of affluence and greatness. Perhaps the most opulent building in the nineteenth century closely associated with American architecture was designed in Collins Street for the Equitable Life Assurance of the United States, remembered until a few year's ago, prior to the wrecker's hammers, as a very distinguished landmark in Melbourne. It followed a pattern of Americanised Renaissance design for city buildings already establishing in downtown Manhattan, New York, with a 'solid' front of granite behind which the affluent institutions of finance impressed their customers.

But we find no evidence in those early days of architects coming here to practice, for Americans like the great Louis Sullivan in Chicago were too busy designing their new skyscrapers and creating their own great cities to think of a far off land across the Pacific. It seems that we had to wait until the new capital, Canberra, was created back in 1910 for an international competition among architects and townplanners—mainly boycotted by our own profession at home—to bring forth an American architect, young Walter Burley Griffin from Chicago, who won the first prize of $A3,500.

Griffin had been a protegé of Frank Lloyd Wright, and collecting his pencils, and a brand new wife who worked alongside him in Chicago, set sail for Australia.

Although frustrated in his efforts to have Australian officialdom accept and implement his plan for Canberra, he did practise here and, with a definite design touch, produced some notable and charming buildings. It was in Melbourne that he produced his most imaginative results.

The name of Walter Burley Griffin has now been indelibly inscribed on Australia's Capital through the sympathetic understanding of the National Capital Development Commission, formed in 1958 with a vigorous Chairman, John Overall, to shape finally many elements of the Griffin plan and to build a worthy national centre.

Griffin, in those far off days on the site for Canberra, while studying the lazy plains and rolling hills with their dramatic mountain backdrop, surely dreamed no little dreams. The lake which now bears his name anchors the two parts of Canberra and serves as some reminder of Walter Burley Griffin. Yet it can be hoped that a more emphatic recognition of Griffin may emerge— Australians should not forget that he gave us the plan for Canberra, and spent the best years of his professional life among us.

On the original Griffin plan for Canberra, on one point of the central triangle, was what was known as the Market Place, at the foot of Russell Hill. This served merely as a grazing area for sheep until the 1950's when the simple shafted Australian-American Memorial for World War II was placed there. The area was later selected as the site for a new complex of defence buildings, and was site-planned by the most distinguished American architects, Skidmore, Owings and Merrill, with the buildings designed by Buchan, Laird & Buchan.

I well remember talking with the late Eero Sarrinen whose untimely death removed one of the greatest architects in the United States. I was at his home one summer's evening in Detroit in 1962, and he told me that his illustrious architect father, Elial, who gained the second prize for the Town Plan of Canberra, always dreamed of visiting Australia. Had Eero Sarrinen lived, he might well have been persuaded to enter for some future competition to design one monumental building in Canberra which would vindicate the absence of any Griffin-designed building there. This was one reason why Eero willingly accepted a position on the panel of architects to judge the designs submitted for the Sydney Opera House.

Today we can see the mushrooming metropolitan aggregations of the 1950's and 1960's now common to both our countries, although more dispersed in America. The apparently uncontrollable suburban growth of Los Angeles, and insatiable city development in New York could have their counterparts soon in Sydney and Melbourne. We have become the third most motorised country in the world after the United States and Canada.

The overcrowded cities, clogging up of highways, and atmosphere filled with smog and grime are grim reminders, even in an affluent society like the United States that the price for progress may be very high if, in the process, human health and happiness are to be sacrificed.

Why, then, do we not pool all our knowledge and utilise the available American experience to help us avoid what might become a megalomania of urban life in Sydney, Melbourne and the rest? The oft repeated suggestion that our individuality in town-planning, architecture, even traffic engineering will be swallowed up or unduly influenced by America gives us no credit for discrimination. Architecture here, unlike advertising, recognises no Madison Avenue. We have seen no evidence yet, as in the accounting profession, of large American architectural firms waiting to takeover their Australian architectural counterparts.

True it is, in some few city buildings, hotels and shopping centres, a direct participation with Australian architects has been invited from American architects during the 1950's and 1960's, but to say that we have not benefited by their wealth of experience and generous co-operation is to adopt an immature viewpoint and a very limited outlook.

Shopping. Perhaps nowhere has the direct influence of American design been more apparent than in the fast emerging suburban shopping centres in so many Australian cities. For many years our department store interior designers have beaten a well-worn track to the United States to discover the most up to date and alluring layouts for merchandise. And it was as far back as 1949 that Mr Kenneth Myer saw the trend which had begun there toward shopping centres, and realised that the development of regional shopping in Australia on those lines was inevitable.

I remember the late Sir Charles Lloyd Jones invited me to Sydney in 1950 to talk over with him some of the exciting new American shopping centres and their application to Australia. Sir Charles had many times travelled far and wide through America studying the best in store design. Our great commercial enterprises such as Myers, David Jones and others have all drawn heavily on the expertise of American design trends in regional shopping, and have adopted these to our economic needs and, perhaps, less sophisticated requirements.

As yet we have seen no evidence, as in the long-term planning for some American cities, of shopping malls freed from city traffic. But this will come and a gathering together of all available American talent to work with planners in Sydney and Melbourne could be one of the most productive, stimulating experiences.

If American design influenced shopping centres have helped to make a new way of life in our big cities, it is motels which have changed the accommodation pattern over the entire continent. And not before it was time, for no hardy traveller who endured the grim rigours of the Australian country hotel will regret its passing in favour of the new smart American design influenced motel. Those rather crude early American attempts at motor hotels in the 1940's which gave way to the lavish landscaped holiday inns of the 1960's have brought Australian tourist accommodation a little closer to jet age requirements.

Australians have been told to prepare in the 1970's for a fabulous expansion of tourism. Whether we resist the so-called 'intrusion' of American design on the Australian way of life or welcome it, we can be quite certain that, unless we are prepared to match their most highly developed tourist industry and provide the same high standard of service, what we expect as a flood of dollars may well turn out to be a trickle. From Townsville to Twofold Bay, or Albany to Alice Springs, we are beginning to see the counterpart of the American motel tailored to our needs.

Hospitals. I think it was in the 1930's that the present doyen of Australian architects, Sir Arthur Stephenson, discovered what great technical information lay behind the United States Department of Health waiting to be modified and utilised to assist here in a great nation-wide hospital programme.

It could be said that the high standards of planning for health in the United States influenced Australia's great new hospital buildings in the 1940's and 1950's. The Royal Melbourne, setting a tremendously high standard in hospital architecture and completed at the commencement of World War II, appropriately became available to take the first American servicemen casualties of the Pacific War.

Australian planning in the buildings for the treatment of the sick, both young and old, and for the care of the aged, has now reached its own high standard, and the ideas can readily be exported to those countries in the Pacific and Asian basin who seek a helping hand.

Industry. History records that as far back as in 1908, the Australian Government called for the design and installation of a Small Arms Plant in New South Wales. The contract was won by Pratt & Whitney of Hartford, Connecticut, who convinced our authorities of the value of their mass-production techniques. The Lithgow factory thus became the forerunner of buildings engineered for industrial production.

With the advent of Australia's heavy industry, drawings for the design of the first automobile plants in Victoria and New South Wales came direct from the United States, not always with the happiest or most economic results, for the engineering calculations on drawings sent to build Australian plants were made for heavy structural steel to take care of snow loads in Chicago and Detroit!

However, from those early plants, there soon evolved modifications in design and construction to suit our local needs, and it is true to say that we have learned well, gaining much from the experience in industrial planning in the United States.

It was inevitable, with America's vast industrial production skills, that we should want to study closely the buildings planned around those skills. Why should we not take what is best for our purposes? The American way so often has been found most suitable for these purposes.

The Australian plants in the 1950's and 1960's for such American industrial giants as Heinz, International Harvester, General Motors, Alcoa, Ford, Caterpillar, now designed and engineered within Australia, adapted for our conditions, are regarded as of a standard comparable to the best that their affluent parent companies can produce.

Too few eminent American architects and scholars have lectured or taught in Australia, and few exhibitions of American architecture have been available to us here. Dean Burchard of MIT and Ernest Kump of California were two welcome yet widely spaced visitors.

Some Australian architects, including Robin Boyd, have accepted limited teaching or lecture assignments to the United States, and there have been others with scholarship privileges to undertake a Master's degree in architecture who have returned to make a greater impact at home. Others like Seidler have completed their architectural training in America, and have come under the full influence of many of the great teachers such as Gropius, Johnson and Mies Van de Rohe, now to make a major contribution to the skyline of Sydney.

Some young Australian architects who have had this American impact, are reaping a reward in commissions to design whole new towns in the outback country areas of Australia to be built around the exciting mineral discoveries.

But we must also be aware that a number of the older architectural practices in Australia have enjoyed a closeness of access to their counterpart offices in the United States, bringing untold advantages in exchange of thought and stimulation through varying ideas.

The professional bodies themselves in both countries have tended, unlike industry and commerce, to stay somewhat apart. Recognition of status reached or professional standing of the individual is by no means automatically accepted by either country. Our professional bodies perhaps have followed more closely the British tradition where their ties have been very strong. The Schools of Architecture in Australia, where invigorating freshness and a desire for experimenting with the new might be expected, have not shown much evidence of desire for exchange with the great American Schools of Architecture.

The younger Australian architect, however, could himself well become a pace-setter. There is already a confident relaxed attitude to the design of houses, institutional buildings and the like where he is beginning to obtain his share.

Those who have returned from the United States have found in their American architect office experiences an enviable dedication to good design. In many of the offices such as Skidmore, Owings and Merrill, Edward Stone, Philip Johnson, Vincent Kling, John Warnecke, there is a studied approach to architecture which is carried through eventually to the smallest detail in a building and its surroundings.

This, unfortunately, has been missing in some of our prominent Australian buildings of the 1950's and 1960's, and the full value of the American influence in this respect is not being realised.

Yet, in other buildings, we can already see on the skyline of Melbourne, Sydney, Perth and Adelaide, the total approach to architecture so recognisable in the buildings of Skidmore, Owings and Merrill, Mies Van de Rohe and the others.

Our Australian architects have never enjoyed overly much contact within Australia from visits, either public or private, with their American counterparts. It is only natural that American architects should turn to Europe, and particularly to Scandinavia or South America, or even Mexico, for their relaxation and professional refreshment. There has never been much to draw them across the Pacific, although one who did come in the late 1940's was Ernest Kump of California.

For over a decade Kump has produced a delightful human touch in his design for schools, houses and civic buildings in California. No American architect, apart from Frank Lloyd Wright, in recent times has adopted with greater success the natural beauty of materials such as timber, brick and stone and produced a pleasing series of buildings each of a scale and modesty particularly appealing to Australians.

One could not say that during Kump's visit here Australian architecture influenced his design outlook, but it is certain that his simple philosophy of architecture and the example of his building, which he described during his visit, indicated their supremely high taste and gratified all Australian architects who were privileged to hear him speak. Some Australians later visited his buildings in California.

It is worthy of note that in this present period there is emerging in Sydney what might be termed a new outlook in Australian architectural design, and some buildings are reminiscent of Ernest Kump. One in particular is the delightful straight-forward, and down to earth New South Wales Award winner—the C. B. Alexander Presbyterian Agricultural School designed by Ivan McKay.

The successful visit to Sydney and Melbourne in 1967 of the exhibition of Contemporary American Paintings arranged by the Museum of Modern Art may once again encourage another type of exchange across the Pacific, photographs of the best of each of our countries' architecture. This requires leadership, and above all hard cash, but it would be a worthwhile enterprise, and perhaps some of the major Australian and American industrial giants at present engaged in the greatest mineral and oil explorations in all history, who have joined in mutual partnerships, may give this lead.

Although one can foresee more and more young Australian architects seeking higher education in the United States at the leading schools of architectural design such as MIT, the only way to ensure a very wide influence of American teaching talent for our young Australian architects is to make available liberal visiting lectureships in architecture, town planning and all the allied design subjects. This would require a new approach to endowments, and a 'welcome' sign from the Universities, and strong encouragement from the professional bodies. There could well be support forth-coming from cultural organisations in Australia, and the lively Cultural Section of American Department of State.

Already a few American professional men in Arts and architecture have come down to spend their sabbatical leave by living and working with us. Landscape architecture, as yet a 'Cinderella' profession here, has attracted some visiting professors to investigate our flora and fauna.

I think that with a little subtle salesmanship, many other notable American architects could be attracted to view the Australian scene. More Australians would eventually be invited as distinguish-ed Architectural 'Lecturers in Residence' to Universities in the United States, and it is my belief that many opportunities exist to widen this very useful avenue of contact and understanding. Through such methods, we can develop a more invigorating, more positive outlook for Australian architecture.

This is no way connotes 'Austericanus'. We have proven that Australia does not have to be a follower in many other professions. In a country such as ours with so many natural materials, beneficial climatic conditions and, we hope, still a large degree of pioneering spirit, we should be able to produce uninhibited architectural design which will not only be satisfying to ourselves, but of great interest to our American colleagues and to all who, with us, should rejoice in belonging to this Pacific region.

Part Three

8 A Historical Perspective

Over the centuries, British and European emigrants have turned their backs on their homes to move into new continental areas. Of these, two of the largest were the United States and Australia, almost identical in size and similar in shape. The United States, physically closer to Europe and resembling it in climate, was settled a century and three quarters before Australia, which was cursed by the 'tyranny of distance' and remote from the main reservoirs of migrants. In a sense both were 'virgin continents' where a new society could be built. George Frederick Vermont expressed a view that was shared by pioneers in both countries:

We are free from the clogs and accumulated hindrances which act as drags upon the progress of older countries. And while at the same time we have all the experience their countries afford, we can make more use of it than they; for while they have to knock down and root up the misshapen structure of the centuries before they can build as their experience teaches them, we, having nothing to undo, can, if we will, make the last page of their history the first of our own, and complete to its finished perfection the temples of which they have but laid the solid foundation.[1]

In the two continents, relatively virgin, two mutations from the British norm developed. Each was shaped both by environment and by the people who strove to dominate that environment. The tribulations of the first Pilgrims in Plymouth Bay were matched in Jamestown but in few other colonies, and the climate and resources of the United States far exceeded the hopes of the earliest settlers. The rivers on the Atlantic and Pacific coasts and the vast Mississippi net-work in the great Plains provided highways to the sea. Soil fertility was high and relatively small part of the country was desert. The Alleghenies and the Rockies ensured good precipitation in the forested areas of the country. The variety of natural life made it easier for the early settler and the later western pioneers to survive:

Formed by a beneficent Creator, to be the world's 'last treasure and best hope', He has extended to it every clime and afforded it every natural advantage for composing a great and mighty people. It abounds with luxurious plains, filled with the spontaneous productions of the earth, groaning under the weight of majestic trees. Broad, mighty and navigable rivers intersect the country on whose placid bosoms the riches of the interior float to the seaboard . . . (1819).[2]

While Mawyer's lyrical enthusiasm for his environment was not shared by the farmers who fought drought and fire and grasshoppers on the High Plains, it was typical of the view of millions of other American farmers.[3]

Australia, by contrast, was a grimmer and more formidable continent a thousand miles closer to the equator. The Great Dividing Range, parallel to the eastern seaboard, resembled the Alleghenies in that it ensured a relatively good rainfall to the fertile crescent on the southern and eastern seaboards. Beyond the mountains, which had no western counterpart to the Rockies, lay the vast interior which resembles the Sahara rather than the American Great Plains. Eighty-seven per cent of the country has an average annual rainfall of less than thirty inches, much of it falling irregularly and in the wrong places and often at the wrong time. Arid land with a rainfall of less than ten inches is five times as extensive as in the United States. The arid zone begins some 450 miles east of Sydney: 'back of Bourke' lies the dry sun-burnt country of little use to farmer or pastoralist. Only large-scale capital investment and modern technology have made possible twentieth century settlement in the remote areas where extensive mineral resources have been discovered. As H. C. Allen has pointed out, large parts of Australia resembled rather the South-West than the Great Plains region of the United States.

The optimism of early Australian settlers was quickly modified by the harsh realities of this sombre country. As Marcus Clarke puts it:

[T]he Australian mountain forests are funereal, secret, stern. Their solitude is desolation. They seem to stifle, in their black gorges, a story of sullen despair. No tender sentiment is nourished in their shade. In other lands the dying year is mourned, the falling leaves drop lightly on his bier. In the Australian forests no leaves fall. The savage winds shout among the rock clefts. From the melancholy gum, strips of white bark hang and rustle. The very animal life of these frowning hills is either grotesque or ghostly. . . . All is fear-inspiring and gloomy. No bright fancies are linked with the memories of the mountains. Hopeless explorers have named them out of their sufferings—Mount Misery, Mount Dreadful, Mount Despair. As when among sylvan scenes in places made green with the running of rivers, and gracious with temperate air, the soul is soothed and satisfied, so, placed before the frightful grandeur of these barren hills, it drinks in their sentiment of defiant ferocity, and is steeped in bitterness.

In time, however, Clarke admitted that 'the dweller in the wilderness acknowledges the subtle charm of the fantastic land of monstrosities. He becomes familiar with the beauty of loneliness.'[4] He could have added that it makes men frustrated, sardonic and tough.

European immigrants colonised these two largely dissimilar lands. While Virginia and Massachusetts had provided outlets for English settlers, the thickening of population brought with it ethnic diversity. In 1790, 60·1 per cent of the people were English and another 17·6 per cent Scots and Irish; 14 per cent were German, Dutch or French.

During the nineteenth century 'great' migration before the Civil War, the new settlers were predominantly British and Irish, German, Dutch, and Scandinavian. As the 'new' migration replaced the 'old', the ethnic balance changed dramatically. Italians and

Greeks, Hungarians and Poles and Russians rapidly outnumbered the Anglo-Saxons moving across the Atlantic after 1890. The easy assumption that 'the huddled masses, yearning to be free' would quickly become assimilated, boa-constrictor fashion, leaving equally little impact, became untenable. Immigration restrictions gradually closed the flood-gates and tried to strengthen the older balance between Anglo-Saxons, Mediterranean and Slavic peoples. Positive measures were adopted to ensure Americanisation. It was not for more than a generation that 'cultural pluralism' began to replace the crude assimilation of the 'melting pot' objective. Mr Dooley's succinct reply to Mr Hennessy's question, 'What wud ye do with th' offscourin' iv Europe?' 'I'd scour thim some more', became irrelevant.

The Australian people were always more homogeneous than the American. This was inevitable in the early stages as 'the prisoner's country' was settled by convicts, soldiers and officials, all of whom by definition came from Great Britain. The trickle of free settlers became a flood with the gold discoveries of the 'fifties but, despite the influx of some thousands of Chinese, the ethnic composition of the population changed hardly at all. Restrictive immigration policies, State and then Federal, ensured that the population would be overwhelmingly Anglo-Saxon leavened by a substantial Irish minority. The 1947 census showed that 99·3 per cent of Australians were of European stock. Australian had nothing comparable to the Negro and non-white minority of 10·6 per cent in the United States in 1940. After 1945, the picture changed dramatically with the large influx of immigrants to Australia. Between 1945 and 1955 three-quarters of a million people entered the country, and another 800,000 came in the next decade. Approximately half of these were non-British. A positive policy of effective integration had to be devised, largely drawing upon later American experience. With it went a positive attempt to strengthen the national identity: Australia Day (26 January) was placed alongside Anzac Day (25 April) in an attempt to give the new and changing population deeper historical roots. Myths and symbols appropriate to the national image were created or developed.

In both countries the process of exploration and internal colonisation began very early in their history. The early settlers at Jamestown pushed up the river valley and venturous Puritans crossed the near hills into Connecticut and beyond. The swarming of New Englanders and Virginians had begun and the moving frontier continued to advance across the Alleghenies and the plains to the Mississippi; beyond the Mississippi to the Rockies as Lewis and Clark, Long, Pike and Frémont explored the semi-arid and arid regions of the west. Free men and convicts from Port Jackson inched their way across the Blue Mountains into the interior grasslands, pointing the way to the squatters and their sheep. But Australian settlers landed at several points along the rim of the continent and began to push their way into the interior, following the lines of the explorers until they petered out in the dry interior. While the early explorers like Mitchell may have discovered 'Australia Felix' and Cunningham the Darling Downs, Eyre reached Mount Hopeless beyond Lake Eyre and Sturt found himself in the parched north-west of New South Wales 'locked up in this desolate and heated region as effectually as if we were ice-bound at the Pole'. Further north beyond Cooper's Creek, he reached a stony desert where 'not a feature broke the dead level, the gloomy purple hue; not a blade of vegetation grew on this forbidden plain'. Conestoga waggons crossed the semi-arid western American plains to Oregon and California, but Burke and Wills and Leichhardt died trying to cross the Australian continent. The American frontier moved irresistably westward. As John Randolph put it: 'We became a great land animal dragging its bulky form across a continent towards the setting sun.' The Australian pioneer pushed into the 'outback' and often retreated, unable to master his environment.

Internal colonisation and migration fluctuating in volume gradually produced the American and the Australian mutations. Frederick Jackson Turner has suggested that 'what the Mediterranean Sea was to the Greeks, breaking the bond of custom, offering new experience, calling out new institutions and activities, that the ever-retreating Great West has been to the eastern United States directly, and to the nations of Europe more remotely'.[5] He claimed that the frontier experience had an immediate and residual effect in producing a democratic, nationally minded society, a society that was egalitarian and promoted initiative. Whether it was the rural or urban frontier which produced the American mutation is a matter for the historians to settle: millions of Americans came to believe that the frontier had changed their outlook and created a clear path from 'Log Cabin to White House'.

Frontier influence on the Australian outlook and character is more difficult to assess because of the more difficult environment and the different patterns of migration and settlement. Australian settlement was concentrated early in its history in the towns strung along the coast: they became reservoirs of population from which a small overflow moved into the rural areas. The gold discoveries of 1851 made Melbourne an important town. It quickly overshadowed in population and resources both the farming and pastoral areas and developed by 1868 a sophisticated and relatively complex society, which led Francis Adams to comment that 'It has what might be called the *metropolitan tone*. The look on the faces of her inhabitants is the *metropolitan look*.'[6] In 1890 it possessed one of the great libraries of the world. Sydney developed as a commercial centre and by 1910 passed Melbourne in size. The other State capitals tended to dominate the back country and their States. By 1965 the majority of the Australian people was living in the capital cities. At a time when the Australian frontier was moving unevenly and in a jagged line towards the interior, the country was one of the most highly urbanised in the world. In 1960, 81·94 per cent of Australia lived in cities compared with 69·9 per cent in the United States. Allowing for different definitions of towns and cities, tighter in the United States, the difference between the levels of urbanisation between the two countries is not very significant. The high degree of urbanisation in Australia must be largely correlated with the sharp rise in overseas immigration as well as to the world-wide in-immigration to cities characteristic of every industrialised country in the world.

Colonisation brought large cities to Australia in the early stages of settlement. In rural areas there was a sharp difference in the pattern of occupation as compared with the United States. The typical Australian settler was the squatter-pastoralist rather than the small farmer who dominated the American Middle and Far West until the later development of the large ranches. The Australian frontier was a big man's frontier requiring extensive capital; the farmer followed the squatter and sought to break the monopoly of the wealthy pastoralist. A battle to 'unlock the lands' had to be fought and won before later immigrants could take up farms. Australian land legislation differs substantially from American to 1860. After 1860, as homesteading and 'free selection' policies were adopted, similar tactics were employed by squatters and ranchers to circumvent the attempts of settlers to obtain small lots of free or cheap land.

By 1890–1900, the geographical limits of effective settlement in both countries had been temporarily reached: to use the American phrase, 'the frontier had closed'. Subsequent settlement involved a minor expansion or contraction of existing areas as a result of technological changes (e.g. the use of trace elements on the Ninety Mile Beach area in South Australia) or climatic fluctuations. The patchy occupation of the High Plains areas as frustrated farmers trekked back to the cities can be matched by the advance and retreat of farmers along Goyder's Line in South Australia.

With the increase of population and rapid urbanisation came a search for a national identity and an attempt to create national unity as awareness developed of differences between Australians, Englishmen, and Americans. What was the typical Australian?

Francis Adams, the young Englishman who spent five years in Australia from 1884 to 1889, found him in the outback:

. . . the gulf between colony and colony is small and traversable compared to that great fixture that lies between the people of the Slope and of the Interior.

Where the marine rainfall flags out and is lost, a new climate, and in a certain sense, a new race begin to unfold themselves.

The 'fancy stations' on this side of the great Dividing Range produce something just different enough from anything in England to make the Englishman accept the *dictum* of the Australian cockney that this is at last the typical example of 'the bush life'.

People in the country districts of Illinois and Kentucky doubtless talk in the same way of 'the West'.

It is not one hundred but three and four and five hundred miles that you must go back from the sea if you would find yourself face to face with the one powerful and unique type yet produced in the new land....

Frankly, I find not only all that is genuinely characteristic in Australia and the Australians springing from this heart of the land but also all that is noblest, kindliest and best. . . .

The one powerful and unique national type yet produced in Australia is . . . that of the Bushman. . . . The Anglo-Saxon has perished or is absorbed in the Interior much more rapidly than on the sea slope and in the towns. . . .

The West was the heart of the country, the genuine America, and the Interior is the heart of the genuine Australia, and if needs be, will do as much for the nation and the race.[7]

Many Australians believe that the back country did, in fact, 'for the nation and the race' what Francis Adams claimed that it would do: that the Australian national image became identified with that of the bushman. Russel Ward has examined the development of the Australian bush legend and has shown that there is a connection between legend and reality. The harshness of the country where '. . . sheep, lying dead everywhere, with agonised back-cast heads, have not perished from thirst',[8] the immense distances and the isolation, led alike to that individualism and initiative which were also characteristic of American pioneers. They also led to an irreverence and a sardonic humour, to a collectivism stronger than the more tenuous community spirit that produced the American cabin raising. 'Mateship' became an essential part of the bush ethos and of the Australian character. It was reflected in the close companionship both of the bush-worker and of the urban 'push'. It was reinforced by the penal background of early settlement, with its dependence on government support, and by the scarcity of private capital for the development of a difficult country.

The Australian tradition was essentially democratic, more belligerently so than the American. The Australian bushman of the 'nineties was an itinerant worker rather than an expectant capitalist. The shearer who 'arrives on a horse leading another, and with a bank-book in his pocket' could not become a squatter in his own right. The nomadic tribe was aggressively egalitarian and class conscious. In writing to the editor of *The Bulletin* in 1897, Joseph Furphy described his classic Australian novel, *Such is Life*: 'temper democratic; bias, offensively Australian'.[9] The interior had destroyed the British traditions and caste lines to produce a new type. 'When a member of the class takes to his bosom that unclean thing in its naked reality, he thereby forfeits the title of "a gentleman" and becomes a mere man. For there is no such thing as a democratic gentleman; the adjective and the noun are hyphenated by a drawn sword.'[9]

In his *Song of the Cities*, Kipling described a Sydney where

> My birth stains have I turned to good,
> Forcing strong wills perverse to steadfastness.

Strong radical wills in Melbourne had become

> Loud mouthed and reckless as the wild tide race
> That whips our harbour mouth.[10]

There was a boastfulness about the Australian that would match the swagger of the Texan and the Californian: Mike Fink belonged spiritually to both sides of the Pacific. But the passionate belief of the bushman in democracy and equality was a belief that in a virgin country a man could make his own way and should be helped to do so by a levelling power exercised by the state. This was a view shared largely by the conservatives who dominated governments during the nineteenth century. As James Service put it, 'every man should start fair in life and have the same chance of making his way through the world'.[11] That proletarian egalitarianism did, however, overlay an earlier aristocratic tradition which is now being re-discovered by the cultural historians. The early squatting tradition of Neil Black and the other 'men of yesterday' in one sense paralleled the Bostonian traditions of the Lowells, the Cabots and the Faneuils, and the patrician Virginian outlook of the Randolphs, Dabneys and Seldens. Australian intellectuals, tired of the levelling tendencies of a primitive bush anarchy, are rebelling against it and rejecting the commonplace and the mediocrity which often appear to be an essential ingredient of 'mateship'. There is a growing awareness that radicalism had roots in cities, that social democracy was spawned in the trade unions developing in the new urban industrial complexes. One of the fascinating problems facing Australian historians is to explain why the bush legend should have been adopted as the central part of a national ethos in a country that was so strongly urban.

Two similar and yet different societies and national types developed in the United States and Australia as Europeans moved into new environments. These mutations from the British or European norm, however, did not take place wholly independently, and over almost two centuries there have been contacts, sometimes close, more often tenuous.

The first contacts between Australia and the United States were commercial. The United States opened its Far Eastern trade with the *Empress of India* in 1784, and found it extremely profitable. When the first settlement was made at Port Jackson, American merchants and consular officials quickly realised the possibilities of using it as a port of call to Canton. King's suggestion to Patrickson when they met by chance in Cape Town that mixed cargoes might fetch good prices in New South Wales led to the arrival of the *Philadelphia* at Port Jackson on 1 November 1792. During the next eight years, thirteen American vessels entered the port and developed a casual trade in 'dry goods' and spirits. The uncertain food supply in New South Wales and the shortage of grain for conversion into spirits led to a steady demand for both provisions and rum. British merchants were prevented from trading with New South Wales because of the East India Company charter which gave it 'exclusive rights from the Cape of Good Hope to the Straits of Magellan'. The American trade was thus illicit, and from time to time governors sought to prohibit it by threatening confiscation of the cargoes. But, in fact, the needs of the administration and the thirst of the colonists kept the trade open until the outbreak of the War of 1812. An infant triangular trade developed between the United States, Australia and China. American ships carrying mixed cargoes of merchandise and spirits sold the cargoes for cash or letters of credit that could be used for purchases in Canton: it was no longer necessary to travel in ballast or half loaded to China.

The trade was, however, a spasmodic and speculative one depending on the whims of the American sea captains or merchants. Between 1800 and 1809 some thirty-three American ships visited Sydney: as many as five ships a year arrived from the American Atlantic coast, but in some years no ships called. Whaling and sealing vessels occasionally put in to Port Jackson as the whaling industry expanded rapidly. Nantucket and Bedford men were quickly attracted by the large numbers of sperm whales in Australian and New Zealand waters, and American captains soon came to dominate the growing whaling industry. American ships put in to several Australian harbours for bay whaling or sealing. Clashes occurred at times over promising sealing grounds. In 1804, Joseph Marrell of the sloop *Surprise* was attacked by American sailors from the *Pilgrim* and *Perseverance* commanded by Amasa Delano (an ancestor of President Franklin Delano Roosevelt). The American dominance of the growing fishing industry aroused concern in New South Wales. Governor King told London on 1 November 1805 that 'if the most decided checks are not given to the introduction of Americans and American vessels, any benefit this colony may possess would become the property of Americans at the expense of England'.[12]

It was not until 1813 that the East India Company's trading monopoly was terminated. But the American trade with Australia had stopped with the outbreak of the 1812 War when privateering developed in the Pacific. Direct trade became much more spasmodic with the opening of trade between New South Wales and England. American domination of both whaling and sealing was so marked that fishing vessels out-numbered general American trading vessels sailing to Sydney, Hobart, Perth and other Australian ports. In May 1835, the first American consul, James H. Williams, was appointed to Sydney but did not take up his post until January 1839. Consulates were opened in Hobart in 1843 and Melbourne in 1852. (The first Australian trade commissioner was sent to the United States in 1918.)

When Charles Wilkes visited Sydney in 1839 as part of his long voyage of exploration (1838–42), which took him from Oregon to Antarctica, he observed that 'New South Wales is known in the United States almost by its name alone'.[13] Whalers and sealers had done little to create images in either country. The discovery of gold at Sutter's Mill in California in 1848 and Hargreaves' successful dig at Bathurst in 1851 brought a substantial change in both images. News of the Californian discoveries reached Sydney in December 1848, and in January 1849, the *Eleanor Lancaster* sailed for San Francisco with passengers and cargo. Its record-making voyage of seventy-one days was followed by a steady and then a dramatic expansion of trade and migration between the two countries. In 1849, sixty-five vessels left Australian ports with some 2,700 passengers. During the first five months of 1850, seventy-five vessels sailed to San Francisco and by the end of the year more than 5,000 people had left from Sydney for the gold fields. The trend was reversed as Australian discoveries were made at Bathurst and Ballarat in 1851. A small minority of the Australian emigrants to California were convicts or ticket of leave men who quickly achieved a notorious reputation. 'Sydney Coves' were held responsible for much of the violence in San Francisco. It was perhaps poetic justice that the first victim of the San Francisco Committee of Vigilance was John Jenkins, a Sydney criminal who was lynched on 10 June 1851. The Committee 'sent a boat aboard every vessel that came from Australia to look for convicts. We had a list . . . of all the convict ships that went from England to Australia, alphabetically arranged, extending over several years.'[14] Convict passengers were then detained and returned to Australia at the expense of the Committee. Attacks on innocent Australians in San Francisco as well as the authoritarian methods of the Committee led to some deterioration of relations between the two countries.

The gold discoveries in New South Wales and Victoria led to a dramatic increase in Australia's population. It had almost doubled to 437,000 between 1841 and 1851 and then jumped to 793,000 in 1855 and to 1,050,000 by 1858. Between 1851 and 1861 Australia produced 39 per cent of the world's output of gold, and the United States, 41 per cent. Most of the immigrants who came to Australia were Europeans, but there was a small percentage of Americans and of Australians who had prospected in California. The British Gold Field's Commissioner at Bendigo reported that 'a number of American adventurers, who had come from Californian diggings, were inciting the people to set up Judge Lynch'.[15] Lord Robert Cecil travelled by coach to Mount Alexander with an American passenger whom he described as 'a coarse, hideous, dirty-looking man, without an attempt at ornament or neatness in his dress. . . . He wore a pair of pistols in his belt, and the words, "put a bullet through his brain" were constantly in his mouth.'[16] But there seem to have been few desperadoes among the Californians and the normal sprinkling of card sharps and dishonest traders. Lawlessness was on a very small scale and most of the criminals appear to have come from Europe, Van Diemen's Land or the mainland colonies themselves. Australian police control, despite the unpopularity of the troopers, was much tighter than it had been in California where federal officials belatedly replaced the tolerant Spaniards after statehood was achieved in September 1850.

American influence on Eureka was minimal. While James McGill organised the Independent Californian Rangers' Revolver Brigade and some 200 marched to Ballarat, few were injured and none sent up for trail except the negro, John Joseph. Radicalism at Eureka was more marked amongst English chartists, Italians and Germans than Californian republicans. American political influence during the gold rushes was rather indirect. *The Hobart Daily Courier* (16 February 1850) drew attention to the swift establishment of self government in California, to the quick transition from a territorial status to statehood and contrasted it with the more majestic devolution of power by Britain to the colonists. 'The Americans, accustomed to action, not whining and petitioning, have elected their governors, and accepted their constitutions, without a moment's obstruction; and have offered a practical lesson to these colonies which has produced a profound impression. . . . We cannot but feel mortified to contrast the spirit of that new nation with the still jealous restraints which fetter the enterprise of our own colonies.'[17] In the debate over the New South Wales constitution, W. C. Wentworth attacked political proposals that smacked of Yankee republicanism. Henry Parkes, just as vigorously repudiated the idea of introducing a 'Yankee' constitution but equally vigorously declared that he for one would never consent to have a 'Norfolk Island' constitution. The American influence contributed peripherally to the climate of liberal opinion which influenced the framing of Australian State constitutions in the 'fifties; de Tocqueville was however more important than Bancroft or gold.

American influence was more marked on urban than rural development despite the rapid spread of American know-how in prospecting for alluvial gold. Melbourne's population rose from 39,000 in 1851 to 139,916 in 1861 and both Ballarat and Bendigo became new provincial towns. American business men quickly moved in to develop a trade with the gold fields. The repeal of the Navigation Acts and the colonial reduction of tariffs freed the Australian trade of many restrictions and the new clipper ships, designed by Donald McKay, gave American merchants a competitive advantage. In 1853, 134 American ships anchored in Hobson's Bay. Dry goods ranging from rugs to suits, watches and sewing machines as well as portable houses were unloaded on Melbourne wharves. The most enterprising of the Yankee merchants was George Francis Train who arrived in 1853 and who was made a member of the Chamber of Commerce three days after he landed. He organised a fire brigade equipped with Boston fire engines, promoted a railway between Sandridge and Melbourne, and converted the Criterion Hotel into the best in the city: its new bars and the luxurious 'Diggers' Nuptial Suites' catered for the thirsty diggers and their brides. Roe's American Circus and American minstrel shows, Edwin Booth and Laura Keene as well as Lola Montez contributed to the new theatrical life of a metropolitan Melbourne.[18]

One of the greatest liabilities of the Australian colonies had been their poor system of communications. Samuel McGowan of Boston built the first magnetic telegraph line from Melbourne to Geelong and American experts operated it. Freeman Cobb, another Bostonian, brought Concord coaches to Melbourne and opened the first coaching service between Sandridge and Melbourne and quickly extended it to Bendigo and other gold-mining towns. Cobb and Company built up a communications net-work that extended to all the eastern States and rivalled the Butterfield Overland Express and the Wells Fargo Company in the United States. Cobb's coaches continued to play a vital role in inland communications long after the American stage companies had been relegated to feeder services for the transcontinental railways. The American 'bush coach' in a sense was the precursor of the Holden car. Clipper and steamship services between Australia and New Zealand and San Francisco were developed in the generation after the discovery of gold. H. H. Hall, the acting American consul in Sydney from 1867, and W. H. Webb pioneered trans-Pacific mail and passenger services which were subsequently taken over by the Union Steamship Company of New Zealand and the Oceanic Company of the United States.[19]

The fifty years between the gold rushes and federation saw a steady expansion of trade between Australia and the United States, a trade, however, that always left Australia with an unfavourable balance. Only between 1849 and 1851 when Australian flour and other provisions fetched high prices in California was the trend reversed. American ideas exercised a marginal influence on the Australian labour movement but had a more direct impact on Australian federation and the framing of the federal constitution.

During these years Australian society was becoming at once fluid and yet at the same time more class conscious. The older lines of division between the 'pure Merinos' and the 'emancipists' had been obliterated by the gold rushes. The majority of the diggers were working-class people with a sprinkling of professional and small business men. The economic boom of the 'fifties and 'sixties and the expansion of trade saw the beginnings of the campaign to sub-divide the large pastoral estates: the middle class was strengthened by the addition of the small farmers and merchants of varying status. At the same time the need for capital for sheep and mining meant that few of the shearers and other bush workers could hope to become capitalists. Australian business men believed in competitive individualism but an individualism tempered by an acceptance of equality of opportunity. The ruthless *laissez faire* of the Rockefellers and Armours, the Carnegies and Vanderbilts did not take root in Australia where governments exercised an increasing power of supervision over social development and introduced compulsory secular education.

The strong trade union movement in Australia was a response to the growth of Australian capitalism after 1851. It was compounded of a determination to improve working conditions in a buoyant society and of that optimism that produced so much of the emigration from Britain. It was strengthened by the feeling of mateship and by a Utopian belief in the future of an Australia that they could help to shape. Henry George's *Poverty* was serialised by a Sydney newspaper within a year of its being published in the United States, and George himself visited Australia in 1890. Bellamy's *Looking Backward* had 'a prodigious circulation throughout Australia. There the workers are a reading class and Bellamy's solution of the problem of living, his combination of Socialism and individual liberty, won the enthusiastic assent of all. The book was read and discussed in workshop and on station, in the mining camps and amongst the timber getters, in fact wherever a few workers were gathered together, there Bellamy was discussed and approved.' [20] Gronlund's *Co-operative Commonwealth* also contributed to what J. D. Fitzgerald described as 'a wave of socialistic hope' and profoundly affected William Lane's thought. But while George, Bellamy and Gronlund all helped to develop the socialist climate of opinion, their direct influence on the Australian labour movement was limited. The fall in wool prices and the deepening of the world depression at the beginning of the 'nineties led to a series of bitter strikes throughout Australia: tactics and strategy became more important than idealist socialism.

The Australian trade movement was influenced more profoundly by English than American experience. The Knights of Labour, with its emphasis on industrial rather than craft unionism, attracted some attention amongst union leaders in Australia after it passed its peak in the United States, but its effect was very short lived and limited. The proliferation of socialist ideas in the United States culminated in the founding of the Industrial Workers of the World in Chicago in June 1905. iww locals were quickly founded in Australia and strengthened the swing towards militancy when arbitration was gaining wide support as a means of resolving industrial conflicts. V. G. Childe believed that the IWW was 'the first body to offer effectively to the Australian workers an ideal of emancipation, alternative to the somewhat threadbare Fabianism of the Labor Party'.[21] Its appeal lay in its demand for industrial unionism, and unionism that would draw into the movement the nomadic semi-skilled and unskilled workers in rural areas, for revolutionary action. This reflected Chicago rather than the more moderate Detroit influence on the Australian branches of the IWW. With the outbreak of war in 1914, the IWW challenged the established leadership and adopted an anti-militarist policy that culminated in vigorous opposition to conscription. It was dissolved under the Unlawful Associations Act of 1916. Subsequent American influences on the Australian labour movement were slight and conservative rather than radical.

By the 'nineties national feeling was growing and the sense of national identity more precise. The foundation of the Australian Natives' Association in 1872 was a symptom of this new-found nationalism and the move towards federation a political recognition of the need for greater security for Australia's standard of living and culture. When the first Commonwealth Parliament was opened on 9 May 1901, the six Australian colonies had 3,773,801 people as compared with the 3,929,214 Americans who lived through the inauguration of the federal government of the United States. The new political entity was born in an industrial age with problems akin to, yet different from, those of the frail republic that came into being in 1787. That republic, however, dwarfed in population, resources and economic development the new Australian Commonwealth.

Australian national culture lagged behind the federalist movement and had its roots deep in the British tradition. De Tocqueville's comment that in America there existed 'an instinctive distaste for the past' applies in large measure to Australia. Joseph Furphy's socialist agitator had warned that 'from the present social system of pastoral Australia—a patriarchal despotism, tempered by Bryant and May—to actual lordship and peonage is an easy tran-

sition'.[22] Australia, unlike the United States, was reluctant to cut
the umbilical cord which tied it to Great Britain: 'Going home'
was as much a cultural as well as a physical experience as it was for
the Virginian or South Carolinian colonist. Australian graduates
migrated naturally to Oxford, Cambridge or London and some
undergraduates by-passed the Australian universities altogether.

At the end of the nineteenth century, *The Bulletin* school of
writers broke definitely with the 'truculent, narcotic and despotic
past' or tried to ignore it. Henry Lawson, A. B. Paterson and
Joseph Furphy developed a new bush tradition that was 'offensively Australian' in bias. Bernard O'Dowd and Furnley Maurice
were less belligerent rebels.[23] Some of the more sophisticated Australian writers like Ethel Richardson (Henry Handel Richardson)
and Christopher Brennan still preferred to be expatriates in Europe
surveying the Australian scene from abroad just as did their
American counterparts. British influences persisted as Australian
writing matured. The American impact was relatively slight
(although Henry Lawson had read the stories of Bret Harte) and
it was not until the 1930's that American literature came to influence Australian novelists. The literature of social protest during
the depression years gained an increasing acceptance by the Australian reader. At the popular level the trickle of American books
reaching Australia became a flood at the beginning of the twentieth century. Ruth Megaw has made a detailed analysis of American cultural influences in Australia to 1914. Visiting American
actors and variety troupes have attracted wide support since the
burgeoning of a colonial theatre during the gold rush. It is not
without significance that the firm of J. C. Williamson which dominated the Australian professional theatre was American rather
than British.

The new nationalism and federalism at the end of the nineteenth century reflected a growing Australian awareness of external threats. Just as the United States had become 'a great land
animal dragging its bulky form across a continent', ignoring
Europe and adopting a Monroe Doctrine which rested on the
broad back of the British navy for almost three-quarters of a
century, so the Australian people concentrated on internal coloni-

sation. British troops—until their withdrawal in 1870—and the British navy provided both local defence and a shield behind which the economic development of the country could take place. Isolationism was deep rooted in both Australia and the United States. Australian concern about French convicts escaping from New Caledonia and McIlwraith's annexation of New Guinea in 1883 were not attempts to promulgate 'a new Monroe Doctrine (which) would prevent old Europe, in the name of the United States of Australia from setting foot upon a single isle of the Pacific' (Prévost-Parabol, 1868).[24] Australian concern at German activities in Samoa and the extension of Hamburg shipping lines into the Pacific was partly allayed by the tripartite arrangements made over Samoa between Britain, Germany and the United States between 1877 and 1889.

The extension of Australia's oceanic frontier in the Pacific brought a rising concern at clashes between rival imperialisms in Asia and the Pacific and a fear that Australian interests might be ignored by Great Britain in a global horse deal in real estate. The Melbourne *Argus* demand in 1895 foreshadowed the Evatt position during World War II: 'No treaty development in the Pacific should be allowed to take place without our claim to participation in it being allowed.'[25] The Spanish-American War of 1898 brought the United States into the Western Pacific with the annexation of the Philippines. Both Russian and Japanese expansion in Asia increased Australian and American fears about a possible 'yellow' peril. The Anglo-Japanese alliance in 1902 temporarily relieved these fears, but tensions over Japanese immigration to California revived them. It created both a sense of community interest between Australia and the United States and at the same time posed for Australia the policy dilemma of its course of action should war break out between Japan and the United States. The conflicting pulls of sentiment and interest which tended to bedevil Australian policy makers for the next half century were then evident.

Australia's move to develop its own defence system and to create an Australian navy after federation was one symptom of its rising national feeling. Alfred Deakin, the Australian Prime Minister, forced the hand of the Colonial Office to invite the American fleet in 1908 to extend its Pacific cruise to Australia. 'The closer the alliance between us the better, for although I am fully alive to the many objectional features of their political life, after all they are nearest to us in blood and in social, religious and even political developments.'[26] Admiral Sperry called his fleet's visit a 'monumental success'. Its emotional impact was striking and it did much to temporarily allay Australian concern at the reduction of the British fleet in the Pacific following the Anglo-Japanese alliance. Australian fears of Japan persisted to the outbreak of World War 1 and were not allayed by the assistance of Japanese cruisers to escort Australian troops to the Middle East.

Australian nationalism was immensely strengthened by the ANZAC landings at Gallipoli in 1915, by participation in the military campaigns in France and Palestine and by her separate representation at the Paris Peace Conference in 1919. Sharp clashes of policy and personality developed between William Morris Hughes, Prime Minister of Australia, and President Woodrow Wilson at Paris. Australia's demand for the annexation of German colonies south of the equator was diametrically opposed to the American war aim of 'no material gains'. The compromise proposal for a mandate system failed to meet Australian objections.

'Mr Hughes, am I to understand that if the whole world asks Australia to agree to a mandate in respect of these islands, Australia is prepared still to defy the appeal of the whole civilised world?'

'That's about the size of it, President Wilson,' replied Hughes.[27]

The final solution came with the creation of the C class mandates under which New Guinea could be administered 'under the laws of the Mandatory as integral portions of its territory . . .'. A further difference occurred over the question of a Japanese amendment to the Covenant of the League of Nations recognising the principle of racial equality. W. M. Hughes helped to mobilise West Coast opinion in the United States against President Wilson in an attempt to prevent what he regarded as a threat to Australia's restrictive immigration policy. Woodrow Wilson declared the amendment lost because the vote was not unanimous.

Friction between Australia and the United States over the details of the Versailles settlement were short-lived. Continued Japanese pressures on China, during and after the war, again posed the problem of political stability in China and in the western Pacific. The Anglo-Japanese Alliance, renewed on several occasions since 1902, still created policy problems for Australia and the United States as well as for its signatories. Australia's insistence on proper representation at the Washington Conference 1921–22 received tacit support from the United States. The State Department agreed that the presence of Dominion delegates 'would be very acceptable' but the British Foreign Secretary, Lord Curzon, was more reluctant. The Australian Defence Minister, Senator Pearce, was finally added to the British delegation. The Four Power Treaty (Britain, France, Japan, and the United States) signed at the conference formally renounced the Anglo-Japanese Alliance. The network of Washington treaties was designed to stabilise the situation in the Far East. In fact it established Japanese naval preponderance in the Western Pacific and left the Pacific east of Honolulu as an American sphere. The newly established British base at Singapore assumed an increasing importance in Australian defence thinking during the next generation. After the breaching of the Washington Treaties by Japan in Manchuria and China in 1937, the need for a new Pacific security system became imperative.

Norman Harper

[1] R. M. Crawford, 'The Australian National Character: Myth and Reality', *Journal of World History*, vol. 2, 1954–55, p. 705.
[2] cit. M. Curti, *The Roots of American Loyalty*, New York, 1946, p. 41.
[3] H. C. Allen, *Bush and Backwoods*, Michigan, 1959, pp. 14–15, 123.
[4] R. M. Crawford, *An Australian Perspective*, Madison, 1960, pp. 42–3.
[5] F. J. Turner, *Early Writings*, ed. Fulmer Mood, Madison, 1938, p. 83.
[6] C. M. H. Clark, *Sources of Australian History*, Oxford, 1957, p. 453 (Francis Adams).
[7] Francis Adams, *The Australians: A Social Sketch*, London, 1893, pp. 144, 154, 165, 166, 171.
[8] Ibid, p. 145.
[9] Tom Collins, *Such is Life*, Chicago, 1948, pp. 395, 205.
[10] R. Kipling, *Collected Works*, New York, 1898, vol. XI, p. 191.
[11] R. M. Crawford, *An Australian Perspective*, p. 30.

[12] Gordon Greenwood, *Early American-Australian Relations*, Melbourne, 1944, p. 69.

[13] C. Hartley Grattan, *The United States and the South-West Pacific*, Cambridge, 1961, p. 94.

[14] W. Levi, *American-Australian Relations*, Minneapolis, 1947, p. 40.

[15] Jay Monaghan, *Australians and the Gold Rushes*, Berkeley, 1966, p. 214.

[16] E. Scott, (ed.), *Lord Robert Cecil's Goldfields Diary*, Melbourne, 1935, p. 13.

[17] Monaghan, op.cit., p. 155.

[18] Ibid. pp. 230-1.

[19] L. G. Churchward, 'American Enterprise: the Foundation of the Pacific Mail Service', *Historical Studies*, vol. 3, 1944-49, pp. 217-24.

[20] T. A. Coghlan, *Labour and Industry in Australia*, Melbourne, 1918, vol. IV, p. 1836. See generally, L. G. Churchward, 'The American Influence on the Australian Labour Movement', *Hist. Studies*, vol. 5, 1951-53, pp. 258-77.

[21] V. G. Childe, *How Labour Governs*, Melbourne, 1964, pp. 104-5.

[22] T. Collins, *Rigby's Romance*, Sydney, 1946, p. 98. cit. R. Gollan, *Radical and Working Class Politics*, Melbourne, 1960, p. 113.

[23] R. M. Crawford, *Australia*, pp. 35-8.

[24] E. Scott, *A Short History of Australia*, Melbourne, 1947, p. 294.

[25] W. Levi, op.cit., p. 82.

[26] J. A. La Nauze, *Alfred Deakin*, Melbourne, 1966, vol. II, pp. 490-1.

[27] W. Levi, op.cit., p. 108.

9 Two Federations

The Commonwealth of Australia came into existence on 1 January 1901. By that time the American federation was more than a hundred years old and it had already weathered severe storms. It was born in difficult times; in the aftermath of a victorious war of independence the separate and insecure American colonies had need of increased strength and the federal form of government devised by them offered a more secure defence, so that they might face the world with more assurance and confidence. Less than a hundred years later, the American Union faced a critical challenge, and the federation survived only after a protracted civil war. The scars of war remained unhealed for a long time: when the Commonwealth of Australia was established less than forty years after the civil war came to an end, the wounds inflicted on the body politic of the United States were still evident.

No such drama attended the birth of Australian federation, nor has it faced any comparable threats. The very fact that the Commonwealth of Australia came into existence by authority of a United Kingdom Act of Parliament was significant. In the United States, federation had come about by the constitutive act of the people of the newly *independent* States; in Australia existing British colonies, maintaining their British links, agreed that it was appropriate that there should be closer constitutional bonds between them, and having done so asked the mother government and parliament of the United Kingdom to take the necessary constitutional steps to give legal form to the federation.

The pressures on Australians to make their federation were

certainly less urgent. Federation was an achievement of enthusiasts, Australian nationalists, able to persuade a majority of the Australian people than an *Australian* political entity was desirable. One of the main arguments in favour of federation was the need for a common defence in face of possible external threats and there were persuasive arguments in favour of common policies on such matters as tariffs and immigration. But while the Australian founding fathers looked to larger horizons they did not contemplate, as did their American counterparts, a federal government for an *independent* nation. The Australian founding fathers anticipated and expected internal autonomy and during the nineteenth century the Australian colonies peaceably developed the institutions of internal self-government without too much interference on the part of the mother country. But it was not envisaged then by the Australian founding fathers, even the most ardent nationalists among them, that Australia should be an independent nation. On the contrary, it was assumed that the external relations of Australia should still be conducted by the United Kingdom government.

This can be readily illustrated by a comparison of the two federal constitutions. The American Constitution has much to say on the subject of treaty relationships; it provides for the making of treaties by the President and for their ratification by the Senate. When ratified, it is provided that treaties shall become the supreme law of the land. There is only one oblique reference to treaties in the Australian Constitution, and in addition a provision authorising the making of laws by the Commonwealth Parliament with respect to external affairs. In writing this clause into the Constitution, our founding fathers had a very uncertain picture of what they were doing. But they were well aware of what they were doing when they did not transcribe from the United States Constitution —which in so many other respects provided a powerful and persuasive model—the various provisions relating to the making and operation of treaties. They saw treaty making as no part of the activities and responsibilities of a *colonial* Commonwealth. Circumstances changed, and at a later time, though still within the framework of continuing membership of the British Commonwealth, Australia became an independent state with independent external policies. Precisely when this happened no one can say, but it certainly happened, with the consequence that a constitutional apparatus which allowed an Australian government to conduct independent international relations had to be found in a Constitution which was never designed for this purpose. As a matter of judicial interpretation of the Constitution by the High Court of Australia, an independent treaty-making power was discovered on the face of the instrument and the obscurely worded legislative power with respect to external affairs was found to be an ample source of constitutional power to implement the terms of such treaties.

There are other indications on the face of the Australian Constitution which bear testimony to colonial beginnings. Some of them have a curiously anachronistic appearance in the late twentieth century: provisions, for example, which refer to the supervisory role of the Queen over certain types of laws enacted by the Commonwealth Parliament. But they are meaningless survivals, atrophied by constitutional developments. There are clauses in the Constitution providing for judicial appeals to the Privy Council, a court which sits in London and is manned for the most part by United Kingdom judges. Some found it difficult to accept the need for this jurisdiction, even when the Constitution was made at the end of the nineteenth century, and in fact one of the major disputes with the British government, when it was asked to secure the passage of the Australian Constitution Bill through the United Kingdom Parliament, was over clauses designed to restrict these appeals. But it is only in the very recent past that the Australian Commonwealth Parliament has declared its intention to abolish appeals from the Australian High Court to the Privy Council. It is a matter of no earth-shaking importance, but it must seem to many strange that right up to this point of time in our constitutional development, it should have been thought sensible to allow such matters to be dealt with at such a remote distance from Australian shores.

In a more general sense, however, the American Constitution exercised a powerful influence over our founding fathers. While the Australian Constitution was given the constitutional form of a

United Kingdom Act of Parliament, it was in substance a home-grown product, for it was drafted in constitutional conventions in Australia in the 1890's and the Bill prepared by the 1897–98 Convention with a few modifications was approved at constitutional referenda in all six Australian States. There were long and protracted debates in the conventions over many questions, but the broad principle was generally accepted that the desirable form of government for the new Commonwealth (a title proposed by the father of Australian federation, Sir Henry Parkes) was federal. This was a pragmatic solution; it was never contemplated that the States and the State constitutions should be obliterated. On the contrary it was assumed that they would continue to have a vigorous existence. It was thought appropriate to constitute a new entity, the Commonwealth, with executive, legislative and judicial arms and to give the Commonwealth limited and specific powers, preserving State institutions and powers save so far as they were modified by the existence and operation of the new Commonwealth.

It was not surprising then that our Australian founding fathers, some of them distinguished lawyers, should have turned again and again to the American Constitution and its interpretation for guidance in the drafting of the Australian instrument. One of the greatest of Australian judges and lawyers, Sir Owen Dixon, wrote some thirty years after federation that 'the framers of our Federal Commonwealth Constitution (who were for the most part lawyers) found the American instrument of government an incomparable model. They could not escape from its fascination. Its contemplation damped the smouldering fires of their originality.' Indeed as references to American constitutional provisions and interpretations came thick and fast in the Convention of 1897–98, one impatient and harassed delegate burst forth: 'We have heard too much about the example of the United States all through the meetings of this Convention. If the Constitution of the United States had been burned before the Convention met we should have done more practical work, and we should probably have evolved a Constitution quite as suitable, if not more suitable to the people we represent.'

There are certainly many evidences of transcription from the text of the American Constitution on the face of the Australian instrument. Some of them are of the most obvious sort: we call our federal legislative chambers the House of Representatives and the Senate, though we preferred Parliament to Congress as a description of the whole. There are legislative powers in each Constitution couched in virtually identical terms; in the judicature chapter of the Constitution there is copying which, in some respects anyway, does not make very good sense. It is a fascinating exercise to speculate why in some instances our founding fathers copied without asking whether there was any sound reason for doing so, while in other cases they very consciously and deliberately departed from the American model.

I have already spoken of some of the differences in the two Constitutions which are partly to be explained by our colonial origins and our continued commitment to imperial and monarchical links. There were other, more significant, differences. The United States Constitution coupled with a federal form of government the doctrine of the separation of powers. This doctrine provides for a separation of legislative, executive and judicial powers and functions. No member of the executive government—the President and his executive officers—may at the same time be a member of the legislature and vice versa. The climate of political thought at the time of the making of the American Constitution strongly favoured such a separation; it was seen as a guarantee against the tyranny which threatened when different governmental powers were joined in one pair of hands.

The Australian situation was quite different in this respect. As a matter of constitutional practice, there had emerged in the United Kingdom the institution of the parliamentary executive. The principal members of the executive government were, and were by practice required to be, members of the legislature drawn from the majority party or grouping of parties in the Parliament. This was so-called responsible government; the government was said to be responsible or accountable to the House of Commons so that when it lost the support of the House, it was obliged to resign and to yield place to another government which could command that support.

This was the pattern which evolved in the Australian colonies, and when at the end of the nineteenth century the new Commonwealth was established, the founding fathers saw no reason for departing from familiar and well-established paths. So it happened that while adopting a federal form of government, they were not persuaded to follow American precedent by adopting the doctrine of the separation of powers. On the contrary the Australian Constitution specifically provided that ministers, the principal members of the executive government, *must* be or speedily become members of either House of the federal Parliament.

Some warned at the time that this would profoundly affect the character of Australian federation. We produced a hybrid: a federation owing much to American influence but with the inherited governmental institutions of our own British history. And there can be no doubt that this has significantly affected our institutions and distinguished them from American institutions. This can be demonstrated by a study of the relationships between the executive and legislative branches of government. What is so striking in the American form of government is the limit on executive power to control the legislature. The President may cajole, threaten, persuade, the Congress; he cannot compel it to do what he wants. It is otherwise in the Australian context: the doctrine of responsible government which asserts the responsibility of the executive to the legislature is in practice one which assures executive domination and control of the Parliament. So long as there is a coherent majority in the legislature, the executive can use that majority to assure the passage of the government's programme through the legislature. Except in very rare cases the legislature is the compliant instrument of the executive will, and the complaints of individual members of the legislature that they are ciphers are valid. Whatever democracy and right of dissent may exist in the party room, the will of government ultimately prevails in the legislative chamber. It is very different in the American form of government. The individual member of Congress is a much more significant figure, certainly in executive eyes, than his Australian counterpart. This serves to explain the power, independence and importance of American legislative committees and their comparative insignificance in Australia. The American position may be productive of frustrations and delay, of great difficulty in securing the passage of controversial legislation. The Australian doctrine assures the predominance of the governmental will so long as there are stable legislative majorities. There are benefits and disadvantages in both systems, and, in my judgment, democratic government is better served by the checks and balances of independent executive and legislative branches of government. But there is no likelihood of change in Australia.

This also serves to explain, in part anyway, the differing roles and authority of the Senates in the two countries. The Australian Constitution followed its American counterpart in providing for equal representation of each of the original States in the Senate. While the composition of the lower house reflected population differences, it was thought proper in a federal system of government to acknowledge in one branch of the legislature the equality of States, however large or small. The Constitution and powers of the Australian Senate were debated very keenly in the Australian federal conventions and the outcome was for the most part favourable to those who supported a strong Senate: they secured equal representation of the States in the Senate and virtually coordinate power with the lower house. There were, however, some notable differences in the two Constitutions: there was no requirement in Australia of Senatorial approval of treaties and of a wide range of presidential appointments.

In the United States the Senate is the legislative house of preponderant significance. It is certainly not the case in Australia: indeed few Australians would pass the test of being able to name all ten Senators from their own State. The face is that the doctrine of responsible government, with its United Kingdom roots, emphasises responsibility to the *lower* House. In the British context, there was good reason for this: the House of Commons was the *elected* House and the House of Lords was wholly non-elective. This was not the case in Australia where Senators were popularly elected by a State-wide constituency. Yet it came about, largely I believe as a matter of inherited doctrine, that primacy was accorded in executive-legislative relationships to the lower house, certainly in the field of financial legislation, but also more generally. I believe that it is because of doctrines and the interpretations of *British* doctrines of responsible government that the Senate in Australia has been viewed as a House of subordinate authority and significance. It is not the only reason of course, but it is a very important one. Whereas in the United States independent Senate activity and initiatives are accepted and expected, government in Australia meets Senatorial obstruction of legislative measures with cries of constitutional outrage. But if it be assumed that bicameral government makes sense, especially in a federal form of government, such outrage, in the case of a popularly elected Senate, has precious little constitutional justification.

The Australian Constitution differed from the United States instrument in other notable respects. What stands out is the strong emphasis on 'Bill of Rights' provisions in the United States and their virtual absence in the Australian Constitution. 'Bill of Rights' provisions are those which impose limitations and restraints on legislative and executive action to secure protection for various liberties and rights conceived to be of major importance. The climate of political thinking in the late eighteenth century was conducive to the imposition of such restraints on governmental authority, and as time passed, additional provisions of this sort were written into the American constitution by way of constitutional amendment. So it was that the Federal and State authorities were restrained from action which impinged upon fundamental freedoms of speech and writing, religion and association; there were also prohibitions on acts which restricted various aspects of privacy and upon acts which denied 'due process' and the 'equal protection of the laws' to citizens. These prohibitions on governmental action have been given sweeping operation by the Courts so that there is an area, a very important and extensive area, into which no government in the United States, Federal or State, may intrude in the exercise of legislative or executive power.

In the United Kingdom context, this made no sense. Only one constitutional doctrine was unquestioned, and that was the competence of the United Kingdom Parliament to make and unmake laws on any matter whatsoever. It was of course a legal and not a political doctrine in the sense that there were practical restraints upon the exercise of legislative authority. In the United Kingdom context, such protection of liberty as existed was assured by a climate of opinion, to be sure buttressed by Acts of Parliament and by judicial procedures, doctrines and attitudes. But all of these safeguards were, as a matter of law, at the mercy of the omnicompetent legislature.

In the Australian Federal Constitution there was no notion of an omnicompetent legislature. Indeed the very notion of federalism denied the possibility of any unlimited authority. Federalism contemplated the distribution of limited and defined powers between Federal and State authorities. But when the question of safeguarding fundamental liberties was raised in the Australian Federal Conventions, as for example, when it was proposed to write 'due process' and 'equal protection' clauses into the Australian Constitution, there was a strong and unfavourable reaction. It was said that this was not the British way of doing things; that such clauses imported unnecessarily vague, uncertain, and unsatisfactory doctrines into the political and constitutional institutions of a country which was accustomed to doing these things in the British way. It was better to leave such matters to the good sense of Parliament, to the inherited traditions and values of the common law courts and to the ultimate judgment of the electorate. This was the view which prevailed, though with one or two odd exceptions. The most notable of these is contained in a clause of the Constitution which restrains the Commonwealth from taking action which affects religious freedom. It is limited in its operation; it restrains action by the central authority, though not by the States. The reasons which led the founding fathers to deal with this particular (and important) freedom, and to neglect others of certainly equal importance are curious and not very convincing. There are other provisions in the Constitution which impose restraints on governmental power in the interest of the individual, but for the most part they are weak and not very meaningful. Perhaps the most important, as things have turned out, has been the well-known section 92 which provides in substance that trade, commerce and intercourse among the States shall be absolutely free. As interpreted, this has come to provide assurances of protection against governmental action which directly impinges on this freedom.

The presence of such provisions in the American Constitution has had a profound effect. Over a long period the courts, and particularly the Supreme Court of the United States, have been called upon to pronounce upon the conformity of Federal and State governmental action with various Bill of Rights provisions. In very many cases the Court has been called upon to give definition to terms as large and unconfined as 'due process' and 'equal protection of the laws', and the Court has also been required to define the scope of provisions assuring the freedom of the individual in the context of spoken and written expression, association and religion. It is not at all surprising that interpretations by the Courts of these provisions have given rise to great controversy, not to say rage and frustration. At one time, Supreme Court decisions emphasised the unconstitutionality of social welfare and regulatory legislation, such as laws imposing restraints on hours and conditions of work and labour. The view of the Court at that time was that these were unconstitutional interferences with freedom of contract. Different views on these matters prevailed at a later date, though this in itself draws attention to historic shifts in the interpretation of unconfined and very general words which, on the face of the Constitution, are expressed in absolute terms. In other cases, from early times and right up to the present day, the Court has been concerned with the lawfulness of governmental action which is said to constitute unconstitutional interference with the fundamental freedoms assured by these provisions of the Constitution. This has occurred in the context of racial issues and discrimination; it has also arisen in a religious context, and in recent years there has been acute controversy over Court decisions holding unconstitutional various police and Court practices which are said to deny fair trial to persons accused of criminal offences.

The major impact of the decisions asserting the unlawfulness of governmental action has been on the States. The great Supreme

Court decision of 1954, holding that segregation in the public (state) schools on ground of race was unconstitutional, provoked strong resistance on the part of State authorities who were strongly opposed to the decision. This opposition on occasion led to the exercise of federal authority and the use of federal troops to secure compliance with what the Supreme Court had declared to be the law of the land. This brought the United States in the 1950's and 1960's to a situation in some respects comparable with that which had produced civil war a century earlier. At this later date overwhelming force was available to the federal government so that the security of the Union was not directly threatened, but the situation dramatically and unhappily exposed the bitter tensions and the acute differences which had arisen between the federal authority charged with the maintenance of the law of the Constitution and States which were bitterly opposed to that interpretation of the Constitution.

The decisions restraining police action have also given rise to sharp and angry controversy, though this has not attracted the world-wide attention which has been focused on the race issue. State governmental authorities have roundly declared that the decisions impose impossible burdens on police forces already overtaxed, and that the restrictions imposed by the courts make it virtually impossible for the police to do their job in a society bedevilled by disorder and criminal activity. Once again the decisions are often seen by the States as an unjust and unreasonable intrusion by central authority into the state sphere of responsibility for the maintenance of law and order.

This has no counterpart in Australian federal experience. The interpretations of the Australian constitutional provisions of this character are few in number and certainly provoke no comparable feelings and passions. But this leads to some important general considerations relating to the umpiring of a federal system. The Australian and American federal systems alike impose restraints on governmental authority at various levels and the distribution of powers and responsibilities between Federal and State authorities raises questions of limits of power and authority. It obviously cannot lie within the competence of one or other governmental authority in a federation to decide on the constitutional validity of its own or its counterpart's actions: this would involve an exercise of judgment in one's own cause. It is necessary therefore to provide for an independent umpire. This, it is long established, is a judicial role. It was not, at first, readily or generaly accepted that the Courts had power to pronounce on the constitutional validity of Acts of the Congress of the United States. That power was declared and asserted by the Supreme Court of the United States by Chief Justice John Marshall in the great case of *Marbury* v *Madison*, and while the issue remained within the realm of controversy for some time, it came to be settled doctrine. The power of the Courts to declare federal acts unconstitutional was the great issue in that case, and the jurisdiction of the Courts of course also extends to the acts of State and local authorities. By the time the Australian Constitution made its appearance, the matter was settled: no one has ever questioned the authority of the Australian Courts to pronounce on the constitutionality of the acts of the Commonwealth and the States, and their consistency with the Constitution.

The power so conferred is an enormous, awesome, one. A court consists of a small group of men who are, in practical terms, accountable only to their own view of the law. The only appeal from their reading of the Constitution is to the constitutional amendment process, and formal amendment of the United States and Australian Constitutions is difficult and comparatively rarely achieved. Judicial decision making in the constitutional area is therefore a responsibility of major importance. In the 'Bill of Rights' area it has aroused great passions and anger. It has sometimes made people unhappily aware of the *margins of obedience*: that is to say of the point at which opposition to the proposition of law stated by the Court is so strong that overt resistance is threatened. It happened at the time of Little Rock in the late 1950's, in the context of racial segregation; it has happened since. This is damaging to the fabric of law, and damaging to the consensus on which any democratic society must rest if it is to survive as a democratic society. This is not to say that a court may in any case shirk its high responsibilities: it points however to the danger which it faces when it is called upon to measure governmental action by constitutional rules expressed in terms of extreme generality and vagueness. Commentators in America have praised the role of the Supreme Court in this area; they have said that the Court has become the voice of conscience and high principle and standards, and has become the great educator of the American community. There is justice in the statement, and one is stirred by the noble and high principled judgments of the great judges of the Supreme Court of the United States. But the role is a difficult and troublesome one, and one, which in my view, calls for self restraint on the part of judges. One recalls the words of a distinguished judge warning against the dangers which flow from judgments which are the idiosyncratic interferences of a few judicial minds, and there is abundant testimony in judicial history to the justice of the warning.

These 'Bill of Rights' provisions highlight special American problems. In other respects, the Courts in America and Australia share common problems in discharging their responsibility for constitutional interpretation. Both Constitutions are short documents, general in terms and inevitably the creatures of their own historical times. As already noted, formal amendment has been difficult and infrequent. The Courts, particularly the Supreme Court of the United States and the High Court of Australia, have done much to update the Constitutions in the course of interpreting them; that is to say, they have endowed them with capacity to provide for situations, problems and conditions never contemplated by the founding fathers.

I have already instanced the interpretation of the Australian Constitution to endow it with the means to take its place as an independent state in the international community. There are many other examples. Both Constitutions assigned war and defence powers to the central authority. The powers thus given in the language of earlier times have been of great importance in the twentieth century when both countries have been involved in wars which have made the greatest demands on national resources. War and defence powers have been held by the Courts to support a complex and wide embracing regulation of the economic and social fabric of nations engaged in total war. Profound changes in technology, the invention of the aeroplane, wireless and television have had to be taken account of by the Courts. In the United States perhaps the most striking example of the effect of technological change has been the interpretation of the interstate trade and commerce power conferred by the constitution on the Congress. Over more than fifty years, the Supreme Court of the United States has given sweeping interpretations of this power, so that the reach of federal authority has become immense. It is interesting to note that a power in precisely similar terms was assigned to the Commonwealth Parliament. The Australian High Court has never been persuaded to adopt the wide-ranging American interpretations of the clause, though it has in recent years acknowledged a wider scope for the power. The difference is, in part anyway, attributable to differing patterns of economic development, and a slower growth of national economic activity in Australia. But other powers, originally contemplated as of limited range, such as the Commonwealth Parliament's power to legislate with respect to conciliation and arbitration in interstate industrial disputes, have been given a broad scope which would surely have surprised the founding fathers. The High Court of Australia has twice upheld the Uniform Tax scheme which effectively makes the Commonwealth the sole income taxing authority in Australia. That has effectively and devastatingly changed the face of Australian federalism.

Interpretations of the Constitutions of the two federations have given great accessions of strength to the central authority at the expense of the states. This has been the great feature in the evolution of the two federations, particularly in more recent times. It is not surprising that it is so, for technology and the transport revolution has annihilated distance, great wars have demanded national initiatives, direction and control, and both countries have lived with war and conditions of crisis. The growth of central power has been accentuated by financial predominance. This is the case in both countries, and particularly in Australia. Reference has already been made to income taxing power; since the early 1940's the Commonwealth has been the sole income taxing authority and the States have come to depend for a great part of their revenues on Commonwealth grants. In Australia the States have also, as a matter of constitutional interpretation, been denied direct access to important sources of revenue, since they may not constitutionally impose sales taxes. The financial situation of the States, in terms of *independent* sources of revenue, has become very difficult. The financial situation of the States in America is not so difficult though there too, the financial predominance of the centre is clear.

This has had great practical effects on the working of the two Federal Constitutions, which were never contemplated in the original assignment and distribution of powers to central and state authorities. States were assigned the major responsibilities in various fields; in fields indeed which have come to be of increasing importance. The discharge of those responsibilities has made enormous and increasing demands on resources which have simply not been independently available to the States. A conspicuous example in the Australian context has been education which is, as a matter of constitutional law, a State responsibility. The enormous and ever-increasing demand for education in the last twenty years has imposed impossible financial burdens on the States. So it has come about that the Commonwealth has entered this field, particularly in tertiary education. This has been done through the provision of funds and as an exercise of the constitutional power to make grants to the States on prescribed terms. In the case of education, this has meant that the Commonwealth, in prescribing terms, has increasingly made, influenced, and is increasingly directing educational policy.

There are other examples. In the United States a conspicuous example of federal entry into new fields has been the initiation and support of programmes of urban redevelopment. On the face of the Constitution, these are State responsibilities, but the magnitude of urban problems of living, transport and regeneration has been such that it has been impossible for State authorities to muster resource to deal effectively with them. In recent times this has been given a special dimension of urgency with the outbreak of violence in Negro centres in large northern urban concentrations, and the constant theme in the debate generated by this crisis has been federal responsibility for finding solution to the overpower-ing problems of crowded, impoverished urban centres. These problems are without much doubt the most pressing contemporary internal problems in the United States, and whatever the Consti-tution may say about responsibility for them, it is to the central authority that all turn.

Urban problems exist in Australia, though they do not have the same racial character. In a country in which more than one-third of the population live in two cities and a great majority in a half dozen, it is not hard to see why governmental responses to the complex problems of urban life should be seen as primarily a national problem whatever the attribution of governmental power under a Constitution fashioned for other days and other condi-tions. Certainly State treasuries are incapable of coping with the massive demands or urban planning and redevelopment. Up to the present time however the central government in Australia has shown little disposition to enter this field, though the demands grow more insistent.

There can be little doubt that central or national power will continue to grow, whether because of financial predominance or because of the magnitude and urgency of problems which the State units lack capacity or resolve to tackle, or in any event to tackle adequately. This is not to say that the States readily acquiesce, and indeed they experience many acute frustrations. There are many angry quarrels between State and federal authorities. In the Australian context, this frequently takes the form of angry protest at what is regarded as federal parsimony (or arrogance) in refus-ing to make available resources to the States, either by more liberal grants or by assigning more independent taxing authority to them. There can be little doubt that the want of balance between State political and constitutional power on the one hand and financial resource on the other is productive of serious difficulties and ten-sions. It is by no means clear that a large transfer of authority from State to national hands would advance the general welfare, and while people generally accept the *fact* of increasing central power they would certainly not, in their present temper, agree to con-stitutional change which would institutionalise it by transferring substantial power to the centre. In the United States, in recent years, the sharpest federal quarrels have arisen out of interpretations of 'Bill of Rights' provisions. As already noted, there have been angry protests on the part of southern States against federal implementation of Court orders decreeing the desegregation of schools, universities and other public places. The Court decisions and their enforcement are seen by the States as unwarranted intrusion of central authority into areas regarded by them as State preserves. It does not mollify their anger to point out that the State action which is being restrained is unconstitutional. There is also a strong feeling in many places that the Court restraints on State police action are an unjustifiable intrusion into areas of State responsibility for the policing of crime.

While there are continuing tensions in the relations between central and State authority, it is a distortion to see the development of federalism in the two countries wholly as a continuing contest between these two tiers of authorities. There has in fact been a striking and significant development in both countries of what is called cooperative federalism; that is to say of cooperation between States and between States and the federal authority to secure agreement on particular ends and agreed solutions to particular problems. There are many interesting examples of this in both countries. A notable Australian example has been the growth of cooperation in securing uniform bodies of law in areas where this is very desirable. One important field is company law: since the Commonwealth lacks power to enact a national company law, the same result is secured by an agreement between the States to enact uniform laws. It is a more cumbrous way of achieving a desired end, but for want of national authority, it serves very well. In the United States there has long been machinery for consultation between the States on uniform laws.

The federal model of government has exercised a powerful attraction for other peoples. In some recently independent States, as in India and Malaysia, federalism has worked, though with a strong emphasis on central power. In other areas, as for example in Central Africa, the British Caribbean and Nigeria it has been tried and failed dismally. It is not an easy form of government to operate successfully; in the United States it had to survive the challenge of a long, bloody and bitter civil war. But in Australia and the United States it is now secure, and despite great pressures and significant changes, the federal form of government mirrors the requirements and aspirations of the peoples of these two countries.

Zelman Cowen

10 The American Image in Australia

Image-making takes us beyond diplomacy and relations between nation-states into a new and largely uncharted area of what has been crudely if appropriately called 'informal penetration'. The difference between a nation's image—how it is 'seen'—and what used to be called its reputation or standing—how it is 'known'—takes us into a world where appearance contributes to reality, where words change meaning, where vision is guided by persuasion, even a world where justice is seen to be done and not done at all. Blame Einstein, Goebbels or the skilful men and women of Madison Avenue: we have to deal with this shadowy world. I have assumed some integrity in it, for this chapter, not out of courtesy or even innocence, but because the basis of relations between America and Australia is so strong that the need to manipulate or distort the reality of the relationship is at a minimum. The hidden persuaders are always there but their need to contrive a relationship in the case of America and Australia is minimised by the fact that the relationship itself is so explicit.

The American image in Australia, as perhaps elsewhere, is formed in three main ways: by the President, through external policies (especially defence and foreign policies) and by the quality of American life. Australians have traditionally depended for their impressions of America on the third category. Partly because the impressions were second-hand, in the sense that Australians tended to rely on British and European interpreters of the American scene, and partly because American self-projection relied on the mass media and the entertainment industry, when bizarre and ultra-human America received more than its due, Australians were late to take the United States seriously as a political force. America seemed an undisciplined, polyglot, violent and peculiar place, where the buildings were taller than anywhere else and the people more desperately in transit between wealth and poverty. It was a society which fascinated Australians, as it exhibited so uncritically the fantasy of discovery that drives all immigrant, frontier societies, including their own. But despite the exploits of the United States cavalry and the obviously growing industrial power of the United States, Australia's political interest remained glued to Britain. It was a substantial interest, including a full range of loyalty on Australia's part, and it prevented Australia from seeing the United States as a potential world power.

A graph of America's standing in Australia in the twentieth century would probably show a correlation with the evidence of American power—the visit of the United States Fleet in 1908, rising through the problems of the Anglo-Japanese alliance and World War I to the Washington conferences of 1921–22, a dip during the trade disputes and American isolationism of the late 1920's and 1930's, a sharp rise after the Japanese attack on Pearl Harbour brought America into World War II, and a steady increase until the controversy of Vietnam. It is only recently, however, that Australians have been sufficiently free of British attachment to look closely at the political sources of this power, in other words, at American society, as distinct from watching the fantasy world behind the use, or non-use, of American power externally.

It is largely since 1945 that Australians have begun to study American history, and to read American newspapers and magazines for political information and analysis rather than for entertainment. Only recently have they begun to attend American universities in preference to British universities. The first full-time Australian newspaper correspondent in Washington, as distinct from New York, was not appointed until 1964. The effect of expanded political relations between Australia and America has brought an increased seriousness in the consideration which Australians now give America. This has been accelerated by the tortured fading in Australia of Britain's image, which has now lost its power over all but the most dogged of Anglo-Saxons and most fervent of teenagers.

There is now in Australia much more understanding of the complexity and richness of American life, the substance behind the oratorical tribute to life, liberty and the pursuit of happiness. Yet intellectual contact between the two countries lacks the fertile exchange of ideas that has at times marked America's relations with Britain and with Europe and can be glimpsed occasionally in its relations with India, Japan and the Soviet Union. Americans still tend to regard Australians as themselves writ early. Australians still hold to the grudging belief that despite America's leadership in industrial Western civilisation, Australians are in fact 'better off' because their lives are 'easier'.

The hustle of America, whether in pursuit of the dollar or the outlaw, whether in the demand for rights or their denial, whether in presidential nominating conventions or mothers' meetings, is warily gauged by Australians. Perhaps the reason for this is that while American life is geared to work, Australian life is geared to leisure. It is not surprising that Australians have coveted most, of the American way of life, its instruments of leisure.

It is fear of American drive rather than what Jacques Barzun has called 'fear of stylelessness' that one finds at the base of much resistance in Australia to the serious image of America. Barzun is perhaps speaking mainly for European critics when he suggests that the image of a pragmatic America means 'the diminishing role of principle and theory, of barriers and distinctiveness, the increasing role of cooperation and good fellowship, the unpolitical, businesslike view, the substitution of the burdensome morality of good intentions for the protecting morality of forms, of etiquette'. Australians do not generally give an important place to etiquette and form. They have a high regard, however, for private activity, even inactivity, and they can point to a tradition of resistance, whether in the board room or the trade union meeting, to the notion that work has a moral value, a tradition which has given Australia a bad name for the cost of its living standards but also produced, before the succession of businesslike governments began in 1949, some of the best welfare legislation in the world.

It needs to be pointed out, before the impression is created that Australians are immune to the pressures of reward, that they are withstanding the affluent society no better than anyone else, and the lives of average Australians are increasingly committed to more money rather than fewer hours of work in order to pay for the pleasures of consumption. But Australians do not intellectualise their experiences as sharply as Americans do. The affluent society has been accommodated in the long weekend and the occasional trip abroad, without the soul-searching and commercial invention of the American experience.

The Australian way of life is hard to define, except in the broadly human philosophy of 'a fair go' which had its origins in the emancipation of the original convict settlement and the struggle of the Labor movement for political control of the society which emerged in the nineteenth century. The image of highly organised America, whether for work or fun, is not therefore immediately relevant to the way Australians think about themselves. Australians retain a love of understatement and subtlety, derived from the British but nurtured by a fairly deflationary history. They notice the odd rather than the obvious; the undertone rather than the explicit statement. They suspect declarations about happiness and destiny as they suspect declarations about decadence and despair. So the fact that Australian society is becoming increasingly more like America has not meant that American culture, in any profound sense, has taken on in Australia. The Australian woman stands as a monument of resistance to the American notion that women have a public role in society. The institutional differences—parliament, the legal system, the press— impose different styles of public assertion in the two societies.

What has happened, perhaps, is that the popular image of America in Australia as a land of opportunity is being gradually replaced by the image of a society on trial. The quality of American life is increasingly seen, not as entertainment but as a lesson in twentieth century survival. So while Australians take America more seriously, they also look at it more critically.

The importance of political America, its external policies and the beliefs and ambitions of its presidents, has begun lately to preoccupy Australians in its own right and not only as a reflection of a society. For it is clear that what is decided in Washington has a direct and sometimes even premeditated effect on Australia. When the consequences of political America were marginal in Australia or suffused throughout the Western world, Australian interest in the detail of American politics was low. But since the war in Vietnam began, taking place as it is against the expected British withdrawal from South-East Asia, Australians have realised that the American alliance is not so much an imponderable bond as a concrete interest, and the decision-makers in Washington have therefore come to have a direct influence on their nation's image in Australia.

When Australia's Prime Minister on 26 December 1941 said that Australia now looked to America 'free of any pangs as to our traditional links or kinship with the United Kingdom', there were startled cries from many influential Australians. The newspapers generally recognised the harsh truth of Prime Minister Curtin's assessment that, with the Japanese sweeping down the Pacific 'Australia can go, and Britain can still hold on'. But they were reluctant to turn away from Britain 'free of any pangs'. The leader of the United Australia Party (W. M. Hughes) thought Curtin implied 'the break-up of the British Empire'. Mr Menzies said: 'The Prime Minister makes a grave blunder if he thinks the ties between Australia and Great Britain are merely traditional.' Editorial writers spoke of the Prime Minister's 'maladroit' or 'unfortunate' references to Britain.

Today the conservative forces in Australia have become the most ardent supporters of the defence alliance with the United States. The attachment to Britain, although retained as ceremony, has almost disappeared in substance. Whether or not Britain enters the Common Market, it is generally accepted in Australia that she will never again maintain in Australia's part of the world the kind of presence which directly affects Australia's security. So what has happened in a remarkably short period as history goes, is that some of the attitudes of loyalty and dependence which formerly characterised Australia's relations with Britain have been transferred to Australia's relations with the United States. These attitudes have not had time to mature and are therefore somewhat brittle. They are based on an appreciation of American power, military and economic, as well as a common commitment to democracy, but they lack, of course, the intensity and intimacy of the attachment to Britain, which although also based on an appreciation of power, was nourished by emotions of racial heritage, loyalty to the Crown and a range of common culture, from the political and legal system and its symbols to knighthoods, cricket and driving on the left.

Nevertheless the succession of conservative governments in power in Australia since 1949 have made the defence alliance with the United States the keystone of their policies and they have done this with political emotion. They have elevated the assumed necessity of Australia's military dependence on the United States into a presumption of virtue. Elections have been fought with this as a prime issue, intending to point out to the Australian public that the government is on better terms with the United States than the Labor Opposition could ever be. The thrust of government electoral propaganda has been that the Australian Labor Party is distrusted in the United States for its tendencies to socialism in domestic affairs and to isolationism in defence and foreign policies, and that if it came to power in Australia the defence alliance with the United States would be endangered. The result of this kind of electoral contest, which became the normal thing during the late Mr Holt's term of office, when the dispute over the military aspects of the Vietnam commitment was intense, has been to concentrate Australia's view of America on security and on the question, always troublesome to Australians, of how to guarantee that protection will be forthcoming when needed.

The consequences have been as one might expect: excessive displays of loyalty on the one hand and, on the other, a resentment that Australian interests should be limited by those, however legitimate, of another nation. For what has happened in the twenty years during which Britain has bowed out of Asia and America has bowed in, is that Australia has itself developed as a nation, gaining confidence in Asia, making striking advances industrially and losing, especially among its younger generations, the attitudes of dependence which characterised its relations with Britain. So the image of the United States as a protector for Australia has had to be formed against a background of questioning of the whole-loyalty-protector concept.

Most nations' attitudes to the outside world are conditioned or at least heavily influenced by considerations of security. But Australians have a special problem. They are racial intruders in their neighbourhood. Ever since the European settlement of Australia, the vision of plundering Asiatic hordes sweeping south has aroused Australians, and they have turned for comfort to a protector who would ensure their safety from aggression and who made no demands on their right to maintain an immigration policy which kept the hordes out of Australia. In return, Australia's loyalty to the protector has been unqualified in the expression, if not always in the act. In the act, Australia learned to watch her own interests, but mainly by establishing the best terms, whether of trade or defence, with the protector. Her national interest, as a nation having relations with other nations, was seen as being determined within the relationship with the protector.

So although Australia is by no means unique in having close military ties with the United States, and is not alone in this being a source of political tension—as the tie with the United States is in Japan—it is doubtful whether in any other country in the world the psychology of protection is so deeply imbedded, and the simplification of foreign relations as loyalty to one's friends so firmly established as a tradition. The difference with Canada is striking—Canada does not have to attract United States attention; she has it, whether wanted or not. Australia's position is probably closer, though the parallel may seen ingenious, to that of Outer Mongolia in its dependence on Russia. But even here the emotional attachment of Australia to a protector is lacking. For Mongolia's racial affinity is not with her protectors, the Russians, but with the Chinese, from whom, oddly enough like the Australians, she is being protected.

I have emphasised the peculiar circumstances of Australia's relationship with America because I believe it explains tension which otherwise is hard to explain. Some of the sharpest criticism of Australia's commitment in Vietnam, for example, is not based on criticism of the commitment in principle, but arises from the suspicion that it was made as an insurance premium; as a contribution, not to democracy in Vietnam or stability in South-East Asia, but to the power and prestige of Australia's new protector. In other words, American influence in Australia has run against the desire of a growing number of Australians to become more self-reliant, and these Australians, in expressing reservations about the alliance with America, are really engaging in self-criticism.

If this analysis is correct, the conservatives in Australia have overplayed their hand in stressing so solemnly a relationship of need. For although the United States may be pleased to have such a loyal ally and may expect to get something in return for its protection—perhaps favourable treatment for investment and support on the big issues, whether in the jungles of South-East Asia or voting tests in the United Nations—it is obvious that a more independent Australia offers no threat to the United States, and might indeed be welcome in a world in which American obligations have multiplied. In fact, the Australian preoccupation with the might and main of the United States is part of a suppliants' chorus in South-East Asia which must at times seem incessant in Washington. It has become clear that with France and now Britain unwilling to share the defence burdens in the region, the United States is saddled with huge commitments unless it can get the non-communist Asian states themselves, and this includes Australia geographically, to contribute more substantially to the provision of a local balance to the rising power of mainland China.

This means that the Australian Labor Party has an opportunity to present a new American image in Australia. For the Australian Labor Party is the traditionally nationalist party, standing for an Australian patriotism as opposed to the past British-imperialism-by-proxy of the conservatives and their tendency today to make loyalty to the alliance with the United States the over-riding objective of defence and foreign policies.

The ALP is split between those who distrust the United States on principle, because it represents an unbridled belief in capitalism, and those who admire the United States for its democratic traditions. Much has been made of this split, but no-one doubts that the Labor Party in power would adhere to the alliance as purposefully as have the conservatives: no Australian political party can neglect what almost every Australian voter assumes to be a fact—that Australia is not yet self-reliant in defence and must, for some years, rely on the United States in the event of aggression. But the ALP would try to project a different image of the United States in Australia in order to justify its association with Washington, and a different image of Australia in the world as an American ally.

It needs to be noted that Mr Curtin was a Labor Prime Minister and that his successors as Parliamentary leaders of the ALP, Chifley, Evatt, Calwell and Whitlam, have all strongly supported the alliance with America. Labor has opposed the Australian commitment in Vietnam but, considering the wealth of opposition to the war in the United States itself and the uncertainty of the outcome, it is difficult to establish that Labor's disapproval, which no doubt would have been modified had Labor been in power when the Americans made their commitment and pressed Australia for support, is a threat to the American alliance, whatever it may seem to the Johnson Administration.

On the whole, a Labor-filtered image contains benefits for the United States, for what has not penetrated Australia is the leaven and ferment of American life, its liberal and humanitarian traditions, its art, scholarship and intellectual endeavour, its social legislation, its education and its philosophy of a pluralistic society. Australians may not find the American model in these things necessarily applicable, but an American image composed of these elements would open Australian eyes to a society more attractive than the combination of business and military acumen and bluntness to which they have become accustomed.

Anti-Americanism would not then occupy the middle ground in Australia, as it tends to when the symbols of the relationship with the United States are the expenditure of American dollars in Australia, military power and popular culture. It would be relegated to the fringe groups, those who maintain the ancient British tradition of the United States as the citadel of philistinism and enormity, and those who oppose America's influence for reasons of dogma and ideology.

Australians recognise that they are fortunate in having a special relationship with the United States. They are fortunate that at the time Britain is retiring from its world role and retreating to Europe, the United States, which happens to be the most powerful nation in the world, is near at hand. The problem is to link Australian aspirations with American power. Australians have not had much experience in charting an independent course. In the days of the Empire, the relationship with Britain was so utterly that of a dependent that you gained independence by occasional defiance. But the assumption of this defiance was your status as an offspring. This cannot be the case with the United States.

The assumption must be that Australia has come of age as an independent nation. Therefore the real dependence which Australia has on the United States in respect of its security cannot be expressed with the simple emotions that were convenient and perhaps even appropriate during the British period. This is why Mr Holt's 'All the way with LBJ' was such a disastrous phrase, which dogged his career. It is not that Mr Holt misjudged the importance of the United States to Australians, or the importance of Vietnam, but he expressed it in a way which was offensive to Australian nationalism.

The requirement now is for hard-headed and long-sighted planning of mutual interests. The inability so far of Australian leadership to make this clear has been the reason that the American image tends to be resisted in Australia, why American protection is seen as a threat to Australian independence, whether this independence be asserted in foreign policy, in attitudes to communism or socialism, or in the control of Australia's natural resources. Knowing Australia's real need of America, Australians fear that Canberra will be too subservient to Washington.

The American presidency has only recently become an important focus of the American image in Australia. Until President Johnson, Australians had accepted their impressions of American Presidents from the common Western view, so that Roosevelt's impact was strongly favourable, without much attention being paid to his domestic critics, Truman was considered forthright, without arousing deep respect, Eisenhower was admired for personal qualities rather than for political leadership, and the sense of commitment to Kennedy as a leader of the West, rather than just another American president, was as keen and hopeful in Australia as it was shown, after his death, to have been in other Western countries.

With President Johnson, who became the first American head of state to visit Australia and who made the journey again within a year, the American presidency has been brought directly into Australia's own framework of controversy and drama. The Vietnam war and the death of Mr Holt exposed Australia and Mr Johnson to each other in indelible outline, and Australians will not have to rely on others, whether American or non-American, for an opinion of the thirty-fifth president of the United States.

It is too early to be sure of President Johnson's contribution to American image-making in Australia. His style and that of his first Ambassador to Australia, Mr Clark, reminded many Australians of the frontier image they had of the United States before they began to take it seriously as a world power. His presidency has been entirely shadowed by Vietnam and therefore by the most bitter dissension in Australian politics since the depression or, to find a closer parallel, the conscription issue in World War I.

Some Australians are concerned that the American effort in Vietnam has isolated the United States in the Western community and that eventually there will be an American reaction against the commitment in Asia which will include Australia. Others, of course, fear the opposite—that the United States, responding to Australia's expressed need of a protector, will withdraw from South-East Asia and set up base in Australia, as it did during the fight-back against Japan. When Walter Lippmann aired this possibility late in 1967, it was not favourably received by the Australian press, although its appeal in the circumstances of a major setback in Vietnam should not be underestimated. Other Australians fear a major war.

So until the Vietnam controversy has settled, President Johnson's own image in Australia will remain clouded. He has managed, however, to give a clearer expression of America's interest in Australia than any other President and sometimes, looking ahead to a more powerful Australia and listening to official affirmation of a special relationship now between Australia and America, it has been possible to imagine a Pacific link between the two like the Atlantic alliance between Britain and America, which was so important to the strength of Western democracy in peace and war.

Clearly this will not be possible until Australia develops greater power in its own right, but the importance of President Johnson's special interest in Australia is that it does now seem possible. His administration has never ceased to tell Australians they inhabit a great country, with an unlimited future. The exhortation has fallen on fertile soil, as Australians are beginning to sense the excitement of growth, and excitement abetted by recent mineral discoveries, which have shown that what was a dead heart in an agricultural era is a lively source of wealth in an age of technology.

Under President Johnson the American image has become more personal to Australia. Since Roosevelt, America has developed a network of responsibilities and, the Cold War following so soon after World War II, has striven to appear as the leader of a team. Johnson's period in office has been marked by a loss of this spirit and a fragmentation of what seemed, in a bipolar world, to be a Western bloc. The process had begun during Eisenhower's time, but it has been emphasised by America's unpopular (in Europe) Vietnam policy. In Asia the United States has clients and satellites rather than allies, as the major nations of non-communist Asia, especially India, Indonesia and Japan, have so far resisted American appeals to show the flag in Vietnam.

This has given Australia a peculiar advantage. We are the only nation of European culture, except for New Zealand, with our primary interests in Asia. We have therefore provided a ready ally for President Johnson, as our democratic tradition, our Pacific alliance with America in World War II and our readiness today to fight alongside the Americans in Vietnam, help to counter American critics who tend to look toward Europe and conclude that Johnson's foreign policy has isolated the United States from the world. The effect of this in Australia has been to project the

United States less as a Western leader and more as a powerful nation with its own national interests to pursue. Mr Johnson's personality has intensified the effect. He has a little of Roosevelt's idealism in world affairs, but he does not convey so convincingly Eisenhower's anxiety to avoid war and he does not have Kennedy's precise, almost courteous, sense of the limited uses of power. He seems, in his fifth year of office, to be neither in control nor in concert with America's allies and in belligerent stalemate with its adversaries. But he expresses without doubt the raw power and authority of the world's most formidable nation and it is this image with which the Australian public is being forced to come to terms.

America's image in Australia then has become more political and controversial. At the same time, Australians have become more knowledgeable about the United States and recognise it, for better or for worse, as the nation in the world most disposed to be helpful to Australia. It still remains for this realism to define the relationship between the two countries, avoiding, on the one hand, attitudes of dependence and loyalty in Australia and, on the other, American assumptions that because Australia must rely on the United States for its ultimate defence it is open to cultural and commercial domination.

Bruce Grant

11 The American Image of Australia

Is there such a thing as an American image of Australia? Surely there is, and yet it is not a single clear picture, but rather a composite of many overlapping impressions, some of them extremely vague. Searching for the American image is a little like trying to find the kernel of an onion; one has to keep peeling off layers of outer tissue in order to try to penetrate to the heart of the matter.

To begin with, most Americans are inadequately informed about Australia, as I am sure our Australian friends are aware. This is not due to any lack of interest, for Americans think of Australia as a glamorous country, which they would very much like to know better. The problem is rather lack of sufficient contact. Australians know a great deal about the United States, for they are accustomed to meeting Americans, to seeing American films and television shows, to reading about our country in books and magazines and newspapers, and, in the case of the business and professional classes, to spending some time on our soil.

The reverse is unfortunately not equally true. As a nation, we just do not see or hear enough of Australia and her people. This is obviously not an ideal state of affairs, and for the sake of a better Australian-American relationship, we must make a major effort to remedy it. Certainly American interest in Australia is increasing steadily, and I believe that we are making very real progress in becoming better informed about it.

The problem of insufficient contact is not basically one of geographic distances, although of course we would know more about Australia if she were as close to us as Canada. The real cause of our lack of familiarity with the lands and peoples Down Under is rather the disproportion in the sizes of our respective populations. There are more than 200 million Americans, but not yet twelve million Australians. Probably more Americans have visited Australia than vice versa, but in proportion to population our percentage of well-informed people is much smaller.

Americans, like Australians, are great international travellers, and each year some three million of us travel abroad. But most travel is to Europe, Asia, and Latin America; not many of us venture down into the South Pacific, although the number is increasing each year. Many Australians, especially of the business and professional classes, visit the United States, but the pattern is to follow a Great Circle route across our continent, with stops only in a few major cities. These visitors from Down Under do not stay with us long enough, or spread out widely enough over our broad expanse of territory, to contribute greatly to the remedying of our ignorance.

The result is that most Americans have never met an Australian —a shocking statement, perhaps, but nevertheless a true one, for most Americans also have never met an Argentinian, a Brazilian, a Pakistani, an Egyptian, a Rumanian, or a Swede. In my own case, although I had spent much of my life in international affairs and had travelled widely, I could count on my fingers the number of Australians I had met until a happy turn of events sent me to Melbourne in 1960. Yet I should think that most Australians must have met one or more Americans, for there are so darned many of us, including several thousands permanently resident in Sydney, Melbourne and other major cities.

Aside from the question of face-to-face meetings, there tends to be, as Robin Boyd points out (p. 145 above), a one-way flow of the products of our mass media. American films, comic strips, and other products of our entertainment industry, far though they may be from representing what we like to think of as the normal and wholesome aspects of American life, flow from our country to Australia. And on a somewhat higher cultural level, many American books and plays get to Australia, a fair number of musicians and other performing artists visit there, and newspapers and other periodicals in the Antipodes carry a goodly amount of American materials.

The reverse flow is regrettably meagre. Such a film as *The Sundowners* fascinated American viewers, particularly for its beautiful shots of Australia scenery and wild life, and many Americans have read one or more novels about Australia by such writers as Patrick White, H. H. Richardson, Arthur Upfield and Nevil Shute, to name a few examples. Almost every American knows the tune of 'Waltzing Matilda', and I was pleased to discover recently, while entertaining Australian guests at Washington's Cosmos Club, a musician who could sing the entire song from beginning to end—'jolly swagman', 'billabong', 'jumbucks', and everything. Perhaps some day there will be more of this sort of impact, but it will come slowly.

Because Australia is a relatively tranquil country, which rarely generates dramatic news stories, normal news coverage in the American press and over radio and television is rather meagre. We get reports on Australian elections and on Australian decisions relative to Vietnam, and we see special features from time to time in our Sunday supplements, such as a recent story out of Sydney by Richart Tregaskis on American immigration, advising American girls to 'come to Australia and find a husband', and reporting that Americans not only find economic opportunity Down Under, but enjoy the 'slower, easier pace' of Australian life. And such a world figure as Sir Robert Menzies has always been newsworthy in our country.

But there is certainly no lack of American interest in things Australian. When the late Prime Minister Harold Holt disappeared in the treacherous seas off Portsea, the American public was deeply stirred, and the story received top billing in all news media over an extended period. This would have been true anyway, but the story was given additional stimulus, of course, when President Johnson flew across the Pacific to attend the memorial service in Melbourne. These services were telecast to America by satellite, and we were able to watch them in tens of millions of American homes. The question of who would succeed Mr Holt as Prime Minister was also fully covered, from Mr John McEwen to Mr

John Grey Gorton. Several feature articles on the personalities involved appeared in American newspapers, along with explanations of the Australian political situation.

Year in and year out, however, Australia is given much better coverage in the sports news than in other categories. There are frequent stories on Australian happenings in tennis, golf, swimming, track-and-field events, and such occasional dramas as the Australian challenge for the America's Cup. Only the good grey *New York Times* would report an international cricket test match or a Melbourne football final, for these are not sports which Americans normally follow. Business news from Australia is given substantial coverage, for Americans think highly of the Australian economic potential.

In spite of our paucity of information, the general reputation of Australia is extremely high in the United States. Even though the picture of Australia that the stay-at-home American carries in his mind's eye is usually vague, fuzzy, and incomplete—and also sometimes confused with what he has heard of New Zealand—he is sure that Australia is a wonderful country, inhabited by a vigorous and hospitable people, which he would very much like to visit. It has romantic appeal for him even though the appeal is based on scandalously inadequate information.

We said in our first paragraph that searching for the American image of Australia would be a process like peeling off the successive layers of an onion. Let us, then, begin to peel. We shall start with the American who has never visited the Antipodes, who has rarely met an Australian, and even then has had only a casual encounter, and who has had no special reason to read up on Australia and inform himself on its history, geography, or economy.

If we were going to do our research properly, I presume we would need to send out several thousand questionnaires, or hire a team of public opinion experts to interrogate a scientifically chosen sample of representative American citizens. But I don't propose to be all that serious—after all, I learned in Australia that it is much better to be entertaining. So rather than collect a lot of monotonous statistics, I have simply undertaken in recent weeks to go around asking all sorts of people: 'What is your mental picture of Australia? What do you think of Australians?'

If I found out that my subject had had any first-hand experience with things Australian, I was only mildly interested, for I already know many such people. He was not the kind I was looking for. If he said, 'Look, I don't know much about Australia. But my Uncle George was down there during the war. You ought to talk with him,' then I knew he was my man. To heck with Uncle George—an admirable type, no doubt, but filled with sentimental memories of an entirely predictable character. I was looking for an average American—one of the 199 million or so Americans who has never visited Australia, and who has obtained all his impressions second or third-hand. I wanted to find out what sort of ideas had filtered through to him.

To begin with, most Americans are aware of the extensive area of Australia—that it is a continental country, the size of the United States. After all, they can see it on every world map. They are also aware that it has a relatively small population. What they are not so likely to know is the extent of the vast expanses of aridity in Australia's interior, for our own arid areas are a great deal smaller, and limited to a few western and south-western States. They have heard that most of the population is concentrated along the coasts, but they tend to imagine the Outback as a huge area capable of development as people become available to settle it. There must be a great deal of desirable land there, they think, just waiting for population.

Thus one receives such comments as these:

Australia is the new frontier, a land of great promise. . . . It has vast virgin lands awaiting settlement. . . . A man could go out there and settle with a few dollars in his pockets and grow up with the country, as Americans did in the Old West a century ago. . . . It must have absolutely unlimited possibilities, with all that land and so few people. . . . It would be a good place to go and get rich, not like the United States where all the natural wealth already belongs to somebody.

If you ask your typical uninformed American how he visualises the part of Australia which is already settled, again he thinks of the old West. He supposes that there are lots of farms and ranches, and that the country is very rural in character, perhaps something like Kansas or Oklahoma. If you remind him that the population is along the coast, then he thinks of a less densely populated California, or perhaps an area like our South Atlantic or Gulf coasts. Or it might be Oregon. Anyway, he thinks of small towns dotting the landscape. Victoria's Western District or the southern part of New South Wales would fit into his stereotype, for if he has read books about Australia, or seen films, they describe this kind of country.

He would have very little idea of tropical Australia; the banana plantings and cane fields of Queensland would not have occurred to him. He would be surprised to hear of the citrus groves of the Murray River valley, or the vineyards of South Australia, or the apple orchards of Tasmania, just because he has not heard about them. But a man on horseback, watching over a flock of sheep extending as far as the eye can see, would fit right into his mental picture, for he has seen such pictures in his grade school geography book. Also, of course, he can hardly think of Australia without conjuring up visions of koala bears, emus, and duck-billed platypuses, or of playful kangaroos that run alongside of cars and jump over them from time to time.

The most surprising thing for many stay-at-home Americans is to learn how urbanised Australian life is in the areas near the capital cities. They are astounded to hear of the huge populations of Sydney and Melbourne, and they can hardly conceive the endless suburbs stretching on for miles and miles, as for example in the area of dense settlement extending south-eastward from Melbourne to Frankston and beyond. Such lesser cities as Bendigo, Ballarat, Shepparton, Albury, or Launceston would be much more like his expectations. And the towns in the back country of New South Wales would delight him, for they would fit his preconceptions exactly.

It would be difficult for an American to envisage the Australian landscape—the beautiful gum trees extending endlessly over the rolling hills of south-eastern Australia, for example. Perhaps a Californian would be able to imagine this sort of landscape, for that State has a fair number of eucalypts—imported, I believe, from Australia. But a Virginian like me, accustomed to the pine and hardwood forests of the Atlantic seaboard, could hardly imagine anything so exotic or so fascinating.

Many Americans think of Australia as having glorious mountain scenery, but here they are more likely to be thinking of films and photographs they have seen of New Zealand's South Island. They are, in fact, inclined to expect a more spectacular mountain terrain than Australia actually possesses. The name 'Great Snowy Mountains' conjures up visions of 15,000-foot snow-capped peaks such as we have in the Rockies and the high Sierras, and such as many Americans have seen in the Alps or the Andes. Films made in Australia tend to reinforce this conception, for all photographers like to show mountain scenery and ski-ing scenes, and one could quite easily get the impression that Australia is a land of high mountains.

The scenic features of Australia which the average American is most likely to have heard about or seen pictures of would include the surf beaches, the great sheep and cattle stations, Ayers Rock rising out of the central Australian plain, Sydney Harbour with its imposing bridge, Mount Wellington rising back of Hobart, the Great Barrier Reef, the hydro-electric developments in the Great Snowies, and the great expanse of the Outback. One of the questions I have been asked most frequently is: 'Did you get out into the Outback? It must be fascinating.'

What one hears least about is the appearance of the major cities with their sturdy stone and masonry buildings and their strong Victorian flavour. One colleague of mine who comes from Wisconsin was thunderstruck upon his arrival in Melbourne to find how much the city reminded him of Milwaukee. His first reaction was that he had travelled halfway around the world and yet had not really left home.

One also hears little in the United States about Australian industry. Any reasonably well-read American knows that Australia is developing industrially, that she has mines and factories and railroads and harbours, and that she has a high standard of living resembling that of the United States. Yet the image of a rural

Australia is the dominant one. When you ask an American, what is your picture of Australian industry? he will respond: 'I hadn't thought much about that. But I suppose there must be many factories nowadays.' And he will mention that he has seen a picture of an Australian steel mill or of a hydro-electric plant.

So much for Australia, the land, in its physical appearance. What sort of mental picture does our stay-at-home American have of the Australian people and their way of life?

We can have some fun with this question, because Americans tend to have quite exaggerated images of what Aussies are like, and how they conduct themselves. The popular stereotype of an Australian is a large, brawny man, at least six feet tall, bronzed from constant exposure to sun and wind. He is a great athlete who plays several sets of tennis every morning before breakfast, or otherwise engages in strenuous physical activity, and an avid sportsman who follows cricket, football, golf, tennis, swimming, surfing, sailing and horse-racing. He is an enormously cordial and friendly person, this brawny Australian, and will make friends easily with Americans, whom he regards as kindred spirits.

One characteristic of Australians which has received wide publicity in the United States is their extraordinary prowess in the consumption of alcoholic beverages. The Americans who were in the South Pacific during World War II brought back many stories of Australian beer-drinking which have no doubt improved in the telling over the years. For the American servicemen of 1942-45 were overwhelmed with Australian hospitality and friendliness, and the monumental consumption of beverages during this experience with mateship left an undying impression. Perhaps the boys from Yankeeland were over-modest about their own exploits in thirst-quenching, but they seem to have felt that during World War II they were clearly over-matched. The Australian capacity inspired admiration bordering on reverence.

At any rate, the American impression is that the typical Aussie drinks whisky with his meals, and beer all the rest of the time—especially on his way home from work, when he stops off at his neighbourhood pub and joins his mates in consuming large quantities of the sudsy stuff in gregarious elbow-tilting. The American is led to believe that he cannot hope to match an Australian drink for drink, for an Aussie can easily drink a person of any other nationality under the table—and then go out and play several sets of tennis before the evening meal.

I may be exaggerating a little, just for the fun of it, but not very much. My little private inquiry brought forth many comments about the fabulous capabilities of the Australian beer drinker. One respondent, for example, told me a story about being in Capetown during the war when a shipload of Australian troops landed for a day of shore leave after a long, dull trip across the Indian Ocean. The Aussies drank every pub in Capetown dry, and when the overwhelmed South Africans ordered another truckload of beer to replenish supplies, the Aussies met the truck on the street, unloaded it themselves with whoops of joy, and consumed the entire quantity right then and there.

In the popular American stereotype as I discern it, Australians are thought to be breezy, informal, imaginative, lively, and colour-ful, and to display great gusto in every activity. They command a delightfully exotic vocabulary, express themselves articulately in the idioms of Down Under, and employ rich vowel sounds which fascinate the American ear attuned to the much flatter and less musical accents of the United States.

As sports competitors, our impression is that Australians are talented in track and field competition, highly competent in yacht racing, excellent in golf and swimming, and virtually unbeatable in tennis. One reason for all this excellence is believed to be the determination of Australian athletes, which motivates them to train very thoroughly, and when in competition to go 'all out' to win.

Aussies in the military services are considered to be matchless fighters, demonstrating technical competence, high morale, great personal bravery, and in the heat of battle an enormous amount of high-spirited dash and gallantry. Australian achievements at Gal-lipoli, at Bardia and Tobruk and El Alamein, and in the New Guinea campaign are well-known and much admired. Because of the high reputation of Australian troops, great value is placed upon them as allies, and current contributions in Vietnam are warmly appreciated.

One meets relatively few Americans who have any very definite images of Australian women. Those who have come to public notice include athletes such as Margaret Court (née Smith) in tennis and Dawn Fraser in swimming, and we may hazard the guess that many in our country hold an image which includes elements of the legendary Amazons, or perhaps a bit of Diana, the classical goddess of the chase. That hardly seems fair to Dame Nellie Melba or to the modern Joan Sutherland, whose excellence in operatic singing is fully recognised in American cultural circles, nor does it take into consideration the richness and variety of women's activities in Australian cities and rural communities. But thanks to the mass media, and especially to the inclinations of photographers, the average American would be more likely to picture in his mind's eye, not the fashionably dressed woman social leader of Sydney or Melbourne, but a golden-haired beauty on the beach at Surfer's Paradise, clad in the scantiest of bikinis.

Regarding the nature of Australian social and political life, most Americans have heard that trade unions play a dominant role in the Antipodes. They tend to envisage a fully developed welfare state, with socialised medicine, highly developed welfare services, and great blocks of public housing. They also associate with trade unions a great deal of labour activity, with strikes, lock-outs, long-drawn-out contract negotiations, and extremely high wages. They may wonder if considerable sections of Australian industry have been nationalised, as under Labour governments in Britain. Yet it does not seem to occur to them that there may be in this welfare state a complex network of social laws and regulations. The tendency is rather to think of Australia as a place where one might go to escape this sort of thing, for many Americans dream of an escape into the simpler life of an earlier America. In any event, it is difficult in the United States, a country where all sorts of activities go on continuously, seven days a week, twelve to twenty-four hours a day, to envisage the shutdown of filling stations, movie theatres, and even restaurants which occurs on an Australian Sunday, or the legal restrictions which close many stores and pubs at an early hour in the evening.

Americans have heard, of course, that Australia is a land where leisure is greatly prized, and that it is a great country for sports and outdoor living. But most of my countrymen with whom I have conversed have been surprised to hear of the huge crowds which turn out in Australian cities for horse-racing, cricket matches, and Saturday football. This is partly because they do not realise how large Australian cities are, and partly because spectator sports, although popular in the United States too, are not followed quite so avidly as they are Down Under. The extent to which Australians live outdoors on week-ends would also surprise many Americans—not those of Southern California, perhaps, but certainly those from parts of our country where the climate is less inviting, and where most people are just too busy to enjoy a great deal of leisure.

This seems like the point to leave behind us the discussion of the images of the Americans who have never visited Australia, and to turn to the far more tangible images and attitudes of those who have at least spent a few days or weeks there, seen a little of what Australian life is like, and reacted to their observations. Let us, then, peel another layer from our onion.

The short-term visitor is invariably impressed with the friendliness of Australians, with the vigour of Australian social and cultural life, with the differentness of the Australian landscape from anything he has seen in the Northern Hemisphere, and with the bustling modernity of the major cities. He feels immediately at home in his host country, and if he is there for business or professional reasons—as a high proportion of visitors are—he quickly establishes rapport with his Australian colleagues. It does not take him long to discover that these colleagues are highly qualified in their fields of endeavour, and that they are educated and articulate people with a sophisticated awareness of the outside world. He will meet many Australians who are leaders in their fields who have read widely in British and American publications, who have travelled extensively overseas, and who are well-informed on the state of their business or profession in other countries. He will also find that they are well-acquainted with the personalities of interest to them in other parts of the English-speaking world.

Typically, the short-term visitor to Australia is a good deal better informed than the 'average American' we have been discussing, but even he is likely to be much more pleased and impressed than he had expected to be—not because he did not have favourable expectations, but because he is glad to have his rather vague pre-conceptions clarified and amplified. Yet even he will have many minor surprises, and sometimes major ones. Some are surprised to find so much modernity in Australia, because they had not realised how prosperous and advanced the country is. Others are surprised —as many European visitors to America are surprised—to find how much of nineteenth century architecture has survived into the twentieth century, and how well-worn much of the man-made landscape has become.

'I was surprised to find so much Victorian British atmosphere still existing in Australia,' one American lady told me. 'Somehow, I had expected that this young, independent country would have developed a totally new culture of its own, and that this new culture would be expressed in new cities, new buildings, new everything. Every one I met seemed very British to me, in their speech, their attitudes, their social standards. I had expected people to be a great deal more like Americans.'

And yet most Americans find that they are quickly at home with their Australian cousins. They find Australians friendly, natural, easy to get to know and to talk with. The strong egalitarian tradition in both countries eases the way to effective communication, and leads to excellent rapport between persons of similar social background and professional interests. The American finds warmth in his Australian relationships, and responds with warmth, even on very superficial acquaintance.

He also develops an affection for the country and its way of life. If he has visited countries in which English is not the native language, he is relieved to be among people with whom there are so few communication-bafflements. He may not always under-stand at first just what an Australian means by some Australian or British expression, but the differences in speech patterns charm and please him. I have known Americans to jot down in a notebook some of the idiomatic words and phrases which they find novel, with the thought of trying them out on their friends when they get home.

Despite these minor differences, the area of overlap between the Australian and American 'cultures' is so great that all around him, the American visitor discovers the familiar and the reassuring. If he reacts by saying, as a first superficial reaction, that 'Australians are just like Americans', he intends this to be an expression of pleasure and esteem. And when he goes home, he tells his friends that Australia is a fascinating land, with wonderful people, and helps to perpetuate the pre-existing favourable image.

Because the cost of trans-Pacific transportation screens out most low-income travellers, the American visitor is likely to be a person of some affluence, who makes most of his contacts with the business and professional classes. He stays at first-class hotels, and is entertained in prosperous homes and clubs and restaurants. His contact with Australians in working-class circumstances are relatively slight. He sees large numbers of people driving automobiles, wearing good clothes, eating good food, and drinking good beer, and tends to take home with him the impression that Australia is a relatively rich country, in which the standard of living is somewhat higher than in fact it actually is.

Let us peel the onion some more and consider next the American who settles down for a sojourn of several months or years, and who acquires a much more balanced picture. He begins to realise after a time that life for the average Australian, while thoroughly healthy and wholesome and happy, is characterised by fewer of the household comforts and luxuries which are taken for granted in the United States even by white-collar workers and wage-earners in the skilled trades. He notes that while the daily necessities of life often cost less in Australia, and amusements are particularly cheap, there is a tendency for machines, electrical appliances, and other manufactured goods to cost more. He finds that the family budget in Australia covers less than it does for the equivalent family in America.

During my years in Melbourne, the Consulate General was often called upon to answer letters from Americans interested in coming to Australia to 'seek their fortune' in a land of unlimited riches. We felt obliged to warn such inquirers that although they could live well in Australia, they would not find it easy to save money and accumulate capital, for wages and salaries were well under American levels. But if an immigrant brought capital with him and invested it in the fast-growing Australian economy, we said, he might do very well indeed.

The long-term American resident comes to learn after a while that Australia does rather a better job than the United States in dealing with poverty and unemployment, and in providing social services. He is impressed with the relative absence of city slums and urban overcrowding, and sees little or none of the kind of rural poverty found in the American south and in the hills of Appalachia and the Ozarks. He will note that Australia's capacity to absorb untrained labour is superior to ours, and that welfare problems do not loom so large in the social picture. Thus even though the median income level is lower than it is in the United States, there is better economic security for the people at the bottom of the scale, and social strains are not as severe.

These statements are made without benefit of computerised statistics, and are open to dispute. But they represent the impressions of many Americans who like me have lived in both countries, and are therefore a part of the American image.

Our experience was that Australia, if not so plentifully endowed as our own country with the newest technological improvements, has reached quite a satisfactory adjustment to the mechanical side of twentieth century life. Houses are not so well-heated in winter, nor so well-cooled in summer. But repair and maintenance services are efficient and reasonable in an Australian city. If one engages a plumber or an electrician, he will come promptly and do an honest and intelligent job, even though he may work at a more leisurely pace than his American counterpart. We also found that one could have an appliance repaired without being pressured to save money by discarding it and buying a later model.

In his social relationship in Australia, the American resident will find much to enjoy and admire. He will find the Australian a generous host in his own home or club, but a stern believer in equality when friends are drinking together in a place of public entertainment; the American can do nothing that will make him unpopular more quickly than to try to grab the check when it is not his turn to 'shout'. He will learn something about the Australian's pride in standing firmly on his own feet and paying his own way.

He will also learn something about the ancient Australian tradition of mateship, and what it means in terms of loyalties and expectations of loyalties. My Australian friends tell me that the concept of mateship has been overplayed by social commentators. I can only say that as an American living in Australia, I found the loyalty of Australians to old comrades in arms, to former companions at work and at play, or to other old friends, a vast improvement over the tendency of restless urbanised Americans to be continually changing their friends as their circumstances are altered in a country where so many people are continually on the move. I was deeply touched to observe the work of such an organisation as Legacy, in which surviving war veterans take responsibility for the welfare of the widows and children of their fallen or departed comrades. Surely this is a loyalty of which any nation could be proud.

It always seemed to me that the Australian concept of mateship entered into the Australian-American relationship in a way which caused certain difficulties. Since mateship arises out of associations of men who have worked together, played together, or fought together, the Australian has tended to place a high value on the wartime association of Australian and American fighting men in the critical days of World War II. The American values this relationship, too, but it does not loom quite so large in his consciousness. Not being rooted in the same tradition, he does not quite understand the Australian expectation that mates will always put their loyalty to one another ahead of other relationships.

Carry this thought over into international relations, and it seems to me that one finds a certain bafflement on the Australian side, and a certain embarrassment on that of the American. The Australian, perhaps quite unconsciously expects to be given a priority position in American affections, to be expressed in terms of military protection, preferential arrangements in international trade, and understanding for Australia's desire to maintain herself as a country of Anglo-Saxon heritage in the far-away South Pacific. American policy, however, is not oriented toward special relationships with other nations even when they share our language and ancestral descent. As a world power, we tend to think in world terms, and as a government to avoid any suggestion that we value one friend more than another. However much individual Americans may come to prefer Aussies to their other friends and relatives, Washington policies are conducted with a certain cosmic impartiality. Intellectual Australians understand this, but I never felt quite comfortable in Australia because of a feeling that our country was somehow not meeting the full expectations of the mateship relationship. In my public speeches, I often could not quite say the things that I felt my audience wanted to hear.

Another factor that enters into this situation is the long historical dependence of Australia on the world power of Great Britain, and the feeling of security that she had because of her position in the worldwide British Empire and Commonwealth. It was a great jolt to Australians when the hard-pressed British were unable to protect Australia from Japanese encroachment in 1941–42, and a corresponding relief when the American and Australian navies were able successfully to halt the threatening advance in the Battle of the Coral Sea. Since that time, Great Britain has given up more of her one-time military power, and a good deal of economic strength as well. The United States has moved into the position of being both the world's greatest power and the world's richest economy. Australians would be less than human if they did not to some extent transfer to the United States their hopes and expectations that our country would be their shield and protector. Yet the typical American really does not look upon the relationship in this light. We think rather of two equal powers—two countries which because of common language and heritage get along extraordinarily well together—which have common interests in working for the same kind of world.

During my years in Melbourne I went through three Coral Sea celebrations. In each of them I listened to a series of Australian and American speeches. It always seemed to me that in these speeches, our two nations were talking past each other, and not quite communicating. Australian speakers, among them the distinguished Sir John Latham, at that time president of the Australian-American Association, stressed Australia's dependence upon American power in the Pacific. American speakers invariably stress the idea of equal partnership in working toward common goals. I always felt that what the Australians wanted to hear was some such statement as: 'Don't worry, pals. We'll always protect you and support you, no matter what happens.' And what the Americans wanted to hear was: 'You can count on us, mates. We'll always be fighting at your side, to the limit of our ability to do so.' The Australian talk of dependence baffled the Americans, who failed to realise the depth of Australian insecurity, and the American talk of partnership puzzled the Australians, who never seemed to realise what a high estimate our Armed Forces placed on their military capabilities.

The same American image of a strong Australia, sturdy and self-reliant, is involved in economic relationships between our two countries. The American business man, to be sure, thinks of Australia as not yet fully developed in the industrial and technological sense. But he also thinks of her as a country of boundless resources, populated by a competent and vigorous people, and enjoying a high standard of living. He looks at Australia's modern agriculture, highly developed pastoral industries, extensive mining operations, and mushrooming factories, and his mental picture is that of a rich and prosperous country, well able to stand on her own feet economically.

What he does not realise is Australia's deep concern over her access to world markets for products of her primary industries, and over her ability to maintain a satisfactory trade balance with the rest of the world. Nor does he, until he penetrates more deeply into the facts of the Australian economy, discover how difficult it is for Australia to export the finished manufactures turned out by her industrial plants in competition with other manufacturing countries which by reason of much greater volume can hold down unit costs and sell more easily in export markets.

The Australian feeling about export markets was dramatised for me in the crisis that loomed in 1962, when it appeared that Great

Britain would enter the European Common Market. I had not realised until then how strongly rooted was the tradition of dependence upon the British mother country, which was still the major market for a long list of Australian products. Deep emotions were aroused by the fear that the British, in seeking to solve their own economic problems, would leave Australia in the lurch. And the United States was held partly responsible, for our government was encouraging British entry into the European Economic Community. I well remember Australians saying: 'You Yanks put the British up to this. So how about giving us, in common justice, preferred access to the American market?'

At this juncture I attempted one day, in a speech to a Chamber of Commerce audience in Melbourne, to explain why the United States, with its world-wide responsibilities and commitments, does not, as a matter of policy, enter into preferential tariff arrangements with specific nations. If we should admit Australian products at preferential rates, I said, we would have difficulty explaining this to competing countries in Latin America and elsewhere, in whose economic welfare we were also interested.

This speech was given wide publicity, partly because it was written up by a reporter who rearranged the sequence of all my sentences in order to get a more sensational effect, but partly, I believe, because I struck a raw nerve. I suggested, in effect, that a sturdy, self-reliant Australia could look to the United States for a brotherly friendship, but it would be unrealistic of her to think of our country as taking over the traditional economic functions of Great Britain, which had always cherished and assisted Australia in a very special historic relationship.

For several days after this I was subjected to a barrage of critical comment. Yet all that I was doing, as patiently and sympathetically as I knew how, was to present the American image of Australia as a strong, mature, and resourceful country which needs no special help from us, and which, in view of all our worrisome responsibilities elsewhere, should be willing to shoulder a bit more of the common burden. But Americans are only too likely, I discovered, to fail to appreciate Australian anxieties. As a large and powerful country, it does not come natural to us to be sensitive to the

Australian awareness of inadequate population, limited capital, geographic isolation from other countries of European heritage, and huge problems of defence and development.

Another factor here is that Australians themselves have more than one self-image, and in presenting their self-images they sometimes confuse Americans. To begin with, Australians are not in the least a humble people. They will look anyone else squarely in the eye, and dare him to consider himself any better than themselves. They conduct themselves in tennis and other international sports with jaunty and confident air, they will fight like tigers in any international context to win political, economic, or military advantages, and they will express themselves vigorously on any issue.

The American therefore finds himself operating on two levels with his Australian friends. On one level the Australian strongly asserts the equality or even superiority, of his country's strengths and virtues. But then there is another level on which the Australian suddenly says: 'Your country is much stronger than ours, so we look to you to be our military protector. Also, you are much richer and have a more advanced technology, so we very much need your economic support. And don't forget that we're a small nation, all alone down here in the South Pacific, with many problems which we do not have the resources to solve without your help.'

The problem the American has, then, is to know which is the correct image. Is Australia a strong and vital country, fully on top of her own problems and able to render valuable support as America's Pacific ally, or is she a weak and dependent country which is greatly in need of American assistance? The truth undoubtedly lies somewhere between these two extremes, but it is surely understandable if many individual Americans have difficulty at times in determining just what they should think.

Another complicating factor is the more leisurely pace of Australian economic life. The American business or professional man very much envies the Australian his freedom from the worries and tensions of the much more demanding American pattern, but is capable at times of wishing he could discover more drive and ambition. And this introduces a paradox which never ceases to amaze Americans. How is it, they wonder, that Australians can be so relaxed about the daily business of making a living, so free from the compulsions of more competitive societies, so unwilling to accumulate ulcers and coronaries, and yet become such ferocious competitors in the field of sports? How is it that they are so scrappy in wartime, such gallant fighters as they have shown in two World Wars, plus Korea and Vietnam and yet so ready to enjoy long hours of leisure in time of peace?

And yet Australia is changing. Australian life was changing noticeably during our years in Melbourne, and according to all accounts it has continued to change since our departure in 1963. This is partly a matter of technological change which speeds up the Australian tempo, partly a matter of population increase and rapid economic development, and partly a matter of the changing mood of the Australian people as the outside world more and more intrudes upon the tranquillity of their lives. Some of these changes have opened up new opportunities to Australia; some have added new burdens of responsibility and anxiety.

And as Australia changes, the American image is changing, at least for those Americans who know and love Australia and are sensitive to her moods. It appears that from now on, life Down Under will be increasingly less isolated, less tranquil, and less carefree as Australia is brought more and more into the mainstream of world events. Who would have thought even ten years ago that Australia would be playing such a key role in her part of the world that the tragic and untimely death of her Prime Minister would stir world-wide interest and concern, and that a bevy of world statesmen, including the President of the United States, would be converging on Canberra and Melbourne to pay a final tribute?

To conclude this essay, I shall undertake to present one American observer's analysis of the challenges now confronting the Australian people. This obviously brings us to the last layer of our peeling onion. We have started with the images of Australia held by a vague and amorphous American public, moved on to a consideration of the reactions of short-term American visitors, and then tried to look at Australia from the point of view of long-term residents. The last image will be a personal one, representing what this writer has come to think about Australia over a period of years.

The essence of this image is that Australia is a country in transition from a comfortable, easy-going past to a future which is rich in promise but also laden with problems. This transitional period is one of rapid maturation and great challenge. It is Australia's time of testing, which is arriving more suddenly than expected.

Every nation lives by its dreams of the future. The Australian dream, it seems to this observer, is one of demographic and economic development as a prosperous Western civilisation in the South Pacific. Australians are keenly aware that they are a nation of moderate size lightly occupying a huge and largely unpeopled continent. They know that the shortage of rainfall over most of this continent imposes severe limitations on the population it can support, but they also know that they are sitting on a storehouse of riches. They aspire to a population of thirty to fifty million people of European ancestry, living in the more habitable portions of their territory and exploiting its very considerable resources.

With this many people, Australians could greatly increase the populations of South Australia and Western Australia, develop Queensland and the tropics, and exploit the seasonal rainfall areas of the northern and north-western coasts. They could also, they hope, expand their secondary industries and become an important producer of high-quality manufactured goods for much of Asia and the Pacific basin.

Thoughtful Australians know that it will be difficult for them to realise their dream because of population requirements. The country has more than twelve million people now, and even if the present rate of immigration is maintained or speeded up, it will take a long time to reach twenty million, much less thirty or forty or fifty million. And yet Australians want very much to maintain their racial and cultural homogeneity, and to avoid the problems which other countries, including the United States, have had with populations of mixed ethnic origins.

To continue to increase their population, Australians know that they must expand economically in such a way, as to make opportunities attractive to the immigrants they want to bring in. To do this, they need more development capital than they can obtain from their own resources, and a higher level of technology than they can produce from their own capabilities in scientific research and industrial development. But they look to capital-exporting nations with very mixed feelings, for they urgently want to remain masters in their own house, and not to become the subjects of development controlled by other nations. Their dilemma is uncomfortable, and it is one which the United States should look upon with great sympathy.

Another dilemma facing Australia is how to maintain a strong defence establishment and fully meet her commitments to her allies, and yet find funds for her own internal development. No other nation is trying to develop such a huge area from the savings and resources of such a small population. Even Canada, with her vast northern territories, is better off in this respect, and has a far more secure geographic position next door to the United States. Australia feels that she must contribute substantially to her military partnership with America, because she lives close to Asia and far from her ethnic cousins, and therefore is very dependent upon the protective shield provided by our Pacific power. But both development and defence must be financed out of the same national resources, which can be stretched only so far. Again, our Australian friends have a right to expect us to be sympathetic.

Faced with so many problems, can Australia continue to be a country which lives at a leisurely pace, which spends much of her national energies on sports and amusements, and which maintains a traditional way of life which is easy-going, relaxed, and unworried? Most contemporary Australians have not grown up expecting hardship and sacrifice and struggle. It is not easy for a nation to re-orient itself overnight. The American cannot help but wonder if these attractive and charming people would be willing to work longer hours, tax themselves more heavily, discipline themselves more rigidly, deny themselves some of the consumer goods and pleasures they now enjoy, and strive more determinedly to build up their manufactures and make them competitive in a free-trading world.

Difficult years lie ahead for Australia. And yet Australians have risen to crises in the past. They have a great fighting tradition, they are a tough and hardy and competent people, and when they have been faced with war, they have not hesitated to march into deserts and jungles in the name of the loyalties they believe in. If their situation ever becomes truly dangerous—which I devoutly hope it will not—it is an enormously good bet that they will rise to the occasion, thrust aside their quest for a pleasurable life, and do whatever they may have to do.

For after all, there are two Australias. There is a relaxed and pleasure-loving Australia, represented by the football fans, the race-goers, the beach-lovers, and the social beer-drinkers; and there is also the scrappy, high-spirited, competitive Australia, which rises to challenges on the sports field or in the thick of battle, and which is quite capable of acting in an inspired manner to control her own destiny.

Civilisations survive and thrive when they can successfully meet and overcome the challenges to which they are subjected. Challenges to the Australian people will, I believe, bring out their finest qualities and enable them to marshall all their resources in response. The exact nature of the challenges which may develop over the remaining years of the twentieth century cannot yet be forseen. To some extent they will be determined by the problems of a difficult world, to some extent by the policies which Australia herself pursues, and to some extent by the support which she receives from loyal friends and allies.

It may be to Australia's advantage to be more challenged in the future than in the past, and to become tougher and more self-reliant, stronger and more prosperous. It will not be to the advantage of her friends to see her pushed too far too fast, or to encounter greater difficulties than she can overcome. The American image of Australia, then, needs to be well-informed, up-to-date, understanding, and sympathetic, for the people of the United States place a high value on Australia, hold her in warm esteem, and want to see her strong, healthy, and successful in her world historical role.

Frank S. Hopkins

Appendix

'We stand on the edge of a great new era, with both crisis and opportunity, an era to be characterised by achievement and by challenge. It is an era which calls for action . . . a time for path-finders and pioneers.'

These words by the late President John F. Kennedy may also aptly be applied to the historical period covering the growth of the Australian-American Association since its early beginnings in 1936. Who could have believed, at that time, that the world stood on the edge of such a great new era as since experienced, or visualised the opportunities and challenges which lay ahead?

The work and significance of the Australian-American Association can only be understood in the light of the rapidly unfolding historical events of the past thirty years—in many ways the most remarkable period in Australian history. First came World War II and more especially, for Australia, the war in the Pacific. Then followed the post-war era leading on to the jet and space age with fantastic developments in aviation; the rapid growth of swift air travel and mails across the Pacific; incredible progress in communications by radio and telephone; increasing business contacts and substantial American investments in Australian industry; and scientific co-operation between Australia and the United States in the pioneering period of space-tracking. More importantly still, in the political sphere, came the ANZUS and SEATO treaties; strategic and international developments in the Pacific area and South-East Asia; and further military alliances in Korea and Vietnam.

All these developments opened up an almost limitless field for Australian-American co-operation. At all times, the Australian-American Association was ready to take advantage of these opportunities as they arose, profiting from them on the one hand, and contributing to them on the other. For a small voluntary organisation its influence was considerable and its contribution outstanding. Throughout, it helped to create in the public mind an atmosphere favourable to a rapidly expanding Australian-American partnership, and provided a national focal point for the implementation of its objectives.

In Australia before World War II, America was a little known country far away. Personal contacts were few and far between. It took two months for a letter from Sydney to receive a reply from New York. To most Americans Australia was a place unknown, while in Australia there was a strong anti-American feeling in many quarters.

In such an atmosphere the Association had its genesis at a representative meeting held at the Millions Club in Sydney on 15 July, 1936 when the British and American Co-operation Movement was established, with Sir Henry Braddon as first President. The initiative in this move was taken by Brigadier H. A. Goddard and Captain E. K. White, veterans of World War I, who were convinced of the need for a close and strong alliance between the British Empire and the United States of America.

A branch of the movement was formed in Adelaide in 1936 with Sir Henry Newland as first President, while in June 1937 a group of Melbourne men launched a similar movement for British-American Co-operation. Meanwhile, the organisation in New South Wales concentrated upon presenting its message to the public, with the support of the press and the encouragement of the Federal Government. A monthly magazine was produced, and a continuous series of broadcasts was maintained until 1939. From the outset, the movement advocated the exchange of diplomatic representatives between Canberra and Washington, and was overjoyed when in 1940 Mr R. G. Casey (now Governor-General of

Australia) was appointed Australia's first Minister to the United States and Mr C. E. Gauss became the first American Minister to Australia.

Thus, by the outbreak of World War II the stage was set for the establishment of a nation-wide organisation to foster British-American unity and develop a close Australian-American partnership in the Pacific area. Steps to this end were taken in 1941 which is a landmark year in the history of the Association. Sir Keith Murdoch had been appointed Director-General of the newly formed Federal Department of Information with Mr R. J. F. Boyer as Head of its American Section. With the support of the Commonwealth Government, they encouraged the formation of State organisations to enlist popular support for these objectives. At the request of Mr Boyer in February of that year, Mr P. M. Hamilton took the initiative in establishing an Australian-American Association in Queensland at a representative meeting in the Brisbane City Hall. This was the first time that the title Australian-American Association was used, subsequently to be adopted by all other States and by the federal movement. Later in the year, Mr A. W. Campbell was elected Queensland's first president.

In March, 1941 Dr Grenfell Price and Mr W. Queale set up a provisional committee in South Australia and at a meeting in the Adelaide Town Hall on 6 May a Branch of the Association was established with Sir George Nicholls as first president. In April, Sir Keith Murdoch took the lead in forming an Australian-American Co-operation movement in Victoria which was formally constituted at a meeting on 1 August. Sir Keith Murdoch became the first president, supported by an influential group of business and professional men. An Australian-American Association was formed in Western Australia on 23 June 1942 with Dr T. Meagher as first president.

All these new state organisations received substantial public support, and with New South Wales already well established the Movement was ready to accept the challenge when the United States entered the war in December 1941 and American troops commenced to pour into Australia.

During the war years the Association performed an outstanding task in catering for the needs of the American troops stationed in, or passing through, their midst. Informative 'Welcome' booklets were prepared and distributed; hospitality centres were established and staffed; financial and other relief was provided for evacuees and others in need; functions and entertainments were organised; and assistance was given to wives and fiancees of American servicemen. In addition, special functions were arranged for 4 July and Thanksgiving Day. But the most important contribution was in providing home hospitality and individual private entertainment. In this field the women's auxiliaries, already established in 1941, did a mammoth task. In Brisbane alone, with the greatest concentration of American troops, the permanently staffed, voluntary AAA Hospitality Centre numbered those catered for by the thousands.

Important steps were also taken during the war years to weld the various independent state organisations, at that stage with differing names but similar basic objectives, into a truly national body. On 10 November 1943, an inter-state conference was held in Sydney, at which it was decided to draw up a federal constitution to co-ordinate the various state activities, and to undertake jointly projects of a national nature. Further inter-state conferences were held in 1944 and in 1945 when a federal constitution was formally adopted, with Mr E. K. White as first federal president. Subsequently the first federal council meeting was held in Sydney on 21 August 1945. At this meeting, on the motion of Mr W. A. Ince of Victoria, seconded by Professor E. J. Goddard of Queensland, it was agreed 'that steps be taken for the observance of the Anniversary of the Battle of the Coral Sea', thereby initiating the first major activity of a national character—the Coral Sea Celebrations. This decision established an important link between the Association's war-time activities and the post-war period.

With the end of the war, the Association was faced with a fresh challenge—how to find new fields of endeavour for the implementation of its objectives. There was a feeling in some quarters that the Association's usefulness was ended. In Western Australia the Association was disbanded, to be revived again in 1950. In both

Queensland and South Australia similar action was discussed, but wiser counsels prevailed. Both New South Wales and Victoria continued their activities unabated and soon two major projects were evolved which provided a new challenge and a fresh incentive. These were the annual Coral Sea celebrations and the American Memorial at Canberra.

From small beginnings in Melbourne and Sydney in 1946, the Coral Sea celebrations were to prove of inestimable value in fostering Australian-American friendship and understanding in the years ahead. Initially, the celebrations were established to commemorate American and Australian naval co-operation in the Coral Sea battle of 4-8 May 1942, which saved Australia from the threat of invasion and proved to be the turning point in the war against Japan. But within a few years they assumed a much wider significance and had become a recognised feature of our national life. They combined thankfulness to the United States for our deliverance at a fateful period in Australian history with an annual occasion upon which to pay tribute to the joint co-operation of all arms of the American and Australian services throughout the war in the Pacific, and to stress the need for continuing Australian-American unity and friendship. In short, their recurring theme was to use the past to assess the present and look to the future.

From 1947-49 the Association concentrated on spreading its message to all sections of the community. Extensive use was made of press articles and radio broadcasts, with enormous audiences both within Australia and overseas. Displays in shop windows, Coral Sea exhibitions, spectacular service marches, memorial church services, lectures and addresses, luncheons and balls, all helped to stimulate public interest and support. Children's rallies, sporting fixtures, essay competitions and addresses to schools catered for the younger generation.

In 1950 a dramatic new development advanced the Coral Sea celebrations from a local exercise in public relations to a truly national occasion, and ushered in an era of active American participation with the support of both the United States and Australian Governments. In that year, Admiral A. W. Radford, Commander-in-Chief of the United States Pacific Fleet, became the first distinguished Coral Sea guest. His visit was such a success that it initiated a period of seventeen years during which top-ranking United States Navy, Army and Air Force Commanders came to Australia for the celebrations, normally for a fourteen days period, including visits to all States. They brought with them numerous units of the United States Navy, including, over the years, the giant aircraft carriers *Tarawa*, *Coral Sea* and *Bennington*, the heavy cruisers *Canberra*, *Columbus* and *Toledo*, numerous destroyers, and varied other modern craft of special interest. For good measure, American naval bands and drum and bugle teams came in their own aeroplanes on several occasions. The ships visited Australian ports from Brisbane to Perth and the American sailors were welcomed in all centres visited.

The Coral Sea Guests of Honour included such renowned war-time leaders as Admiral T. C. Kincaid, Commander of a destroyer force in the Coral Sea Battle; General R. L. Eichelberger of 'Jungle Road to Tokyo'; Admiral W. F. ('Bull') Halsey, and General J. J. ('Jimmy') Doolittle of Tokyo raid fame. These were followed later by senior service officers including Admiral F. B. Stump, Commander-in-Chief, US Pacific Fleet; General I. D. White, Commander-in-Chief, US Army, Pacific; General L. S. Kuter, Commander-in-Chief, US Pacific Air Force; General H. H. Howze, Commander-in-Chief, United Nations Forces in Korea.

With such support, the success of the celebrations was assured and few people in Australia were unaware of their significance. Whereas previously the Association had to create or seek publicity for its objectives, this now followed automatically. In addition, each state developed special local activities such as 'Coral Sea Sunday' and a Cenotaph wreath-laying ceremony in Sydney; an evening, open-air, flood-lit service at the foot of Queensland's Memorial to the United States in Brisbane; Schools' Day and a full-scale services march through the city in Melbourne; a wreath-laying ceremony at the War Memorial in Adelaide; and a parade in Perth. Highly successful Coral Sea veterans' reunions were also developed. For a voluntary organisation the over-all national result of the Coral Sea celebrations, coupled with substantial official, public and press support, was an outstanding achievement.

The construction of Australia's National Memorial to America at Canberra was another imaginative project of the early post-war years. It provided the Association with a new challenge and a unique task which was undertaken with enthusiasm and determination. Its ultimate success far exceeded the most optimistic forecasts. At a Federal Council meeting in March 1948 it was resolved 'to establish a Memorial in Canberra in the form of a monument or statue, to perpetuate the services and sacrifices of the United States forces in Australia and to symbolise Australian-American co-operation in arms', and a Victorian-based US Memorial committee was appointed to undertake the responsibilities involved. Initially, a small group of statuary to cost £20,000 was envisaged. But it soon became evident that to be worthy of its purpose a memorial of considerable size and striking design was essential. Thus arose the idea of 'something soaring' which would be readily seen from all parts of the national capital.

The whole project proved to be much more complicated than at first envisaged and took six years to bring to fruition. The search for a site took three years; an architectural competition to secure a suitable design took one year; the organisation of the appeal for funds took a year, and the actual construction took over a year. The appeal for funds was launched by the then Prime Minister, the Rt Hon. R. G. Menzies, in May 1950. The target was £50,000, but in six weeks over £63,000 was subscribed. Thousands of donations, large and small, poured in from the Australian people, and all States exceeded their quotas. Later, to meet rising costs the Commonwealth Government made a donation of £50,000. Both Queensland and South Australia erected local memorials of considerable merit in Brisbane and Adelaide.

The memorial itself consists of an octagonal aluminium shaft 258 feet high, surmounted by a symbolic American eagle, with wings upstretched in a victory sign. It stands today in Australia's national capital as a people's tribute to the American nation, and as a symbol of enduring friendship, proved in war and fostered in peace.

It was consequently a proud day for the Association when, on 16 February 1954, with the Association's Federal President, Sir

John Latham, presiding, Her Majesty Queen Elizabeth II unveiled the Memorial in the presence of a distinguished gathering from all parts of the Commonwealth. An actuality broadcast of the proceedings and an enormous press coverage carried the message throughout Australia and overseas. Later, a film of the ceremony was seen by millions of people in Australia, the United Kingdom and the United States.

Thus was achieved the purpose of the Association to establish a lasting memorial to Australian-American unity and goodwill. In the words of General Douglas MacArthur at the time: 'This Memorial is a permanent reminder that in the defence of liberty Australians and Americans find common cause.'

A further national activity of this period was the establishment of the magazine *Pacific Neighbors*. Commencing as a Victorian publication in 1946 it was soon adopted as the Federal Journal of the Association. A high quality, well illustrated publication, *Pacific Neighbors* carries informative articles of special Australian-American interest and reviews in detail the progress and purpose of the Association's work. The journal has proved of inestimable value in linking up the membership in all states and in steadily spreading its message in official and influential quarters. Complimentary copies are distributed regularly to major libraries, public organisations and key individuals throughout Australia and the United States. Copies in bulk are also purchased by the American-Australian Associations in New York, San Francisco, Los Angeles and Honolulu. For many years the magazine was also the official Journal of the New Zealand-American Association.

The American-Australian Association in New York was established by Mr Randal Heymanson at an inaugural luncheon on 7 October 1948, at which Sir Keith Murdoch and the Rt Hon. R. G. Menzies were guests of honour. This kindred Association consists of representatives of the major commercial, financial and industrial companies in the United States. Its main activity is to hold top-line luncheons in New York for visiting Prime Ministers, Cabinet Ministers and diplomatic representatives from Australia, New Zealand and the United Kingdom. In a city the size of New York, with scores of national organisations competing for recognition, these luncheons have commanded a quite remarkable press and radio coverage throughout the United States and overseas.

Similar American-Australian Associations were later established in San Francisco in 1958, Los Angeles in 1965 and Honolulu in 1967. Over the years all the organisations have co-operated with the Association in Australia in a variety of ways. 'Coral Sea' functions have been held; public and business interest has been aroused; hospitality has been arranged; and distinguished visitors have been entertained with much resulting publicity for the aims of the Association.

In 1958 the Association accepted a new challenge when it agreed to act as sponsor in Australia for the American Field Service International Scholarships. This remarkable American organisation arranges annually for over 3,000 teen-age students from more than fifty countries to spend a year in the United States, without charge, as members of carefully selected foster families, to study at American schools for an academic year and to participate in a bus tour of the United States at the end of the period. Here was a wonderful opportunity to foster Australian-American goodwill in a new field and on a scale not envisaged in the early stages of the programme.

The first six students, three from New South Wales and three from Victoria, left Australia in 1959. Within a few years all states had adopted the programme and by 1964 the number of students departing by charter flight had jumped to sixty-three. By 1968, a grand total of 632 Australian students had benefited from this rewarding experience. In reverse, the first five American students arrived in Melbourne in 1961 and by 1968 131 American students had come to Australia for an academic year.

The AFS programme opened many new doors, evoked tremendous enthusiasm and called for much hard work. It created an entirely new interest in Australian-American relations in homes, schools and communities across the nation. It also involved the setting up of active AFS committees in all states; the difficult tasks of selection and home placements; the establishment of returnees' associations and the raising of finance. Largely as a result of the

AFS project, branches of the Association were established in Canberra in 1961 and Tasmania in 1963, and AFS students were selected from these areas.

In many respects the AFS project is the most rewarding activity undertaken by the Association. Its scope is remarkable and its lasting value is inestimable. Life-long friendships are formed; youthful enthusiasm is engendered; knowledge of both countries is widened; and with the numbers now increasing at the rate of over 140 a year its influence will continue to grow. In addition, Australian AFS students have to date given over 18,000 talks about Australia to audiences scattered throughout the United States.

Another rewarding development of this period was the formation of junior associations, which enlisted the enthusiastic support of the younger generation and greatly widened the scope and work of the parent body. These junior associations comprise a representative cross section of young people in the 18-35 age group, drawn largely from business, professional and academic quarters. They brought youthful energy and enthusiasm to the work of the Association, and rapidly spread its message in a field previously untouched.

A younger set had existed in West Australia for some years, but the first more independent and wider junior association was formed in Victoria in 1957. Within a few years similar groups were formed by all other branches, with a total membership of some 1,600. Specific activities include hospitality for young Americans, especially from visiting American naval ships, public speaking, art, music and drama, and help for the aged and for underprivileged children.

These junior associations also rounded out the work already undertaken in this field. The Association has always recognised the importance of spreading its message among young people and in 1947 introduced a pen friends project which forwards annually to US Friendship organisations the names of thousands of Australian children in the 8 to 16 years age group for linking with pen pals in the United States. The total number of names handled by this project during the past twenty years is now over 150,000.

Thus today through its pen friends, the AFS Scholarships and the junior associations, the Association caters in one way or another for our younger people from 8 to 35 years of age.

In addition to the national achievements already outlined, each branch of the Association has developed special projects of considerable merit within its own area. In New South Wales important steps have been taken to spread the message in country districts by establishing sub-branches in Newcastle in 1953 and Grafton in 1957, and by linking up country towns with towns of similar interests in USA through its Community Co-operation project. Commencing in 1961 by linking Bega (New South Wales) with Littleton (Colorado) eleven such affiliations have already been made including Maitland (New South Wales) with Maitland (Florida), Orange (New South Wales) with Orange (California) and Katoomba (New South Wales) with Flagstaff (Arizona). Seven more links are in process of formation by this imaginative project which creates many valuable personal and official contacts. Considerable assistance has also been given to the New York Metropolitan Opera auditions in Australia, and to providing hospitality and entertainment for American servicemen from Vietnam, when on rest and recreation leave in New South Wales. A further recent major task is to establish an Australian-American Centre in Sydney through the purchase and renovation of two historical houses built in 1835 as the headquarters of the Association's activities.

In Victoria, a major achievement has been the establishment by its women's group of an Australian-American centre and club in Melbourne. In 1957 a city building was purchased and renovated. By 1958 an all-purposes centre was in operation and in 1960 the club was officially constituted with a membership of over 1,400. Other special activities undertaken from time to time include an exchange of project books between Victorian and American schools; gifts of valuable sets of Australian books to American libraries; and staffing an information and hospitality centre for American visitors during the 1956 Olympic Games in Melbourne.

Queensland holds pride of place for having erected the first Memorial in Australia to the American people for their war-time help. Unveiled in 1952, the memorial consists of a 35-foot high column of fluted freestone on a granite base, surmounted by an emblematic American eagle. It stands on a historic site at the edge of the Brisbane River in Newstead Park. The inscription at the foot of the memorial carries the simple caption: 'They passed this way.'

A local memorial to America was also established by South Australia in 1953. Situated in the Adelaide Botanic Gardens, it takes the form of twin sandstone pillars, each surmounted by a globe with America and Australia standing out in relief. Western Australia has made special efforts over the years to extend friendship to the many Americans in their midst, either the crews of visiting American naval ships or the large number of American industrial, commercial and official representatives associated with the dramatic developments in that State. In all states and Canberra the Association now has active women's groups, junior associations and AFS committees devoting their time steadily to a never-ending round of useful activities.

All this extensive work outlined could not possibly have been achieved without wise leadership, efficient administration and a devoted membership. Throughout its existence the Association has been able to command these basic requirements for success in full measure. In the federal sphere there have been five federal presidents only during a period of twenty-three years. Each has made his own special contribution to the work of the Association and all have had in common a devotion to the cause of British-American unity and a firm belief in the vital importance of Australian-American co-operation and goodwill.

Mr E. K. White, New South Wales state president during the war years and from 1954-57, and federal president for a total period of seven years, has throughout brought drive, enthusiasm and imagination to the cause he has championed for so long. The Rt Hon. R. G. Casey, federal president and Victorian state president from 1946-50, whose wider work for Australian-American accord in the political and diplomatic fields has been outstanding, gave added strength to the work undertaken during the early post-war years. On his retirement as federal president he was elected federal patron of the Association, a position which Lord Casey still holds as Governor-General of the Commonwealth of Australia.

Sir John Latham, well-loved elder statesman of wit and wisdom, Victorian state president for fourteen years until the time of his death, and federal president for five years, brought a lifetime of experience in international, political, diplomatic and legal affairs to the task. Mr R. Keith Yorston, a foundation member and office-bearer of the early movement, state president in New South Wales for eight years and federal president for four years, has for over thirty years given unfailing energetic and enthusiastic support to the Association's work. Mr Wesley A. Ince, a foundation member of the Association in Victoria, a vice-president since its inception and federal president for three years, has for the past twenty-seven years brought sound business and legal guidance to the cause he has held so closely at heart.

In the state sphere, the Association has been likewise fortunate in the efficient and devoted leadership it has received from its state presidents. Throughout it has secured the support of business and professional community leaders who have voluntarily given many years of whole-hearted service to the problems and work involved. Without such help, initiative and guidance the progress outlined in this review could not have been achieved.

The history of the Association would be quite incomplete without paying a warm tribute to the work of its women's groups for their outstanding contributions to the results achieved. The nature, extent and value of their voluntary services cannot be over-emphasised. With tremendous enthusiasm and energy they have been ever ready to grasp every opportunity to support the cause. Specific activities include endless hospitality for visiting Americans, annual Coral Sea Balls which are a highlight of the celebrations, and fund raising functions of all types. It is estimated that the total money raised for both charity and Association purposes throughout Australia over the years would be in excess of $300,000.

Special reference should be made to the women's American Field Service Scholarships committees which control the complicated tasks of responsibility for American students throughout their year in Australia, home and school visitations, conferences and orientation sessions, and the arrival and departure of all groups, in an endless process as the years go round. Without such devoted services the AFS programme could not possibly function so effectively.

Further, as a corporate body, many thousands of members have, in a wide variety of ways, played a vital part in the progress of the Association. Their genuine devotion to the cause of Australian-American friendship and their work for the realisation of this ideal, have helped to establish a firm foundation for finer fruition in this special field of endeavour.

Throughout its short history the Australian-American Association has been heartened by the encouragement of both the Australian and the United States Governments, the support of the Australian people and the active co-operation of all federal, state and local authorities. In addition, the United States and Australian services and the diplomatic representatives of both nations have given whole-hearted assistance on all occasions. Substantial financial assistance has also been received from business companies which recognise the importance of the Association's objectives.

The Australian-American Association has been the product of its period and the pioneer and spearhead of a popular objective. Fortified by such wide acclaim, and aided by the passage of events, a relatively small voluntary organisation has been able to accomplish quite remarkable results. Its seed has fallen on good ground and has brought forth abundant fruit.

Patrick Hamilton